Modeling Religious Pluralism

Modeling Religious Pluralism

Cultivating Religious Equity in Today's World

Edited by

SIMRAN JEET SINGH

OXFORD
UNIVERSITY PRESS

OXFORD
UNIVERSITY PRESS

Oxford University Press is a department of the University of Oxford. It furthers the University's objective of excellence in research, scholarship, and education by publishing worldwide. Oxford is a registered trade mark of Oxford University Press in the UK and in certain other countries.

Published in the United States of America by Oxford University Press
198 Madison Avenue, New York, NY 10016, United States of America.

Library of Congress Cataloging-in-Publication Data
Names: Singh, Simran Jeet editor
Title: Modeling religious pluralism : cultivating religious equity
in today's world / [edited by Simran Jeet Singh].
Description: New York, NY : Oxford University Press, [2026] |
Includes bibliographical references and index.
Identifiers: LCCN 2025048654 (print) | LCCN 2025048655 (ebook) |
ISBN 9780197745816 paperback | ISBN 9780197745809 hardback |
ISBN 9780197745847 | ISBN 9780197745830 epub
Subjects: LCSH: Religious tolerance | Religious pluralism
Classification: LCC BL99.5 .M63 2025 (print) | LCC BL99.5 (ebook) |
DDC 323.44/2—dc23/eng/20260205
LC record available at https://lccn.loc.gov/2025048654
LC ebook record available at https://lccn.loc.gov/2025048655

DOI: 10.1093/oso/9780197745809.001.0001

Paperback printed by Marquis Book Printing, Canada
Hardback printed by Lightning Source, Inc., United States of America

The manufacturer's authorized representative in the EU for product safety is Oxford University Press España S.A. of Parque Empresarial San Fernando de Henares, Avenida de Castilla, 2 – 28830 Madrid (www.oup.es/en or product.safety@oup.com). OUP España S.A. also acts as importer into Spain of products made by the manufacturer.

FSC
www.fsc.org
MIX
Paper | Supporting responsible forestry
FSC® C103567

Contents

Acknowledgments ix
List of Contributors xi
Introduction xv

PART I RELIGIOUS LITERACY

1. Critical Religious Literacy: Promoting the Public Understanding of Religion in Service of a Just World at Peace 3
Diane L. Moore

2. Cross-Cultural Religious Literacy: A Methodology That Messages the Model 15
Chris Seiple

3. The Benefit of Illiteracy: Navigating Privilege, Fostering Religious Literacy, and Creating Equity 22
Ilyse R. Morgenstein Fuerst

PART II RELIGIOUS FREEDOM

4. Learning to Live with Global Neighbors 31
Knox Thames

5. *In Medias Res*: Religious Freedom and Moral Imagination Forging a New, Pluralistic Nation 38
Keisha E. McKenzie

6. Political Partisanship and Its Effect on the Future of Religious Liberty 48
Asma T. Uddin

PART III ADDRESSING HATE AND POLARIZATION

7. Faith Is a Bridge: Why Engaging Religion Is Essential for Addressing Polarization 61
Eboo Patel and Mary Ellen Geiss

8. Religious Communities and Anti-Asian Racism during the COVID-19 Pandemic 72
Melissa May Borja

9. Hinduism, America, and the Making of a New Pluralism 81
Uma Viswanathan

PART IV RELIGION AND RACIAL JUSTICE

10. Staying in the Spiritual Fire of Equity and Kinship 87
Kaitlin B. Curtice

11. Black American Religious Pluralism: Rethinking a Historiography 92
Randal Maurice Jelks

12. To Fight Racism, We Need to Confront Religion's Racist Past 106
Simran Jeet Singh

PART V RELIGION AND MEDIA

13. Representing the Muslim 115
Hussein Rashid

14. Stories, Stereotypes, and Sitting Shiva: Improving Jewish Representation in TV and Film 123
Esther D. Kustanowitz

15. The State of Religious Pluralism in TV and Film 135
Jody Hassett Sanchez

PART VI RELIGION IN THE WORKPLACE

16. Faith-and-Belief Friendly Workplaces 145
Brian J. Grim

17. Living Interfaith: Applying a Model of Religious Unity in the Workplace 151
Jeremy Fricke and Wendy Goldberg

18. Religious Pluralism in the Workplace: A Conscious Decision 159
Reverend Mark E. Fowler and Megan Leverage

PART VII RELIGION AND PHILANTHROPY

19. A New Path: Pairing Power and Religious Pluralism 169
Jason Garrett

20. A Case for Faith-Integrated Philanthropy 177
Farhan Latif and Catherine Orsborn

21. Let's Talk about It: Philanthropy-Serving Organizations' Role in Promoting Pluralism 187
Allison K. Ralph

References 199
Index 217

Acknowledgments

Neither this book nor the organization's vision are my creation alone. A whole team co-created this vision, and an ecosystem of supporters have helped make it possible. Meryl Chertoff founded the Inclusive America Project, which was the incubator for what would become the Religion & Society Program at the Aspen Institute. The Inclusive America Project laid the groundwork for our work on religious pluralism with two publications, *Principled Pluralism* and *Pluralism in Peril*. The co-chairs for both publications were the late Madeleine Albright and the late David Gergen.

Meryl hired Dr. Allison K. Ralph as editor for the latter publication, and Allison then went on to drive the model for religious pluralism. Zeenat Rahman became the executive director and led the transformation of the Inclusive America Project from a standalone project to a full-blown policy program with a $1.2 million budget. She launched the Religious Pluralism Funders' Circle, extended our networks, and enabled a wide-ranging body of scholarship. It was also under Rahman's leadership that Dr. Ralph worked closely with colleagues, including Rahman and Elizabeth Lynn at the Lake Institute on Faith and Giving, to develop what would become the Religion & Society Program's model for religious pluralism.[1] Dr. Ralph also consulted with Amy McIsaac to clarify definitions and structure for this model.

I first came to know of the Aspen Institute's model in 2019, and I was immediately drawn to it. It resonated with my own professional work and lived experience, and at that point, I had not yet seen any individual or entity articulate the aspects of religious pluralism in such a clear and holistic way. I started working more closely with Zeenat and Allison, and eventually joined the team in 2021 as the executive director of the Religion & Society Program. I served in this role until 2024, and cared about its work enough that I stayed on as an advisor after accepting a position at Union Theological Seminary. It has been an honor to steward and grow this program at Aspen, helping to drive new work and thought leadership on one of the most critical issues of our time. Today, the program continues to flourish under its new director, Josh Good.

The Religion & Society team members contributed immensely to our work and thinking on religious pluralism. Our members of the Powering Religious

[1] Ibid.

Pluralism Network, many of whom contributed to this volume, gave of themselves significantly and generously. Kali Handelman has been a wonderful support in helping me think through the volume and edit the chapters. Ganeev Sachar has also provided invaluable support through the final stages of the manuscript.

The research and framework for this book have been underwritten by our friends at the Templeton Religion Trust. We are grateful for their support and for their continued commitment to advancing religious pluralism.

We remain committed to helping build a world where all people can thrive, no matter what they look like or what they believe. Our earnest hope is that this volume is a resource for those who aspire toward religious pluralism, and that it proves fruitful—and perhaps even inspiring—to anyone and everyone who reads from it.

Contributors

Melissa May Borja is associate professor of American culture and Asian/Pacific Islander American studies at the University of Michigan, where she directs the Asian/Pacific Islander American Studies Program. She is the author of *Follow the New Way: American Refugee Resettlement Policy and Hmong Religious Change* (Harvard University Press, 2023) and directs the Virulent Hate Project.

Kaitlin B. Curtice is an award-winning author, poet-storyteller, and public speaker, and writer at *The Liminality Journal*. As an enrolled citizen of the Potawatomi nation, Kaitlin writes on the intersections of spirituality and identity and how that shifts throughout our lives.

Reverend Mark E. Fowler is the CEO of the Tanenbaum Center for Interreligious Understanding, a secular, nonsectarian nonprofit whose mission is to combat religious prejudice, promote justice, and build respect for religious difference. Reverend Fowler is also an instructor for first- and second-year students at the One Spirit Interfaith Seminary.

Jeremy Fricke is an educator on religious diversity and an independent consultant on improved intergenerational or interfaith engagement. He currently serves as executive director of Camp Naco, a Buffalo Soldier site being rehabilitated into an intercultural and historical US-Mexico borderlands experience.

Jason Garrett has been working over twenty years to bridge, organize, and fund member-based communities, faith groups, and more to bring about justice. He currently serves as the senior vice president of Faith, Bridging, and Belonging at the Freedom Together Foundation.

Mary Ellen Geiss is chief program officer at Interfaith America (IA), overseeing strategy, alignment, and integration across IA's programming. Geiss has over two decades of experience in pluralism and bridgebuilding, nonprofit executive leadership, research-to-practice partnerships, and cross-sector collaborations.

Wendy Goldberg co-founded and previously led the Tri-Faith Initiative in Omaha, Nebraska, fostering interfaith collaboration and community connection. She now leads Curista Collection, a sustainability-driven project that explores storytelling, legacy, and secondhand fashion.

Brian J. Grim is the founding president of the Religious Freedom & Business Foundation and a globally recognized expert on the socioeconomic impact of religious freedom. His work spans continents and institutions, from establishing the first Western-style business school in the Soviet Union to advising the World Economic Forum.

Jody Hassett Sanchez is a journalist and filmmaker. She has reported on religion, culture, education, and foreign policy for CNN, *ABC News*, and PBS. Her documentaries have screened at top film festivals and in more than fifty countries. She is a trustee of the Media Project and founder of the Africa Film Project.

Randal Maurice Jelks is the Ruth N. Halls Professor of African American and African Diaspora Studies at Indiana University, Bloomington. He is an award-winning author, a documentary film producer, and a professor, as well as Presbyterian (USA) clergy.

Esther D. Kustanowitz is an award-winning writer, journalist, and podcaster who has worked with dozens of publications and nonprofit organizations on projects connected to contemporary Jewish identity and representation. Her podcast, *The Bagel Report*, explores the intersection of Jewish identity and popular culture, with an emphasis on television and film.

Farhan Latif is the president and a trustee of the El-Hibri Foundation (EHF), a community-built, intergenerationally focused institution based in Washington, DC. In this role, he leads efforts to invest in leadership, strategy, and action.

Megan Leverage holds a PhD in American religious history. She is a senior workplace program associate at the Tanenbaum Center for Interreligious Understanding.

Keisha E. McKenzie is a multidisciplinary strategist, facilitator, and consultant. Her forthcoming book in the *Building a Moral Economy* series (Fortress Press, 2027) explores how religion and spirituality inspire community experiments in shared memory, collective decision making, and sustainable economics.

Diane L. Moore was on the faculty of Harvard Divinity School for twenty-five years and was the founding director of Religion and Public Life at HDS before her retirement in 2025. She is the author of *Overcoming Religious Illiteracy* (Palgrave, 2007) and is currently the Co-Director (along with Hussein Rashid) of Religion and Public Life at Union Theological Seminary and a Scholar-in-Residence there.

Ilyse R. Morgenstein Fuerst is associate professor of religion and director of the Humanities Center at the University of Vermont. She is the author of *Indian Muslim Minorities and the 1857 Rebellion* (Bloomsbury, 2017), co-editor of *Words of Experience* (Equinox, 2021), and co-author of *Religion Is Not Done with You* (Beacon, 2024).

Catherine Orsborn serves as senior director of programs and public policy at the El-Hibri Foundation (EHF). With an academic background in religion and social change and a track record in nonprofit leadership, she brings a deep commitment to advancing inclusion, belonging, and social cohesion.

Eboo Patel is founder and president of Interfaith America, and author of numerous books on pluralism.

Allison K. Ralph heads Cohesion Strategy, a consulting firm supporting pluralistic nonprofits with strategy, research, facilitation, and evaluation services. She formerly led the Aspen Institute Religion & Philanthropy Initiative and is a recognized expert in religious pluralism.

Hussein Rashid is a free-range academic whose research focuses on Muslims in US popular culture. He is also an award-winning documentary film producer, cultural strategist, consultant, and futurist. With Diane Moore, he is co-director of Religion and Public Life at Union Theological Seminary.

Chris Seiple is the president emeritus of the Institute for Global Engagement, where he founded *The Review of Faith & International Affairs.* He is a former senior advisor to the State Department, and to the first-ever US government summit on strategic religious engagement.

Simran Jeet Singh is assistant professor of interreligious histories at Union Theological Seminary and senior adviser for the Aspen Institute's Religion & Society Program. He hosts the PRX podcast *Wisdom & Practice* and the TV show *Undivided.*

Knox Thames is an international advocate for religious freedom and former US State Department special advisor for religious minorities. He writes and speaks widely on advancing global human rights, faith engagement, and defending the persecuted.

Asma T. Uddin is an assistant professor of law at Michigan State University College of Law and a fellow at the Aspen Institute's Religion & Society Program. A leading scholar of constitutional law and religious liberty, she is also the author of *When Islam Is Not a Religion* and *The Politics of Vulnerability.*

Uma Viswanathan is president of the Samuel S. Fels Fund, and was previously the executive director of New Pluralists, a funder collaborative investing $100 million to grow pluralism in American culture. Her Hindu worldview shapes her two decades of experience investing in and leading for transformational social change.

Introduction

How do we deal with difference? This has become a central question of our time.

Racial difference. Political difference. Cultural difference. Ideological difference.

Scholars, activists, and everyday citizens have discussed and debated these topics at length. Yet despite their clear importance and urgency, there are some forms of difference that have not yet received the attention they merit, despite their clear importance and urgency.

Our capacity to understand and engage with religion and religious diversity is one such issue. Religion is often overlooked, misrepresented, and misunderstood. Many people avoid conversations about religion, believing them to be too messy and too volatile.

On the occasions that people do discuss religion, it quickly becomes apparent that most in our society are ill equipped to deal with the complexities of religious difference.

The stakes are too high to continue operating in these ways. With surges in religious nationalism around the world and across the United States, it is past time that we develop a foundational understanding of how religion operates in our society and how we can engage religious difference in productive and meaningful ways. There are many leaders and initiatives working to advance that vision, and this volume is our humble effort to contribute to these efforts.

For the past two decades, the Aspen Institute's Religion & Society Program has been working to make religious diversity an asset rather than a liability. We have recognized the global magnitude of this challenge and chosen to focus our work on the United States. It's where we are situated, the context we know best, and a country where navigating religious difference remains a real challenge.[1]

Through our convenings and research, we have determined that building a healthy society and democracy in this country necessitates a strong and robust commitment to religious pluralism.

What is religious pluralism? Since 2020, this has been our working definition: "[R]eligious pluralism is a vision of the world in which diverse religious

[1] While our work and this book primarily attend to the domestic context, we anticipate that the insights and lessons we offer might inform questions and approaches in other contexts as well.

Introduction In: *Modeling Religious Pluralism*. Edited by: Simran Jeet Singh, Oxford University Press.
© Oxford University Press 2026. DOI: 10.1093/oso/9780197745809.001.0001

communities and non-believers engage one another in beneficial ways, maintain their distinct identities, and thrive and defend one anothers' right to thrive."[2]

In other words, religious pluralism is neither anti-religion nor pro-religion; it does not favor a particular religion or diminish another; nor is it a call for cultural relativism or an all-inclusive Unitarianism. Religious pluralism is a recognition that religions are different and specific, and that we can view them without assigning hierarchical value or placing them in competition with one another. The goal of engaging with religious difference is not to convince or convert, but instead, to disrupt bias, enhance understanding, and build empathy.

Religious diversity has often been targeted as a problem in this country. Figuring out how to navigate it has been a long-standing topic of debate, from before the United States was founded in 1776 to the present day. Leaders of all stripes have used the presence of religious difference to stoke fear and to advance ideologies of exclusion. This project offers another way forward, one that claims neither religious similitude nor religious supremacy, but instead, a model for appreciating the diversity that surrounds us.

While this book aims itself at the aspiration of religious pluralism, it is also grounded in present realities. This is to say, the authors and I are all keenly aware that not all religions have been able to claim equal footing in the United States of America, and that all religious communities have their own unique challenges. This includes Christianity, which is often centered in how we conceive of religion and religious freedom in this country, as well as minoritized traditions like Hinduism and Buddhism, which have a strong presence in the United States but do not enjoy equal opportunities or freedoms.

As a scholar of religion, I am also keenly aware that religion itself is a problematic category, neither native nor universal in the way we often presume in our modern world. I am also aware that talking about religion in the singular, rather than religions in the plural, can reify presumptions of essentialism and homogeneity, privilege dominant narratives, and marginalize lesser-known traditions. And yet, I am also aware that religion is an operative and important construct with real political consequences. In this volume, we have done our best to remain sensitive to these considerations in conceiving of and writing our chapters. One of the ways we have expressed this sensitivity is in our commitment to defining religion not based on what institutions or textbooks say, but on what it inspires people to do.

[2] Aspen Institute, *Many People, Many Faiths, One Nation: A Primer on Religious Pluralism* (Washington, DC: Aspen Institute, 2020), https://www.aspeninstitute.org/programs/religion-society-program/religion-society-program-publications/many-people-many-faiths-one-nation-a-primer-on-religious-pluralism/ (accessed December 18, 2025).

Implicit in our definition of religious pluralism is our position that the consequences of religious pluralism are positive and desirable. This is not to say that religion is always positive and pro-social. There are countless examples of how it has sown discord and division, hatred and violence. Many of the chapters in this volume speak to the suffering wrought by religious actors. What we believe, though, is that advancing religious pluralism has many positive outcomes that are worth naming explicitly, including enhanced civic engagement, social cohesion, trust, resilience, and belonging.

I have also experienced firsthand and believe wholeheartedly that learning to overcome the insecurities one might feel in proximity to religious difference, and learning to appreciate religious diversity, can be personally transformative. I believe it has made me a kinder, more empathetic, and more understanding person, and that it has made me happier, too. One of my motivations to write this book and to share these ideas with those willing to receive them is to help invite more people into this transformative worldview.

Here's something else I have come to believe deeply: It's not enough to simply observe religious diversity and theorize about why religious pluralism matters. We must also move toward progress through practical engagement. Here is the question that has animated our work at the Aspen Institute and that is at the core of this book: *How can we create the conditions for religious pluralism, so that we might be better equipped to engage with the religious diversity we encounter?*

This question has felt increasingly urgent over the past decade, and it has moved us to work with a wide cross-section of practitioners on the ground to develop key resources and identify best practices for enhancing religious pluralism. Working groups composed of top experts on these topics have collaborated to develop a vision and a theory of change for how to cultivate religious pluralism in our society. Collaboration has been an important aspect of our process, perhaps reflecting the spirit of pluralism we seek to lift up in this anthology.

Modeling Religious Pluralism is a culmination of our collective work over the past decade. It brings forward the model we have developed together—which we have described as a virtuous cycle or ecosystem of religious pluralism—where the outcomes of each area support progress in the larger field.

We do not see this model as the only way to understand and strengthen religious pluralism, but as one approach that can help move us forward. It is my belief that the model we propose and the chapters in this anthology are best understood as starting points that provide us *some* insights and *some* guiding principles upon which we can build together. It is in this spirit of humility that we have assembled this volume, and in this spirit that I have asked the contributors to write their chapters.

In 2020, the Aspen Institute's model consisted of eight component areas of religious pluralism that we identified and focused on in our work: Religious

Literacy, Religious Freedom, Racial Justice and Religion, Thriving Religious Communities, Diversity and Representation in Media, Hate Speech and Hate Crime Prevention, Multi-Faith and Intra-Faith Engagement, and Religion and Philanthropy.[3]

We have iterated our model over time, and for the purposes of this book, we are working with a model that encapsulates seven component areas: Religious Literacy, Religious Freedom, Religion and Media, Religion in the Workplace, Religion and Philanthropy, Religion and Racial Justice, and Religious Hate and Polarization.[4] We renamed a few of these categories for ease and consistency. For example, Racial Justice and Religion became Religion and Racial Justice, and Diversity and Representation in Media is now Religion and Media. We recognized that two of these groupings—Multi-Faith and Intra-Faith Engagement and Thriving Religious Communities—were infused in everything we do, and that therefore they did not necessitate their own categories. And we introduced a new category, Religion in the Workplace, recognizing that corporations are a key driver of culture change in the United States and there are important conversations and work emerging in that context.

Modeling Religious Pluralism is organized into a seven-part structure, with each category from our model serving as its own section for the book. Each section will be preceded with a brief essay from me, in which I will introduce you to the chapters and their authors, along with short reflections from my life and work that pertain to the topics.

We have curated chapters from foremost experts on key issues of religious pluralism, all of whom have worked with us in different capacities. I want to note directly that each author came into this project with their own subjectivities and writes from their own perspective. None of the authors in this book—including those who are scholars of religion and religious leaders—speak for their entire communities.

Moreover, the authors have experienced and engaged religious pluralism in different contexts and have strong divergences in their approaches, their styles of writing, and what they consider important to know. We have asked our contributors to leverage their own diverse perspectives by writing in a voice and style that feel authentic to them.

This, too, is what we mean by modeling religious pluralism.

[3] Ibid.

[4] Allison K. Ralph, "The Multiplier Effect: A Case Study of Faith-Based Community Organizations in Chicago, IL," Aspen Institute, 2020, https://www.aspeninstitute.org/wp-content/uploads/2020/09/FINAL-Multiplier-Effect-Paper-4.pdf (accessed December 18, 2025).

PART I
RELIGIOUS LITERACY

"Why do you wear that thing on your head?" I received this question often growing up as a Sikh in Texas, especially from my classmates and peers. Now that I have young children of my own, I am again fielding versions of this question regularly.

I don't mind providing answers, especially for curious children. But I'm reminded of what I used to wonder as a kid in Texas. *Wouldn't my life be so much easier if people just knew who I was?*

From a young age, I could see that my friends and neighbors had few opportunities to learn about my cultural and religious heritage. I also noticed that we didn't spend much time in school learning about other cultures and religions. What I did learn, though, was what can happen when we don't know and care about one another: bias, prejudice, bigotry, hate.

I encountered these negative consequences of ignorance often, and I had to figure out early how to deal with them. As I grew older—and through my study, community work, and personal encounters—I came to see how detrimental cultural and religious illiteracy could be. Too many times, I witnessed how ignorance enabled harmful stereotypes, misinformation, social division, and violence. I wanted to help people better connect with one another across the lines of cultural and religious difference. Education became central to my theory of change.

I have devoted much of my life and career to the work of enhancing religious literacy. Here's why I feel so drawn to it: Cultural and religious literacy is a social good that makes us better citizens and makes our society healthier. And it's also more than that. For many communities, including my own, being known and understood can be the difference between life and death.

Knowing about one another isn't the sole cure to our social divisions, but it's an important step. When it comes to religious difference, learning how to ask and answer questions about religion and religious difference is generally referred to as "religious literacy." The metaphor of "literacy" captures the fact that our goal is not to know everything. One doesn't have to already know something in order to read about it. The goal is to develop enough fluency in the language of religion to interpret and learn from encounters with religion and religious people.

Religious literacy is an essential aspect of religious pluralism in that it helps create conditions where all people can thrive. Knowing one another makes it easier to care for one another, and understanding the particularities of our traditions can help us ensure that we design norms and policies that account for diverse traditions and practices.

To begin the work of enhancing religious literacy, the definition offered by the world's largest organization of religion scholars—the American Academy of Religion (AAR)—will help us to grasp the work we're undertaking:

> Religious literacy helps us understand ourselves, one another, and the world in which we live. It includes the abilities to:
>
> - Discern accurate and credible knowledge about diverse religious traditions and expressions
> - Recognize the internal diversity within religious traditions
> - Understand how religions have shaped—and are shaped by—the experiences and histories of individuals, communities, nations, and regions
> - Interpret how religious expressions make use of cultural symbols and artistic representations of their times and contexts
> - Distinguish confessional or prescriptive statements made by religions from descriptive or analytical statements[1]

This section builds on the AAR's definition by inviting three scholars who think and work on religious literacy to share their expertise. Their differing perspectives reflect their particular experiences, approaches, training, and professional contributions.

Dr. Diane L. Moore, who is a progenitor of this field, lays out the three-part framework she has developed for how we can better understand and teach about religion without falling into some of the common traps that lead us to oversimplify, flatten, misunderstand, and ultimately dehumanize religious communities.

Dr. Chris Seiple, a seasoned diplomat with decades of experience in conflict resolution around the world, shares his methodology for cross-cultural religious literacy. He emphasizes, among other things, the importance of mutually engaged pluralism, and he shares examples of what these principles look like when applied in real situations.

Dr. Ilyse Morgenstein-Fuerst, a scholar of race, religion, and empire, brings a critical voice to the conversation, peeling back the layers of privilege and power within the discourse of religious literacy. She asks us to consider questions such as: *Who gets to see religious literacy as an intellectual exercise? For whom is religious literacy a matter of survival? And who is hurt most by religious illiteracy?*

Each of these scholars has contributed substantially to my own understanding of religious literacy, and each of them brings an important contribution to this growing field.

[1] American Academy of Religion, "AAR Religious Literacy Guidelines: What US College Graduates Need to Understand about Religion," https://aarweb.org/resource/aar-religious-literacy-guidelines-2/ (accessed December 18, 2025).

1

Critical Religious Literacy

Promoting the Public Understanding of Religion in Service of a Just World at Peace

Diane L. Moore

Overview

Religions have functioned throughout human history to inspire and justify the full range of human agency from the heinous to the heroic. Their influences remain potent here in the twenty-first century despite modern predictions that religious influences would steadily decline in concert with the rise of secular democracies and advances in science. Understanding these complex religious influences is a critical dimension of understanding modern human affairs across the full spectrum of endeavors in local, national, and global arenas.

The form of religious literacy advanced in this chapter is a method for understanding *how* religions function in human experience and was the foundation for the Religion and Public Life (RPL) program at Harvard Divinity School from 2020 to 2025.

Normative Assertions

Though there are many reasons to deepen the public understanding of religion, our focus in RPL is to enhance "religious literacy" in service of a just world at peace. Our commitment to just peace is a normative claim based on the following assertions:

1. Structural forms of inequity are widespread and intersecting.
2. These inequities are harmful to both those in positions of privilege as well as those who are marginalized, albeit in very different ways.
3. Structural inequities are not inevitable.
4. Their eradication is a condition of just peace.

Diane L. Moore, *Critical Religious Literacy* In: *Modeling Religious Pluralism*. Edited by: Simran Jeet Singh, Oxford University Press. © Oxford University Press 2026. DOI: 10.1093/oso/9780197745809.003.0001

In this way, just peace is an aspiration and a guiding framework for engaging in a *process of praxis*[1] in our attempts to mitigate structural inequities in and through our work.

The aspiration of contributing to a future where just peace is realized is one we share with countless others in civil societies in the United States and globally. Our particular contribution or lane of engagement relates to the complex roles that religions play in both promoting and thwarting structural inequities as they manifest in particular social and historical contexts. Understanding these influences can provide fresh insights into understanding the persistence of inequities as well as constructing imaginative strategies for their mitigation.

Foundational Assumptions That Frame RPL

1. Religion is a powerful force in human experience. From the beginnings of human history into our contemporary moment, religious convictions continue to inspire terrible acts of violence as well as profound acts of courage, compassion, and imagination.
2. Despite this reality and for many reasons, few citizens of the world understand the depth and breadth of this power, particularly how it manifests in so-called secular arenas of our lives.
3. This lack of understanding about religion and its power has many consequences. The consequences we are most concerned with are civic consequences. Partial or superficial understandings of religion too often fuel bigotry and prejudice. They also hinder creativity, imagination, and cooperation in local, national, and global contexts.
4. We believe that promoting a nuanced and capacious understanding of religion provides tools to mitigate the destructive power of religion and enhance its ability to generate compassion, beauty, and just peacebuilding.
   a. Mitigate the destructive power by identifying the ways that dimensions of religion function as forms of cultural and epistemic violence.
   b. Enhance the imaginative power by considering what is possible versus probable within particular contexts and recognizing how "*religious worldviews provide alternative frameworks from which to critique normative cultural assumptions. In this way (contrary to popular belief) the*

[1] This understanding of praxis comes from Paulo Freire's explication in *Pedagogy of the Oppressed*, first published in Portuguese in 1968 and translated into English in 1970. The most recent publication is a fiftieth-anniversary edition published by Bloomsbury Academic Press in 2018. Freire defines praxis as an ongoing process requiring the dynamic of action, reflection upon the action relevant to overarching aims of dismantling structural injustices, and further action informed by those reflections in a continuing sequence.

> *study of religion can serve to enhance rather than thwart critical thinking and cultural imagination regarding human capacity and agency.*"[2]

Just like pathbreaking scholarship that has illuminated the pervasive role of class, race, gender, and so many other important factors in addressing issues of civic importance, we believe this approach to understanding religion in context is crucial to understanding the rich complexity of modern human affairs.

Foundational Assumptions Regarding Critical Religious Literacy

1. There is a fundamental difference between the devotional expression of a religious worldview as normative and the study of religion that recognizes the factual existence of diverse devotional assertions.
2. Religions are internally diverse.
3. Religions evolve and change.
4. Religious influences are embedded in all aspects of human experience.
5. All knowledge claims (including religious ones) are socially constructed and represent particular "situated" perspectives.
6. There is nothing inevitable about either violence or peace; both are manifest in three intersecting formulations (direct, structural, and cultural), and both are shaped by conscious and unconscious human agency where religious influences are always operative.

Development of Assumptions Regarding Critical Religious Literacy

For a variety of reasons dating back to the Enlightenment—including Christian-influenced theories of secularization that were reproduced through colonialism—there are many commonly held assumptions about religion in general and religious traditions in particular that represent fundamental misunderstandings. Scholars of religion are well aware of these assumptions and have articulated some basic facts about religions themselves and the study of religion that serve as useful foundations for inquiry.[3]

[2] Diane L. Moore, *Overcoming Religious Illiteracy: A Cultural Studies Approach to the Study of Religion in Secondary Education* (New York: Palgrave Macmillan, 2008), 5, emphasis added.

[3] See American Academy of Religion, "AAR Religious Literacy Guidelines"; and American Academy of Religion, *The American Academy of Religion Guidelines for Teaching about Religion in K-12 Public Schools in the United States*, April (Atlanta, GA: American Academy of Religion, 2010).

Differentiating between Devotional Expression and the Study of Religion

First and foremost, scholars highlight the difference between the *devotional expression* of particular religious beliefs as normative and the nonsectarian *study of religion* that presumes the religious legitimacy of diverse normative claims. The importance of this distinction is that it recognizes the validity of normative theological assertions without equating them with universal truths about the tradition itself.

Unfortunately, this distinction is often ignored in public discourse about religion. For example, there is a great deal of contemporary debate about the roles for women in Islam. In truth, there are a variety of theological interpretations of the tradition that lead to different, sometimes antithetical practices and assertions. Equally common is that differing communities will have similar practices but with diverse theological or ideological justifications.

It is appropriate for members of a particular community to assert the orthodoxy or orthopraxy of their theological or ideological interpretations of the tradition, but it is important to recognize the difference between a theological assertion of normativity and the factual truth that multiple interpreted perspectives exist. The latter represents the nonsectarian study of religion. This is the approach promoted here and the one most appropriate to advance the public understanding of religion.

There are three other central assertions about religions themselves that religious studies scholars have outlined and that flow from the recognition of the distinction between devotional expression and the nonsectarian study of religion outlined above:

1. Religions are internally diverse as opposed to uniform.
2. Religions evolve and change over time as opposed to being ahistorical and static.
3. Religious influences are embedded in all dimensions of culture, as opposed to the assumption that religions function in discrete, isolated, "private" contexts.

Religions Are Internally Diverse

This assertion is a truism but requires explanation due to the ways that religious traditions and practices are frequently portrayed as uniform. Aside from the obvious formal differences within traditions represented by differing sects or expressions (e.g., Roman Catholic, Orthodox, and Protestant for Christianity;

or Vaishnavism, Shaivism, and Shaktism for Hinduism), there are differences within sects or expressions because religious communities function in different social/political contexts. One example is the debate mentioned above regarding the roles of women in Islam. The following assertions are also commonly repeated: "Buddhists are nonviolent." "Christians oppose abortion." "Religion and science are incompatible." All of these comments represent particular theological assertions as opposed to factual claims representing any given tradition itself.

Religions Evolve and Change

This is another truism but again requires explanation due to the common practice of representing religious traditions without social or historical context and solely (or primarily) through ritual expression and/or abstract beliefs. Religions exist in time and space and are constantly interpreted and reinterpreted by believers. For example, the Confucian concept of the "mandate from heaven" evolved across dynasties, geopolitical regions, and historical eras, and it continues to evolve today. Another example is that the practice of slavery has been both justified and vilified by all three monotheistic traditions in differing social and historical contexts. Finally, in a more specific example, the Southern Baptist Convention in the United States passed a series of resolutions in the 1970s supporting the moral legitimacy of abortion and reversed those resolutions in 2003.[4]

Religious Influences Are Embedded in Cultures

Religions are collections of ideas, practices, values, and stories that are all embedded in cultures and not separable from them. Just as religion cannot be understood in isolation from its cultural and political contexts, it is impossible to understand culture and politics without considering their religious dimensions. In the same way that race, ethnicity, gender, sexuality, and socioeconomic class are always factors in cultural interpretation and understanding, so too is religion.

Whether explicit or implicit, religious influences can virtually always be found when one asks "the religion question" of any given social or historical experience. For example, political theorists have recently highlighted the ways that different interpretations of secularism have been profoundly shaped by varied

[4] For a full-text compilation of all the Southern Baptist resolutions on abortion from 1971 to 2009, see Robert Johnston, "Southern Baptist Convention Resolutions on Abortion 1971–2009," https://www.johnstonsarchive.net/baptist/sbcabres.html (accessed July 28, 2024). To explore all the Southern Baptist Convention resolutions on abortion, go to https://www.sbc.net (accessed December 19, 2025) and type "abortion" into the search field.

normative assumptions about Christianity.[5] This is just one representation of a fundamental shift in political theory that is challenging the legitimacy of the long-standing assertion that religion both *can be* and *should be* restricted to a private sphere and separated from so-called secular political influence.

Modernist claims predicting the steady decline of the transnational political influence of religion that were first formalized in the seventeenth century have been foundational to various modern political theories for centuries. In spite of the ongoing global influences of religions in political life throughout this time period, it is only in the aftermath of (1) the Iranian Revolution in 1979, (2) the fall of the Berlin Wall in 1989 and the subsequent rise versus the widely predicted demise of religion, and (3) the 9/11 and 7/7 attacks that political theorists in the West began to acknowledge the highly problematic ways that religions and religious influences have been marginalized and too simplistically rendered.

This shift is a welcome one and paves the way for multi- and cross-disciplinary collaborations with religious studies scholars across the full range of social science investigations to explore the complex and critically important roles that religions play in our contemporary world.

Definition of Religious Literacy

Given the above principles, RPL utilizes my definition of religious literacy that was adopted by the AAR to help educators understand what is required for a basic understanding of religion and its roles in human experience:

> Religious literacy entails the ability to discern and analyze the fundamental intersections of religion and social/political/cultural life through multiple lenses. Specifically, a religiously literate person will possess 1) a basic understanding of the history, central texts (where applicable), beliefs, practices and contemporary manifestations of several of the world's religious traditions and expressions *as they arose out of and continue to be shaped by particular social, historical and cultural contexts*; and 2) the ability to discern and explore the

[5] See Talal Asad, *Formations of the Secular: Christianity, Islam, Modernity* (Stanford, CA: Stanford University Press, 2003); Janet R. Jakobsen and Ann Pellegrini, eds., *Secularisms* (Durham, NC: Duke University Press, 2008); Charles Taylor, *The Secular Age* (Cambridge, MA: Harvard University Press, 2007); J. Bryan Hehir, "Why Religion? Why Now?" in *Rethinking Religion and World Affairs*, edited by Monica Duffy Toft, Alfred Stepan, and Timothy Samuel Shah (New York: Oxford University Press, 2012), 15–24; José Casanova, "Rethinking Public Religions," in *Rethinking Religion and World Affairs*, 25–35; and Elizabeth Shakman Hurd, "The Politics of Secularism," in *Rethinking Religion and World Affairs*, 36–52.

religious dimensions of political, social and cultural expressions across time and place.[6]

Critical to this definition is the importance of understanding religions and religious influences *in context* and as *inextricably woven into all dimensions of human experience.* Such an understanding requires both the basic understanding of religious traditions described above and an awareness of the complex (and often contradictory) ways in which religion influences human behavior and social structures. A religiously literate person will be equipped not only to recognize religious references, whether to texts, ideas, or practices, but also to critically interrogate how religion manifests in cultural and historical contexts.

Cultural Studies/Critical Theory

The cultural studies/critical theory approach to understanding religion assumes the basic elements of the study of religion outlined above and frames them within a postmodern worldview with the following specific characteristics.

First, the method is multi- and interdisciplinary and recognizes how political, economic, and cultural lenses are fundamentally entwined rather than discrete. For example, economic or political dimensions of human experience cannot be accurately understood without understanding the religious and other ideological influences that shape the cultural context out of which particular political or economic actions and motivations arise. This is the methodological framework related to the third tenet of religious studies above: that religions are embedded in culture and that culture is inclusive of political and economic influences.

Second, the method assumes that all knowledge claims are situated in that they arise out of particular social and historical contexts, and therefore represent particular rather than universally applicable claims. This notion of "situatedness" is drawn from historian of science Donna Haraway's assertion that "situated knowledges" are more accurate than the "god-trick" of universal or objective claims that rest on the assumption that it is possible to "see everything from nowhere."[7] Contrary to popular opinion, the recognition that all knowledge claims are situated is not a manifestation of relativism, whereby all interpretations are considered equally valid. Rather, situated knowledges offer the firmest ground

[6] American Academy of Religion, *The American Academy of Religion Guidelines for Teaching about Religion in K-12 Public Schools in the United States*, 4, emphasis in original.

[7] Donna Haraway, "Situated Knowledges: The Science Question in Feminism and the Privilege of Partial Perspective," in *Simians, Cyborgs, and Women: The Reinvention of Nature* (New York: Routledge, 1991), 191.

upon which to make claims that are defined not by their detachment but rather by their specificity, transparency, and capacity for accountability.

Regarding the study of religion, this understanding of situatedness offers a tool to recognize that religious claims are no different than other forms of interpretation in that they arise out of particular contexts that represent particular assumptions as opposed to absolute, universal, and ahistorical truths. For example, claims such as "Islam is a religion of peace" and "Islam promotes terrorism" are equally problematic and need to be recognized as particular theological assertions as opposed to ultimate truths.

Third, this notion of situatedness applies to the texts and materials being investigated, the scholarly interpreters of those materials, and all inquirers regardless of station. The method recognizes that all forms of inquiry are interpretations filtered through particular lenses. By acknowledging this fact, an essential dimension of the inquiry itself is to identify those differing lenses and make transparent that which would otherwise be hidden.

Fourth, the method calls for an analysis of power and marginalization related to the subject at hand. Which perspectives are politically and socially prominent, and why? Which are marginalized or silenced, and why? Regarding religion, why are some theological interpretations more prominent than others in relationship to specific issues in particular social and historical contexts? For example, what are the factors that led to the Taliban's rise to power in Afghanistan in the 1990s and again in 2022, and why did their interpretation of the role of women in Islam, for example, gain social and political prominence over other competing claims within the tradition itself?

In another vein, what are the converging factors that lend social credibility and influence to some religious traditions over others; which dimensions of those traditions are interpreted as orthodox and which heretical; and by whom? What were the conditions that allowed Muslims, Christians, and Jews to live together in relative harmony in medieval Spain, and what are the religious influences that have contributed to shaping contemporary tensions in the Middle East and more globally regarding the "War on Terror," "Arab Spring," and "Muslim Ban"?

Fifth, this approach highlights what cultural anthropologists know well: that cultural norms are fluid and socially constructed even though they are often interpreted as representing uncontested absolute truths. This dynamic tension is powerfully demonstrated in social science theorist Johan Galtung's three-pronged typology of violence/peace. Galtung's framework provides an excellent foundation for discerning and representing the varied ideological influences of religions in human affairs.[8] What follows is an overview of his typology and

[8] Though his own representation of religion is problematic in that he falls victim to making universal claims about religion based on a specific interpretation of one tradition, the typology itself is extremely useful when a more sophisticated and complex understanding of religion is employed.

examples of how it can be useful for highlighting the significance of religious influences in human experiences across time and place.

Johan Galtung: Direct, Structural, and Cultural Forms of Violence and Peace

Often referred to as the "Father of Peace Studies," Norwegian theorist Johan Galtung has developed a three-pronged typology of violence that represents how a confluence of *malleable* factors merges in particular cultural and historical moments to shape the conditions for the promotion of violence (and, by inference, peace) to function as normative.[9]

- **Direct violence** represents behaviors that serve to threaten life itself and/or to diminish one's capacity to meet basic life needs. Examples include killing, maiming, bullying, sexual assault, and emotional manipulation. Direct violence is also represented when humans exploit other life forms for their own benefit.
- **Structural violence** represents the systematic ways in which some groups are hindered from equal access to opportunities, goods, and services that enable the fulfillment of basic life needs. These can be formal, as in legal structures that enforce marginalization (such as Apartheid in South Africa, gerrymandering in the United States, or the Nation State Law in Israel), or they could be culturally functional but without legal mandate (such as limited access to education or healthcare for marginalized groups). Structural violence is also present in the ways that humans have near-absolute legal and social power over all other life forms.
- **Cultural violence** represents the existence of prevailing or prominent social norms that make direct and structural violence seem natural, right, or acceptable. For example, the belief that Africans are primitive and intellectually inferior to Caucasians gave sanction to the African slave trade. Another example is the assumption that humans are superior to (and thus more valuable than) other life forms. Galtung's understanding of cultural violence helps explain how prominent beliefs can become so embedded in a given culture that they function as absolute and inevitable and are reproduced uncritically across generations.

9 Johan Galtung, "Cultural Violence," *Journal of Peace Research* 27, no. 3 (August 1990): 291–305.

These forms of violence are interrelated and mutually reinforcing. Galtung provides a representation of these intersecting forces in the following commentary on slavery:

> Africans are captured, forced across the Atlantic to work as slaves: millions are killed in the process—in Africa, on board, in the Americas. This massive direct violence over centuries seeps down and sediments as massive structural violence, with whites as the master topdogs and blacks as the slave underdogs, producing and reproducing massive cultural violence with racist ideas everywhere. After some time, direct violence is forgotten, slavery is forgotten, and only two labels show up, pale enough for college textbooks: "discrimination" for massive structural violence and "prejudice" for massive cultural violence. Sanitation of language: itself cultural violence.[10]

The corollary to the violence triangle outlined above is the peace triangle that RPL represents in the following ways:

- **Direct peace** represents behaviors that serve to preserve life itself and to promote human and planetary flourishing. Examples include active expressions of respect, kindness, compassion, empathy, healing, generosity, and humility.
- **Structural peace** represents the systematic ways in which all groups have equal access to opportunities, goods, and services that enable the fulfillment of basic life needs. These can be formal, as in legal structures that enforce equity (such as affirmative action programs or policies that protect non-human species), or they could be culturally functional but without legal mandate (such as equal access to quality education and healthcare, and communal/social supports for life choices based on interdependence).
- **Cultural peace** represents the existence of prevailing or prominent social norms that make direct and structural peace seem "natural," "right," or "good." Examples include recognition of our interdependence with one another and with all of creation, how "injustice anywhere is a threat to justice everywhere," and the importance of imagination, creativity, and critical thinking.

Galtung's typology provides a helpful vehicle to discern the complex roles that religions play in all three forms of violence as well as in their corresponding

[10] Galtung, "Cultural Violence," 295.

forms of peace. The formulations of cultural violence and cultural peace are especially helpful and relevant. *In all cultural contexts, diverse and often contradictory religious influences are always present.* Some will be explicit, but many will be implicit. Some religious influences will promote and/or represent socially normative beliefs, while others will promote and/or represent marginalized convictions.

For example, in Galtung's illustration cited above, religions functioned to both support and challenge the moral legitimacy of the transatlantic slave trade, and religions continue to function to support and to thwart structural and direct forms of contemporary racism. Similarly, religions currently function in particular ways to shape and support as well as to challenge prominent economic theories and their policy manifestations. In another example, normative cultural assumptions about gender roles and sexuality in particular social-historical contexts are shaped as well as contested by diverse religious voices and influences. Finally, diverse representations of religions have promoted as well as challenged assertions of human superiority in creation. One must simply look for these voices and influences—in any context and about any issue—to find the ways that religions are embedded in all aspects of human agency and experience. This framework can serve as a useful tool for analyzing the diverse and sometimes contradictory ways that religions function in all social contexts.

Summary

The following methodological and analytical assumptions about religion that RPL employs have been briefly outlined in this chapter:

1. There is a fundamental difference between the devotional expression of a religious worldview as normative and the study of religion that recognizes the factual existence of diverse devotional assertions.
2. Religions are internally diverse.
3. Religions evolve and change.
4. Religious influences are embedded in all aspects of human experience.
5. All knowledge claims (including religious ones) are socially constructed and represent particular "situated" perspectives.
6. There is nothing inevitable about either violence or peace; both are manifest in three intersecting formulations (direct, structural, and cultural), and both are shaped by conscious and unconscious human agency where religious influences are always operative.

Religion is a powerful force in human experience, but few citizens of the world understand the full range of that power due to a host of intersecting factors. Our work at RPL at Harvard Divinity School from 2020–2025 provided tools to understand that power through our version of religious literacy. Through these tools, our aim was to promote the public understanding of religion in service of a just world at peace.

2
Cross-Cultural Religious Literacy
A Methodology That Messages the Model

Chris Seiple

In life, there is always the "what," and then there is the "how." Today we live in a world where different beliefs, religious or otherwise, are everywhere, even as our global challenges demand new partnerships. This "what" is humanity's second greatest need.

Humanity's greatest need, however, is "how" we will build the partnerships necessary to meet this need. What is the framework, conceptual and operational, through which we engage each other's inherent dignity, across deep, even irreconcilable, difference, in a mutually respectful and meaningful manner, such that enduring solutions result that serve everyone?

Cross-Cultural Religious Literacy

Cross-cultural religious literacy (CCRL) is a leadership tool that provides a practical framework to understand oneself, one's neighbors, and the world as they are—in order to engage them effectively and efficiently but also, more importantly, promptly, elicitively, ethically, and empathetically, pursuant a pluralism that is not only principled and practical, but compassionate and covenantal.[1]

Diversity—the presence of difference—begs the twofold question of how it is engaged, and toward what end. If our global challenges, such as climate change, terrorism, and economic development, defy single-actor responses, can multi-partner responses model and message a mutually engaged pluralism? It would seem that such potential is in our self-interest, since we must address these challenges that will not go away on their own.

[1] For more on covenantal pluralism, please see W. Christopher Stewart, Chris Seiple, and Dennis R. Hoover, "Toward a Global Covenant of Peaceable Neighborhood: Introducing the Philosophy of Covenantal Pluralism," *The Review of Faith & International Affairs* 18, no. 4 (Winter 2018): 1–17, https://doi.org/10.1080/15570274.2020.1835029.

Chris Seiple, *Cross-Cultural Religious Literacy* In: *Modeling Religious Pluralism*. Edited by: Simran Jeet Singh, Oxford University Press. © Oxford University Press 2026. DOI: 10.1093/oso/9780197745809.003.0002

But, no matter our moral point of departure, it would also seem that the "how" of engagement, the process of partnership building, must also be about doing the right thing, the right way, at the right time. It has been my experience across beliefs and cultures that we not only have an obligation to engage across deep difference, but the responsibility to protect and respect it, according to the inherent dignity of every human being, even, and especially, when we disagree with others' beliefs.

And so, we come back to the most basic questions of our times: What is (y) our practical philosophy of partnering with the other? What are the ends we seek—for (y)ourself, (y)our family, (y)our community, (y)our country, and so on—and do (y)our means for getting there message the model of pluralism we want to build?

Such engagement requires preparation. We have a responsibility—to our moral beliefs, to our job, to our country, and to our world—to be prepared. We have to think about how we will engage according to our competencies (personal, comparative, and collaborative); and we have a responsibility to think through the application of our skills in that specific situation as we evaluate the context to include the people, the players, and how we might negotiate and communicate with them.

This process is also known as CCRL—a means toward the ends of covenantal pluralism. CCRL provides a conceptual and operational framework for working with the other in order to address and even solve our common global challenges. CCRL is also a framework that expects and encourages the inclusion of religion as an analytic factor. It calls on us to see religion as a force for good, through faith communities that collectively and individually live and work in every sector of society and the state. Such people of faith will never agree on theology, but they do agree that their values should inform their engagement, just as non-religious people naturally feel that their values should inform their engagement.

So, what does this process of partnership look like? How can we each cross over to—that is, move toward—the other without sacrificing the substance of our own beliefs, or theirs? CCRL is a leadership tool that provides a framework for this discussion, pursuant practical impact.

CCRL anchors in a simple reality: There is you, the other, and what you do together.

The Parameters

Before continuing, however, it is important to say what CCRL is *not*. It is not syncretism. CCRL asks that its participants seek to discern their differences in order to dignify, not demean, the other. Participants in CCRL believe that each human has dignity, even as each human has the capacity and right to disagree with their neighbor's beliefs and behavior.

CCRL is not secularism. For example, for many of my Muslim friends worldwide, secularism means "godless." And most Muslims that I know find it impossible to conceive of a public sphere without God. As a Christian, I feel the same way.

It is also important to say that CCRL is not fluency; nor is it illiteracy. Rather, CCRL is more like humility in action. It is knowing just enough to get the questions right about the other. CCRL respects the inherent dignity and freedom of conscience of each human being, while seeking to better understand why others believe and behave as they do.

In other words, CCRL is about possessing the humility to listen, observe, verify, and then engage, that is, to L.O.V.E., a fellow citizen, a neighbor, for the sake of everyone. In my experience, it is best to listen and observe with your heart, verify with your head, and engage with your hands.

The Competencies

CCRL has three competencies: personal, comparative, and collaborative. These competencies help one to think about the process of engagement, which entails the process of understanding yourself, the other as they understand themselves, and the context in which you might practically partner.

Because we are all humans, we all have stereotypes. Stereotypes are more likely when we rely only on what we've been told about the (religious) other, instead of seeking to understand them as they understand themselves.

Personal competency is understanding oneself, to include the values that guide your engagement of others who do not believe as you do. This process can involve much wrestling, and it is informed and formed by the comparative and collaborative competencies discussed below. If we want to practice that first part of wisdom—naming something properly—we must self-examine our own tools of analysis and understanding. Doing so will help us develop enduring relationships and practical partnership.

For example, in my own case, I had to wrestle with how key areas of my own personal and professional life were transforming from ideology (what I had been told) to identity (what I had reasoned through, in part, due to my own thinking and experience), and how international relations was moving from theory to reality, belief from religion to faith, human rights from tolerance to respect, and American policy from defense to security.[2]

[2] Please see Chris Seiple, "From Ideology to Identity: Building Communities of the Willing," in *Religion, Identity and Global Governance: Ideas, Evidence and Practice*, ed. Patrick James (Toronto: University of Toronto Press, 2010), 292–310.

Comparative competency actively seeks to understand others as they understand themselves, to include the values that guide their engagement with you. I remember traveling to Indonesia in January 2017 and meeting with Dr. Ahmad Syaffii Maarif. It was clear that I had much to learn from him. He gave me his book, which I quote:

> [B]eing religious in a civilized way is the same as being religious in an honest, sincere, and generous way. By "generous" I mean that the principle of pluralism is important; it shows in our willingness to recognize the rights of others to hold that the greatest truth resides in their respective religions, even if we do not agree with them. At the same time, other people must respect the position of Muslims who say that Islam is the truest religion.
>
> The expression "truest" must be understood in the light of the distinct beliefs of each adherent. It is uncivilized and it disturbs the peace to say, "Our religion is the truest and your religion is packed with myths and confused beliefs."[3]

Dr. Maarif captures a fundamental truth: We must respect the right of others to hold that the greatest truth resides in their belief system, even if we disagree with them. How we hold these irreconcilable opinions, however, is essential to social cohesion and stability.

In other words, disrespecting the dignity of the other not only goes against one's beliefs, but it is bad for one's country. When we needlessly insult another's faith, we speak against our own faith because we are demeaning the dignity of someone else—someone who has just as much claim on a (different) conclusion, about anything, really, as we do.

Collaborative competency is understanding the context of potential collaboration among actors of different beliefs. Two questions define this competency. Do I have the will and skill to move toward the other in order to build partnerships that serve all of society? And, do I understand the spiritual, secular, ethnic, and organizational cultures of the partners involved, to include the power dynamic between an ethnic and/or religious majority and ethnic and/or religious non-majorities?

In May 2007, I worked with the chief minister of Pakistan's Northwest Frontier Province to hold a conference on Christian-Muslim relations. To my surprise, the chief minister invited not just Muslims and Christians to his home the night before the gathering, but also the Hindu and Sikh leaders from his community. After the conference, the Hindu and Sikh leaders shared with me that it was the

[3] Ahmad Syaffii Maarif, *Islam Humanity and the Indonesian Identity* (Leiden: Leiden University Press, 2018), 33.

first time that they had been able to share publicly how the values of their faith served all Pakistanis, no matter their beliefs or politics.

At that moment I understood the collaboration process as a model for the ends we seek, that is, a covenanted pluralism engaged across the dignity of deep difference. There had to be a table that fostered a partnered and practical pluralism.

This table could be hosted by anyone. If it is the government, then it should ensure that everyone gets a seat in the name of good governance. If it is a nongovernmental or faith actor, it should do the same, but it should freely share, like those Hindu and Sikh leaders above, what motivated them to host and/or participate in the pluralism table. In setting this example, the chief minister—as a Pashtun-Sunni majority member of his society and government—gave me the great gifts of example and challenge.

Would I do the same in my country and culture, where I am a member of the ethno-religious majority as a Christian of Caucasian descent and a Protestant? Didn't I have a responsibility to make sure that the non-majority has a seat at the table, and to work toward not only engaging them but respecting and protecting them—as a function of my own faith, particularly when I have irreconcilable differences with theirs?

I have always worked closely with my Muslim friends, Sunni and Shia and Sufi. Through these relationships I have a friend from Texas by the name of Rashad Hussain. President Biden nominated him to be the sixth (and first Muslim) US Ambassador-at-Large for International Religious Freedom. He is eminently qualified. He is the former US special envoy to the Organization of Islamic Cooperation. He has worked in counterterrorism and served on the National Security Council. But there are still stereotypes about Muslims in America, and his Senate confirmation was not necessarily a foregone conclusion.

So a Texas pastor and I wrote an op-ed published in Dallas affirming and asking the US Senate to unanimously approve our friend Rashad Hussain as ambassador.[4] In January 2022, Rashad was confirmed by the US Senate as America's Ambassador-at-Large for International Religious Freedom. The majority has a responsibility to support the non-majority as a function of one's faith (the right thing to do), and as a function of working with others on our common challenges.

These three competencies—personal, comparative, and collaborative—provide a framework for how to think through how *you* live out and apply *your* faith in the context of your neighbors' beliefs, religious or otherwise.

[4] Please see Bob Roberts and Chris Seiple, "U.S. Senate Should Quickly Affirm Texan Rashad Hussain as Religious Freedom Ambassador," *Dallas Morning News*, October 21, 2021, https://www.dallasnews.com/opinion/commentary/2021/10/21/the-us-senate-should-quickly-affirm-texan-rashad-hussain-as-religious-freedom-ambassador/ (accessed December 16, 2025).

The Skills

Three skills—applied internally and externally—help implement this framework: evaluation, negotiation, and communication.

Evaluation is a process that takes specific account of self, as well as the other, according to the context in which the relevant parties are seeking to implement their shared goals. I have found that the simultaneous evaluation of internal and external contexts is good for both.

I once met the head of the largest madrassah in Peshawar, Pakistan. He did not like America. But he met with me because we had a common friend (the chief minister mentioned above). We had a conversation that was as candid as it was courteous. He said something to me that I will never forget: "You Americans want respect; we want tenderness." I still think about that. But it was the kind of comment that forced me to evaluate how he had come to that conclusion, which, in turn, made me evaluate myself and my country.

Evaluation is constant.

Negotiation involves mutual listening and understanding, which, in turn, lead to sustainable action through shared goals that often begin with self-interest. It too takes place internally and externally. One time there was an incident in northwest Vietnam, where a local villager had converted to Christianity and had been persecuted as a result. It was receiving much attention in Washington, DC, and, because of the trust that I had with the Vietnamese government, I suggested to them that I should go to the village.

They said, "We can't do that. That's a very sensitive area regarding ethnoreligious minorities, and it's right on the Chinese border." So, we began to negotiate. I told them that I did not pick the place, but rather the place had picked me. I asked, "Do you want to look bad over this incident? You need somebody that Americans in the US Congress trust to visit and see for themselves to verify. The Congress is not going to trust you." The government allowed me to visit.

But one negotiation always leads to another. Once I got there, I had to negotiate with the village elders, looking and listening (evaluating) as I did. Here's what I found: Of course, the person who converted had a right to do so, but he had done so in a manner disrespectful to the village culture and the ancestors they worshiped. The "how" was more important than the "what."

I told this story honestly, such that all parties felt that their side of the incident was told fairly. It was only possible because we were able to negotiate with each other, deciding that everyone could win if an independent observer told the story.

Experiences like this one can't help but make you look inside yourself, asking, "What do I believe? What would I have done? Should I change anything about myself as a result of these negotiations?" In other words, as you engage, you learn more about, negotiate, and refine your own identity.

Negotiations never stop.

Communication is likewise an internal and external process that is verbal and, especially, non-verbal.

One time I was asked to speak in a madrassah. I had no idea what to say. So I prayed. I asked God for guidance, and I felt Him whisper, "Psalm 11:7," from the Zabur, the psalms of King Daoud, King David. It says, "For the Lord is righteous. He loves justice. The upright will seek His face." So I spoke about what that verse meant to me. Did I water down the differences between our faiths? No. But I spoke about a common value that we both had, justice.

Another time, in America, we had a conference panel with Christians and Muslims on it, talking about examples like these. During the Q&A, a Christian man came to the microphone, weeping. He confessed his hatred of Muslims since September 11. The remarkable thing is that we had not discussed the terrorist attacks on 9/11. The non-verbal communication—the visible, on-stage respect among fellow Americans, as Christians and Muslims—convinced this person that his stereotypes were not accurate.

You are always communicating, sometimes with words.

Conclusion

In conclusion, how do we best enable this kind of engagement as progress past polarization, particularly in my own country, the United States of America? I guess the answer begins with how we understand the phrase *e pluribus unum*—out of many, one. What does it mean to be "one"?

One cannot mean dumping everyone into a great "melting pot" so that all the identities get blended and, de facto, reflect the majority culture. Nor can one mean that one identity gets to become an ideology—political or theological—imposing its will on the rest.

Instead, I think we have a choice. From the personal perspective, we have a choice to tolerate or celebrate the other. No one wants to be tolerated. But we can celebrate the inherent dignity of the other because we know them, because we are in relationship with them. We can do this with all people, even when we do not agree with their beliefs.

There is a similar choice from the policy perspective: Will we seek to assimilate or integrate the other? A melting pot yields assimilation. Integration instead invites the best of one's identity to contribute to the oneness of a shared neighborliness. Integration builds a table of principled, practical, and partnered pluralism, a pluralism that is covenanted—a pledge and an obligation to respect and protect the other.

Cross-cultural religious literacy is a means to celebrate and integrate the other, yielding a covenantal pluralism that seeks the best for everyone.

3

The Benefit of Illiteracy

Navigating Privilege, Fostering Religious Literacy, and Creating Equity

Ilyse R. Morgenstein Fuerst

Let's start with the controversy: We must talk about religious literacy because the religious *illiteracy* of dominant majorities necessitates it. Religious illiteracy is not merely a problem of individuals not knowing about other people's religious, cultural, or spiritual histories, practices, or norms. Rather, religious illiteracy is a systemic problem that dismisses, renders invisible, or misunderstands—sometimes willfully—minoritized religions. Practically, in North America and Europe, that translates to "the holiday season" being equated to Christmas; lawsuits required for prisoners to access meals without pork; or parents calling their children out of school, after calling themselves out of work, for holidays like Holi, Eids, Vaisakhi, and Yom Kippur. This chapter addresses the unmarked privilege of religious illiteracy and calls for ways to foster both religious literacy and, more importantly, religious equity.

To be blunt, when a conversation about religious literacy takes place in the "West," we are necessarily talking about and within systems of Christian domination and white supremacy. While it may seem historic or far-fetched to say that imperial and colonial history still impacts religious literacy in the West, the fact is Christian colonizers are part of why religions have been racialized and minoritized—which is to say, why some religions are valued above others. Living in Christian-dominant North America and Europe creates a reality in which minoritized religious people experience hate, regularly, in societies that are explicitly and implicitly structured around Christianity.[1] We have to advocate for religious literacy because of a system of power that privileges Christianity above all else, that devalues accurate and readily available information about

[1] Cf. Talal Asad, *Formations of the Secular: Christianity, Islam, Modernity* (Stanford, CA: Stanford University Press, 2003); Naber Nadine, "'Look, Mohammed the Terrorist Is Coming!' Cultural Racism, Nation-based Racism, and Intersectionality of Oppressions after 9/11," in *Race and Arab Americans Before and After 9/11: From Visible Citizens to Visible Subjects*, eds., Amaney Jamal and Nadine Naber (Syracuse: Syracuse University Press, 2008), 276–304; and Deepa Kumar, *Islamophobia and the Politics of Empire* (New York: Haymarket Books, 2012).

Ilyse R. Morgenstein Fuerst, *The Benefit of Illiteracy* In: *Modeling Religious Pluralism*.
Edited by: Simran Jeet Singh, Oxford University Press. © Oxford University Press 2026.
DOI: 10.1093/oso/9780197745809.003.0003

non-Christian religions, and that structures everything—law, healthcare, education, even calendars—around Christian norms.

Religious literacy, in these contexts, is actually a strategy for safety, for survival, to become legible in a system that would prefer minoritized religions be or remain unreadable, invisible. Religious literacy is often required for members of minoritized religions but seen as a soft or unnecessary or "bonus" skill for members of the majority. Religious illiteracy, on the other hand, is normative for the normative group only: It is, without question, a privilege.

Literacy, Illiteracy, and Privilege

In the United States and Europe, the history of Christian domination and supremacy allows for a lack of knowledge, understanding, accommodation, and acceptance of non-Christian groups. This is not just about the histories of these regions and individual nation-states—though, sadly, we could, without any effort at all, list the abysmal records of antisemitism, Islamophobia, the persecution of Native religions, the legal limits placed on various religious minorities, and more. Religious illiteracy is more than outward forms of oppression, suppression, hate, genocide, and legal frameworks that render some less able to practice their religions than others. Religious illiteracy is also a lack of basic knowledge; the tacit way we accept the Easter Bunny as a universal everyone *should* know but treat Lunar New Year as a special, private, exotic holiday; the reality in which secular corporations and secular governments close for Christmas but Muslims take personal vacation days to mark Eid; the US Supreme Court ruling that a coach's right to pray during a football game on the field supersedes a child athlete's right to not listen to, participate in, or be subjected to that prayer (*Kennedy* v. *Bremerton* [2022]).[2] Religious illiteracy allows for microaggressions—microtransgressions—against anyone who finds themselves outside the pale of Christianity.

That does not mean those who identify as any denomination of Christian or find themselves culturally Christian are always actively doing harm or purposefully perpetuating Christian domination. Rather, while religious illiteracy implicates individuals, it also includes those *systems* that take Christian norms for granted and, importantly, do not or—by virtue of illiteracy—cannot imagine that those norms are, in fact, Christian. The calendar is my favorite example here. We accept that the year is 2026, we treat the idea that weekends are Saturday and Sunday as natural, and we do not question why Christmas and Easter appear

[2] *Kennedy* v. *Bremerton School District*, 597 U.S. 507 (2022), https://www.supremecourt.gov/opinions/21pdf/21-418_i425.pdf (accessed December 16, 2025).

on bank holiday schedules and often not the interfaith calendar. How that happened—how the world decided to agree on *time* despite there (still) being dozens of time systems—is too long a history for this chapter, of course; the short story is about Christian imperialism and how it made sure the sites of global military, economic, and social power were in Christian-majority places. The takeaway is this: We think of our calendars—if we think about them at all—as inherently neutral, when in reality, the year we are in (right now: 2026) is a numerical representation of how long it's been since Jesus was born. That is anything but secular, it is anything but universal, and to not know that is to be illiterate about the presence of religion (specifically Christianity) in our day-to-day lives.

Illiteracy is a privilege because it allows power to go unmarked, uncontested, and unexamined, as it does with calendars. Even religious literacy, as a discursive concept, often maintains Christian-centric framing: Religious literacy has been framed in public discourse as just another intellectual pursuit, knowledge for the sake of knowledge. It has also been framed as a neutral: Muslims benefit from learning about Hindus; Hindus benefit from learning about Jews; Rastafarians benefit from learning about Jains. These are true statements, of course! We all benefit from more knowledge! But thinking about religious literacy as a generic and blanket set of issues that works the same for everyone ignores *power*.

To be clear, many groups advocating for religious literacy—whether that's lobbying governments, holding public fora, petitioning school boards, educating medical students, or training social workers—hold less access to normative society. This is because religious literacy is often driven by necessity. Religious literacy is often framed by minoritized and racialized religious groups as a survival strategy—that is to say, folks like Jews, Muslims, Sikhs, Hindus, Buddhists, Native, or African Diasporic practitioners have learned, often through forced assimilation, lacking protection for their religious practices, or outward violence, that knowing about others' religions, especially the dominant religion, is a necessary requirement to live safely. Beyond these vested groups, religious studies scholars advocating for religious literacy do so, often, in service of the public or, pragmatically, with an eye to programmatic survival as cuts to the humanities proliferate.[3]

[3] Jagbir Jhutti-Johal and Hardeep Singh, *Racialization, Islamophobia and Mistaken Identity: The Sikh Experience* (London: Taylor & Francis, 2019); Simran Jeet Singh, "Why Universities and the Rest of Us Need Religious Studies," *Religion News*, December 4, 2020, https://religionnews.com/2020/12/04/why-universities-and-the-rest-of-us-need-religion-studies/ (accessed December 16, 2025); Brie Loskota, "Understanding Religious Literacy Content Creators and Providers in Education, Journalism and New Media: A Report for the Arthur Vining Davis Foundations," the Arthur Vining Davis Foundations, Aspen Institute Inclusive America Project, and USC Center for Religion and Civic Culture, 2021, https://www.aspeninstitute.org/wp-content/uploads/2021/08/Understanding-Religious-Literacy-FINAL.pdf (accessed March 3, 2022); and Ilyse R. Morgenstein Fuerst, "Survivals: The Stakes of Religious Literacy," *Method & Theory in the Study of Religion* 34, no. 5 (2022): 435–445, https://doi.org/10.1163/15700682-bja10078.

The framing of religious literacy as just knowledge or as a neutral set of information to which everyone has equal access is dangerous, precisely because it renders such literacy as an *extra*, a luxury good, a specific skill for a specific profession, or something to learn about when one is done learning about "relevant" and "important" matters. Religious *illiteracy*, here, is not seen as a contributing factor to religious hostility or intolerance, but rather just a bug of growing up differently than others—something we all experience, regardless of background. The thing is, however, that even if we could all learn more about someone else's religion, the *what* we learn and *about whom* have radically different outcomes for different groups. Religious illiteracy is a privilege in a country that shouts, often literally, "Jesus saves!" or quotes the (Christian) Bible in response to conversations about healthcare. Imagine not knowing who Jesus was, or what that shout meant? Seems impossible, right? And yet when I teach college-level classes on Islam, there are always students who do not know what "Allah" means or who Muhammad is and was. What makes Jesus different?

Spoilers: It's Christian supremacy and domination. One cannot *not* know. One cannot be *that* religiously illiterate, regardless of one's religious background, within Euro-American contexts. That literacy is rarely reciprocated—and that's why illiteracy is a privilege.

It is also a privilege because illiteracy is a luxury good, one that non-Christians truly cannot afford. My Jewish children may have a coach who wants to exercise his right to thank Jesus for the football game, which is his right, according to the Supreme Court (*Kennedy* v. *Bremerton*).[4] It is my job, as a Jewish parent, to both make them aware—as my parents did for me—that the world is not Jewish (i.e., we do not expect our cultural and religious norms to be available, honored, or valued at all times or in all places), as well as prepare them for how to respond to (never-consensual) religious missionizing. Because, given the ruling, my Jewish children can and should expect this disregard, with the full force of the highest court in the nation, even if that seems to this humble author to violate my children's right to freedom *from* religion.

I've chosen a low-stakes example—prayer at a children's sports game—for this little thought exercise on purpose. Even this low-stakes scenario has *real* stakes, especially for people of minoritized religious backgrounds. Children feeling uncomfortable on their own team because of their religion is not *physically* going to harm anyone. Does it contribute to feeling othered, maybe even unwelcomed? Yes, of course, but harm? That's harder to quantify here. But what if *not* participating in that prayer leads to a coach's distaste for that player, fellow players snubbing or teasing them, or less playing time in the future for not conforming? These are, again, relatively low-stakes outcomes. But these low-stakes examples

[4] *Kennedy* v. *Bremerton* (2022).

exist in the real world, where Jewish, Muslim, Sikh, Buddhist, Hindu, Indigenous, pagan, and so many more people have, for centuries, had to navigate legal, physical, sociocultural barriers that have included murder, imprisonment, the removal of children from homes, and placements into Christianizing schools. All of this is to make this important point: Lower-stakes examples of religious intolerance foster and reinforce systems of religious illiteracy. Prayer at a football game without considering its impacts is a form of illiteracy; it demonstrates that one does not know or does not care about the history of oppression religious minorities have experienced, the ways in which that prayer might infringe upon *their* freedoms from religious obligation, the experience of power differentials, and the contexts of forced Christianity that many people from colonized nations experienced. To not know or consider all that? What a luxury.

Combating religious illiteracy—which is to say, fostering religious literacy—has been a strategy for survival for members of minoritized religions, especially in the United States, for decades. Jews, Muslims, Sikhs, Hindus, and other minoritized religious groups have been arguing for religious literacy both for safety purposes and for the ability to live religiously and publicly; this is about their survival. Many religiously affiliated social justice organizations either formed to make themselves legible or in response to enduring hate crimes—that is, as direct responses to what was perceived as ignorance directed toward them. All of the following organizations stress education as a major combative strategy against hate for their specific communities and "all Americans," phrasing that is found on each of their public sites. The Anti-Defamation League (ADL) was founded in 1913 to combat antisemitism and still touts its rootedness in "Jewish values."[5] The Council on American-Islamic Relations (CAIR) expressly seeks to counter Islamophobia, with media, legal, and policy-making branches within its large structure.[6] The Sikh Coalition was founded immediately after 9/11 and in light of growing Islamophobia that targeted Sikh men, in particular, for their turbans. The Sikh Coalition has also been active in religious literacy in schools that center student safety.[7] The Hindu American Foundation (HAF) launched a campaign titled "Fight Hate: Educate" with the express goal of combating rising hate crimes against Hindus and promoting a "deeper understanding and broader awareness of Hinduism."[8]

[5] Anti-Defamation League, "Who We Are," https://www.adl.org/who-we-are (accessed June 28, 2025).

[6] Council on American-Islamic Relations, "CAIR at a Glance," https://www.cair.com/about_cair/cair-at-a-glance (accessed June 28, 2025).

[7] Sikh Coalition, "Creating Safe Schools—Sikh Coalition," April 21, 2023, https://www.sikhcoalition.org/our-work/creating-safe-schools/ (accessed December 15, 2025).

[8] Hindu American Foundation, "Hindu American Foundation Launches 'Fight Hate. Educate.' Campaign," https://www.hinduamerican.org/press/hindu-american-foundation-fight-hate-educate-campaign (accessed June 28, 2025).

Again, these are merely representative and well-known examples; they do not scratch the surface of other supporting examples. Even though these organizations' politics vary widely, the shared commonality is the focus on religious literacy as an explicit strategy to mitigate physical, legal, and social harm. In other words, these organizations view religious literacy as a way to combat religious intolerance and hostility—which stems, in this logic, from religious illiteracy.

While many white Christians can live safely in a bubble of religious illiteracy, their non-Christian and often non-white counterparts are not only learning how to educate everyone else about themselves, but also continuing to learn and teach their communities how to survive in a space that is sometimes dismissive and often hostile to their very existence. Illiteracy, here, is a privilege of your coach's prayers matching your own, of collective and individual mental load, of your foods always being available, of your holidays not requiring explanation and explication, and of your religious heroes and figures being known and understood and respected.

Beyond Literacy: Aiming for Religious Equity

While greater literacy does not inherently mean progress—governments have used and continue to use knowledge about "the Other" as a means through which to oppress, conquer, and dominate—illiteracy is not an option, either. We cannot have religious equity—where all religious beliefs, practices, customs, and priorities (or lack thereof) have equal legal footing and exist in spaces of mutual respect—without religious literacy. We simply cannot achieve equity if Sikhs and Muslims are being asked to remove their head coverings or if taking a sick day is the only means through which a Jewish person can observe Yom Kippur or if traditional, religiously sanctioned hairstyles for Black people can cause someone to be fired.[9] Religious literacy that expressly engages *illiteracy* as an ill to be remedied comes from public scholars attempting to change their publics and, most often, from community organizers. Religious literacy that takes seriously illiteracy does so, perhaps, out of a sense of social justice. And that is a wonderful and necessary step. But it is just a first step. The goal must be religious *equity*, rather than just literacy, in the same way that I would hope that we aim for *acceptance* of religio-racial, linguistic, ethnic difference rather than tolerance.

[9] *Equal Employment Opportunity Commission* v. *Catastrophe Management Solutions*, No. 14-13482, 852 F.3d 1018 (11th Cir. 2016); and Umer Hussain and George B. Cunningham, "Why Muslim Women Choose to Wear Headscarves while Participating in Sports," *The Conversation*, February 23, 2022, https://theconversation.com/why-muslim-women-choose-to-wear-headscarves-while-participating-in-sports-176441 (accessed March 10, 2023).

Religious equity, in a system that is white Christian supremacist by design, is no small feat. Lofty goal or not, there are ways that we can imagine remedying religious illiteracy via religious literacy and moving toward religious equity. As I said above, my go-to example of religious illiteracy hiding in plain sight is our uncontested calendar. Would religious equity in the workplace look like floating days off for religious observance? I can imagine a world where Christmas is not a given day off, where Christians had to choose to spend their religious observance day there—and Jews, Sikhs, Hindus, Muslims, and atheists could choose to take that day off, too, or spend it on days that better suit them. (Yes, even atheists: Because they, too, can have access to the same days off without having to prove their belief or lack thereof.)

Would religious equity in schools look like even less Christian dominance—and, sorry fellow parents, that does indeed mean zero Santa and "Jingle Bells" at public school—and better, more inclusive education about religious systems, religious people, and the ways religion shows up in history? That's a future I can get behind. It might even be naming the religion as we already teach it: What's at stake in *not* naming the founding fathers of the United States as Christians? What's at stake in *ignoring* that we have never had a non-Christian president? That, of course, is about unmarked privilege, including religious illiteracy, but it is also an opportunity to think about literacy and equity.

As it stands, the conversations about religious literacy ignore the problems of illiteracy, the systems that allow such illiteracy, and the steps needed to really move toward equity. Starting somewhere is important, and it will take scholars, educators, activists, community members, politicians, law, and institutional gumption to get there.

PART II
RELIGIOUS FREEDOM

When I was younger, my parents typically described their motivations for immigrating to the United States in terms of educational and economic opportunities. Their story reflected the script of the "American Dream," a young couple seeking a better life for their family. As we grew older, we learned that their decision wasn't just a reflection on the promise of a new home; it was about seeking religious freedom, too.

My parents grew up as Sikhs, a minority religious community in India, and they were starting to notice signs of religious persecution there—stripping of civil liberties, demeaning and divisive narratives, accusations of separatism. My parents left India before the conditions worsened, narrowly escaping a decade of genocidal violence in Punjab.[1]

I learned this story as a teenager, and back then, I assumed it was unique. *How many other people could have such a harrowing experience?* Now, I realize that this is a shared story for so many of us; that religious persecution is a norm, not an exception; and that the dream of religious freedom remains a distant aspiration.

In 2021, the Pew Research Center reported that government restrictions on religion worldwide reached their highest levels since the center began tracking such issues nearly fifteen years prior. The report also announced that religious harassment had increased as well: "In 2021, religious groups faced harassment from governments or social groups and individuals in 190 out of the 198 countries and territories in our study. This was an increase from 2020 but the same number of countries as in 2019, marking a return to the peak level since this tracking began in 2007."[2]

[1] For more on this subject, see Human Rights Watch (Asia), "Dead Silence: The Legacy of Human Rights Abuses in Punjab," Physicians for Human Rights, May 1, 1994, https://www.hrw.org/report/1994/05/01/dead-silence-legacy-abuses-punjab (accessed December 17, 2025); and Ensaaf and Benetech Human Rights Data Analysis Group, *Violent Deaths and Enforced Disappearances during the Counterinsurgency in Punjab, India: A Preliminary Quantitative Analysis*, 2009, https://hrdag.org/indiafaqs/ (accessed December 17, 2025).

[2] Pew Research Center, "Globally, Government Restrictions on Religion Reached Peak Levels in 2021, while Social Hostilities Went Down," March 5, 2024, https://www.pewresearch.org/religion/2024/03/05/globally-government-restrictions-on-religion-reached-peak-levels-in-2021-while-social-hostilities-went-down/ (accessed December 17, 2025).

In 2022, the Pew Research Center confirmed that government restrictions on religion remained at peak levels from the previous year. Pew also noted a correlation between government restrictions and social hostilities.[3]

The on-the-ground realities of religious persecution conflict with a common and pervasive myth about modernity: that as time moves forward, our civilizations progress, and we become increasingly capable of navigating human diversity. Perhaps the arc of the moral universe bends toward justice, but it's certainly not as linear as we make it out to be.

While religious freedom is a principle that many democratic societies agree upon, the mechanics that determine who enjoys religious freedom, in what ways, and to what extent are rife with controversy. Do my religious views enable me to discriminate against you because of your sexual orientation? Should we use our cultural norms of monogamy to criminalize polygamy, even if a religious tradition espouses it? Can politicians give preferential treatment to a majority religious community in order to secure their support?

These are tough, contentious, consequential questions. And the answers are even tougher if we are committed to hearing different perspectives and building a religiously pluralistic society. This is why I'm so grateful to our contributors to this section, three people with experience and expertise on the question of religious freedom and belief.

The author of our first chapter, Knox Thames, has devoted his career to this issue. He has served in multiple presidential administrations, including on the US Commission for International Religious Freedom. Knox's chapter lays out some of the basic considerations in the field, including the global challenges and global standards, and he also guides us to where we might go from here.

Keisha McKenzie draws on Adventist history and advocacy to explore ways in which we might approach religious freedom as a "shield, not a sword." Dr. McKenzie attends to the question of how we ensure that no religion is favored over another, and offers a set of principles that we can apply to ensure that religious liberty is equally available to all.

Asma T. Uddin, a scholar of religious freedom, considers the factors that contribute to social polarization, explores how these factors play into perceptions in and across Muslim-American and conservative white evangelical Christian communities, and offers ideas for how we can build social cohesion.

These chapters bring to the table different perspectives, experiences, and approaches for building religious freedom. What they hold in common is a shared, pluralistic aspiration: moving from where our world is currently to one where all people have an opportunity to live freely, irrespective of what religion they follow or don't follow, and regardless of what they believe or don't believe.

[3] Pew Research Center, "Government Restrictions on Religion Stayed at Peak Levels Globally in 2022," December 18, 2024, https://www.pewresearch.org/religion/2024/12/18/government-restrictions-on-religion-stayed-at-peak-levels-globally-in-2022/ (accessed December 17, 2025).

4

Learning to Live with Global Neighbors

Knox Thames

How can we live together in diversity? Everyone is everywhere. Faiths and peoples are intermixing as never before in human history. In the past, such proximity and religious intolerance brought discrimination, violence, and even mass atrocities. Wars of religion victimized millions when irreconcilable beliefs clashed with claims of authority and power. These old hatreds are nothing new and continue to vex humanity today. Avoiding such tragedies will take intentional work, focusing on building bridges, and respecting the rights of others to hold differing beliefs. In this effort, religious freedom has much to offer if holistically and inclusively applied. Otherwise, it will become another sword in cultural wars.

To chart a path forward, this chapter will discuss current standards on international religious freedom and their purpose, potential, and limitations. It will argue for the importance of protecting international standards while exploring new culturally sensitive avenues to promote the right of individuals to peacefully practice the belief of their choice. Finally, recognizing how twenty-first-century challenges will require new approaches, the chapter will highlight innovative ways to promote diversity, pluralism, and the rights of others.

Global Challenge

Grim headlines constantly remind us about the severe limitations experienced by faithful individuals and religious actors. Humanity's old urges to act against the religious "other" still haunt the globe. Every community is negatively impacted somewhere, either by governments, extremists, terrorists, or all of the above. But despite the potential for severe and painful consequences, billions of individuals continue to search for the divine, desiring to explore life's meaning through faith and belief. As Pope John Paul II wrote in 1979, "[T]hough the routes taken may be different, there is but a single goal to which is directed the deepest aspiration of the human spirit as expressed in its quest for God and also

Knox Thames, *Learning to Live with Global Neighbors* In: *Modeling Religious Pluralism*.
Edited by: Simran Jeet Singh, Oxford University Press. © Oxford University Press 2026.
DOI: 10.1093/oso/9780197745809.003.0004

in its quest . . . for the full meaning of human life."[1] Consequently, the salience of religion is evident in almost every society.

We know this empirically in part thanks to the Pew Research Center, which, beginning in the 2000s, has helped quantify a problem many have observed anecdotally or felt personally when experiencing persecution firsthand. Year after year, Pew's research has found troubling levels of restrictions by government or societal actors, and sometimes both. According to their research, approximately two out of every three people globally live in restrictive environments.[2] While this does not mean everyone faces persecution in these countries, Pew's findings demonstrate how millions live in restrictive environments limiting free inquiry and theological innovation.

One reason limitations have increased is that billions of individuals worldwide hold deep affiliations to belief systems or religious creeds. For example, Pew researchers have documented how approximately 80 percent of the global population believes in God or a higher power that gives meaning and direction to their lives.[3] The remaining percentages also represent individuals with sincerely held belief systems, such as atheism and agnosticism, or new beliefs not fitting into larger molds. While differences often characterize opposing faiths, at their core, they demonstrate a shared human drive to appreciate the divine and to strive for the sacred, albeit defined differently. Religious and belief systems frame many of life's greatest moments. Births and deaths. Weddings and funerals. Games and wars. Hopes and fears. Successes and failures. Belief systems help consecrate, explain, or console.

Faith and belief drive the decisions of women and men around the globe, regardless of society. Philanthropist and philosopher Sir John Templeton understood the importance of freedom of conscience and promoted the discovery of "new spiritual information." In his book *The Essential Worldwide Laws of Life*, Templeton spoke of "universal truths of life that transcend modern times or particular cultures" that "help people in all parts of the world to make their lives not only happier but more useful."[4] Billions still agree.

History teaches and everyday life demonstrates how religion and belief motivate individuals to undertake acts of charity and kindness. Faith actors help

[1] John Paul II, "Encyclical Letter: Redemptor Hominis," March 4, 1979, https://www.vatican.va/content/john-paul-ii/en/encyclicals/documents/hf_jp-ii_enc_04031979_redemptor-hominis.html (accessed December 17, 2025).

[2] Pew Research Center, "Globally, Social Hostilities Related to Religion Decline in 2019," September 30, 2021, https://www.pewresearch.org/religion/2021/09/30/globally-social-hostilities-related-to-religion-decline-in-2019-while-government-restrictions-remain-at-highest-levels/ (accessed December 17, 2025).

[3] Pew Research Center, "The Global Religious Landscape," December 18, 2012, https://www.pewresearch.org/religion/2012/12/18/global-religious-landscape-exec/ (accessed December 17, 2025).

[4] John Templeton, "Introduction," in *The Essential Worldwide Laws of Life* (West Conshohocken, PA: Templeton Press, 2012), xv–xvi.

societies flourish by promoting peace, tolerance, and justice; assisting the poor and sick; and serving as a moral compass outside political considerations. Yet, in too many circumstances, government or society restrictions severely limit faith actors' ability to engage and worship freely. When individuals face penalty or punishment for their deeply held beliefs, it can stir intense resentment, foster the growth of extremism, and create ongoing instability and violence.

Consequently, high levels of religiosity and ever-present repression are a recipe for volatility, violence, and human rights abuses. We know this based on human history. We remember the violence perpetrated by the Nazi regime against Jews because of their religion and ethnicity, as well as other religious, political, and sexual minorities. Today, mass atrocities perpetrated by China and Burma against Uyghur and Rohingya Muslims partly motivated by their distinct religious beliefs result in industrial-scale repression evoking the oppression last seen during the Second World War. And in ungoverned spaces, persecution also thrives—for instance, the cruelty and barbarity of ISIS against religious minorities during their invasion of Iraq in 2014.

To quote sociologist Peter Berger, the world is "furiously religious."[5] Without intervention, these trends will lead to further mass abuses. We must find ways to live together despite our differences. Otherwise, our furiously religious world risks the punishing furies of Greek mythology.

Global Standard

With the founding of the United Nations in 1945, the global community affirmed the inviolability of the human person and the obligation of states to protect their freedoms and rights. The Universal Declaration of Human Rights (UDHR) in 1948 established global human rights standards, including the individual right to freedom of thought, conscience, religion, and belief. For the first time, the community of nations established individuals as rights bearers and placed the obligation to protect those rights on governments. In her book *The World Made New*, Mary Ann Glendon summarized how the UDHR "challenged the long standing view that a sovereign state's treatment of its own citizens was that nation's business and no one else's."[6]

Article 18 of the Universal Declaration addresses religious freedom, and the authors smartly avoided defining "religion" or "belief" as they are inherently subjective terms. What one person may consider sinful, another may consider

[5] Peter L. Berger, *The Desecularization of the World: Resurgent Religion and World Politics* (Washington, DC: Ethics and Public Policy Center, 2008), 2.

[6] Mary Ann Glendon, *A World Made New* (New York: Random House, 2000), xvi.

sacred or salvific. However, the drafters instead established an expansive definition of the right, recognizing the right of individuals to decide for themselves ultimate truth and their ability to practice those beliefs peacefully. Article 18 declares, "Everyone has the right to freedom of opinion and expression; this right includes freedom to hold opinions without interference and to seek, receive and impart information and ideas through any media and regardless of frontiers."[7]

In this one sentence, the Universal Declaration recognizes the inherent dignity of the human person to chart their own spiritual path. Article 18 declares the right of everyone to hold any belief or none, to change those beliefs free from penalty or coercion, to meet alone or in community for worship or prayer, and to educate one's children. Notably, Article 18 does not privilege one faith over others but rather prevents discrimination based on faith. In addition, Article 18 protects freedom of conscience, the right of individuals to critique or criticize belief systems. Article 18 is supported by Article 2, which prevents religious discrimination, noting that states could not limit any rights and freedoms set forth on religion or other grounds. Thus, when properly considered and inclusively applied, the right to religious freedom promotes respect for diversity and requires the state to protect individuals and their communities equally.

While some have viewed these documents as "Western" concepts forced on the world through globalized colonization, their drafting history and intent demonstrate the opposite. The Universal Declaration specifically, and the international human rights movement in general, emerged from the ashes of the Holocaust and the murder of millions because of their religion and ethnicity. Moreover, the multinational and multicultural drafting committee had representation from every region, representing different faiths, philosophies, and political systems.

Had the Universal Declaration existed during the colonial period, it would have provided a devastating critique of those policies. While imperfect, the UDHR established standards to protect the rights of the weak against the strong. It would have made clear the wrongness of British, French, Dutch, German, and other European expansion, as it would have American segregation. In other words, many Western nations supported the creation of the international human rights system in direct conflict with Western imperialism and discrimination at the time. These human rights standards did not promote Western hegemony but were instead built to end it.

[7] United Nations, "Universal Declaration of Human Rights," December 10, 1948, https://www.un.org/en/about-us/universal-declaration-of-human-rights (accessed December 17, 2025).

Global Protection

Though UN General Assembly resolutions are technically nonbinding, the Universal Declaration holds an elevated position, viewed as a "common standard of achievement"[8] against which to measure government actions. It established that individuals—regardless of race, gender, politics, or faith—should be free from harm and free to peacefully live out their lives however they wish. International standards on freedom of religion or belief provide an indispensable tool to encourage conditions conducive to freedom in every country.

These norms have provided unbiased measuring sticks against Russia's invasion of Ukraine, Saudi Arabia's attacks on Yemen, China's social reengineering of Tibet and Xinjiang, and elsewhere. The standard is strong, despite religious freedom being a right frequently respected in the breach.

In the twenty-first century, diversity is an undeniable reality, with people and various faiths mixing and interacting as never before. Dr. King recognized this fifty years ago when he wrote, "This is the great new problem of mankind. We have inherited a large house, a great 'world house' in which we have to live together—black and white, Easterner and Westerner, Gentile and Jew, Catholic and Protestant, Muslim and Hindu—a family unduly separated in ideas, culture and interest, who, because we can never again live apart, must learn somehow to live with each other in peace."[9] Yet, with these trends even more powerful today, fear of the religious other often leads to divisions, hostility, and even violence.

Religious freedom is relevant everywhere because religion is everywhere. The desire of individuals, both women and men, to understand the transcendent is a constant across time and in every society. Human rights norms protect individuals from harm. However, these often fall short, are ignored, or are viewed as imposed by outsiders. I know from my diplomatic work how raising religious freedom in some contexts, both conservative and liberal, can create defensiveness or close communication channels. As a result, new initiatives are trying to chart innovative pathways forward.

For instance, Chris Seiple and Dennis Hoover write about a "covenantal pluralism" that bridges differences and creates solidarity among otherwise competing belief groups. "Covenantal pluralism," as they describe, is "characterized both by a constitutional order of equal rights and responsibilities and by a culture of reciprocal commitment to engaging, respecting, and protecting the other—albeit without necessarily conceding equal veracity

[8] United Nations, "Universal Declaration of Human Rights," Preamble.

[9] Martin Luther King, *Where Do We Go from Here: Chaos or Community?* (Boston: Beacon Press, 2010), 177.

or moral equivalence to the beliefs and behaviors of others."[10] In other words, individuals and groups respect and protect the rights of others to hold differing beliefs on fundamental issues without creating a lowest-common-denominator theology that satisfies no one. As Seiple and Hoover conclude, "[N]o matter our different spiritual epistemologies and/or ethical frameworks, it is in our collective self-interest to find a way to work together."[11]

Brigham Young University's (BYU) International Center for Law and Religion Studies has elevated the foundational concept of individual dignity woven throughout the UDHR. For instance, the UDHR Preamble grounds the entire human rights system on human dignity, saying, "Whereas recognition of the inherent dignity and of the equal and inalienable rights of all members of the human family is the foundation of freedom, justice and peace in the world."[12] The first article supports this, declaring, "All human beings are born free and equal in dignity and rights. They are endowed with reason and conscience and should act towards one another in a spirit of brotherhood."[13]

The notion of "dignity" holds immense power and is a shared concept transcending cultural and religious boundaries. The Punta del Este Declaration, launched by BYU law professors, explores how rights and dignity are co-equal. The Punta del Este Declaration states, "Human dignity for everyone everywhere reminds us to work toward the elimination of egregious abuses of human rights of individuals and groups, including genocide, crimes against humanity, and other atrocities." Focusing on commonalities around human dignity still respects the belief rights of others without specifically relying upon international documents. It does not undercut the UDHR, but rather bolsters key themes. The Punta del Este Declaration continues, "Recognizing that the concept of human dignity emphasizes the uniqueness and irreplaceability of every human being; that it implies a right of each individual to find and define the meanings of his or her own life; that it presupposes respect for pluralism and difference; and that it carries with it the responsibility to honor the dignity of everyone."[14]

And while covenantal pluralism and the Punta del Este Declaration are significant innovations, examining our collective histories can improve our future. For instance, across the Middle East, sacred heritage sites tell of a diverse but forgotten past. They demonstrate a history of living together despite profound

[10] Chris Seiple and Dennis Hoover, "Rethinking Religious Literacy and Pluralism: Crossing Cultures, Making Covenants, and Engaging Globally," in *The Routledge Handbook of Religious Literacy, Pluralism and Global Engagement* (London: Taylor & Francis, 2022), 30.

[11] Ibid., 5.

[12] United Nations, "Universal Declaration of Human Rights," Preamble.

[13] United Nations, "Universal Declaration of Human Rights," Art. 1.

[14] Dignity for Everyone, "Punta Del Este Declaration on Human Dignity for Everyone Everywhere: Seventy Years after the Universal Declaration of Human Rights," December 2018, https://www.dignityforeveryone.org/about/ (accessed December 17, 2025).

differences. While these stories were never perfect, sacred heritage sites provide an indigenous inflection point to discuss the importance of respecting diversity and others' beliefs. Often overlooked, they can build bridges from the past to a brighter future tomorrow. Unrealized synergies exist between freedom of religion or belief standards and cultural heritage protection. These two related but rarely interacting fields of interest present novel opportunities for joint efforts on common concerns.[15]

These efforts are still new, but the theory of change is that sacred heritage can educate an entire society about its diverse past, thus opening conversation channels about respecting contemporary diversity and the rights of others. It builds from a society's history instead of lecturing about international standards that feel imposed upon them from the outside. By partnering with local religious communities, people from different religious backgrounds can learn to promote interfaith peace and preserve a culture of diversity, protect religious traditions, and preserve irreplaceable global heritage. At a time of increasing diversity and intolerance, emphasize how sacred sites can foster interreligious peace by overcoming interfaith amnesia through an appreciation of historic religious pluralism.

Conclusion

The Reverend Dr. Martin Luther King, Jr., wrote in his last book, published before his assassination, "One of the great liabilities of history is that all too many people fail to remain awake through great periods of social change.... But today our very survival depends on our ability to stay awake, to adjust to new ideas, to remain vigilant and to face the challenge of change. The large house in which we live demands that we transform this worldwide neighborhood into a worldwide brotherhood."[16]

Inspired by Dr. King's words, building off the established human rights advocacy methods and finding new approaches can prevent unneeded human rights violations and end persecution victimizing millions. Developing a new trajectory that focuses on inclusion and not exclusion, respect for rights and not disdain for the "other," will take commitment and dedication. But, as Dr. King said, the "fierce urgency of now" requires we forge ahead.

[15] See generally Knox Thames and Emily Scolaro, "Freedom of Religion or Belief and Cultural Heritage Protection: Synergistic Not Competitive," *The Review of Faith & International Affairs* 20, no. 2 (2022): 49–60.

[16] King, *Where Do We Go from Here*, 181.

5

In Medias Res

Religious Freedom and Moral Imagination Forging a New, Pluralistic Nation

Keisha E. McKenzie

Conflicts

Discourse about religious freedom and pluralism in the United States is riven with metaphor and analogy, much of it conflictual. In the Seventh-day Adventist communities I was raised in, for example, the ideal way to present religious liberty was as "a shield, not a sword."[1] This casually martial phrase signaled a foundational constitutional right, one that protected people's consciences, free expression, free association, and freedom of worship. It implied an opposition on the other side of the shield, encouraging us to adopt rhetoric about advantage and defense, and ready ourselves for bureaucratic battles against spiritual antagonists and other humans in the civic sphere as needed to protect the interests of the denomination.[2]

When Adventist public affairs and religious liberty staff have taken this model into their public engagement work and advocated for religious liberty in the United States and beyond, the sword-shield metaphor has enabled two things. First, it has helped them to reinforce the identity boundaries around the denomination's institutions and allies, those who merit the shield of protection. Second, it has also allowed them to define limiting legal principles for navigating contemporary conflicts and protecting groups like the denomination from an overbearing government and more powerful religious groups wielding social influence or dominance like a sword.

At a deeper values-based level, then, "shield, not sword" has created a base for more than mere self-protection. Advocates cite the mantra as they seek to

[1] Washington Adventist University, "The New Supreme Court and Religion: Constitutional and Prophetic Perspectives," YouTube video, September 17, 2022, 1:36:19, https://www.youtube.com/watch?v=_oy_2A6njK4 (accessed December 19, 2025).

[2] Ellen White, *The Great Controversy between Christ and Satan in the Christian Dispensation* (Mountain View, CA: Ellen G. White Estate, 1911/2023), https://m.egwwritings.org/en/book/132/toc (accessed December 19, 2025).

Keisha E. McKenzie, In Medias Res In: *Modeling Religious Pluralism*. Edited by: Simran Jeet Singh, Oxford University Press. © Oxford University Press 2026. DOI: 10.1093/oso/9780197745809.003.0005

preserve public square space for others and not just themselves. As Adventist scholars, hospital administrators, and missions officers trace histories of religiously motivated persecution across the Americas, Europe, and the Global South, they have deduced that it is immoral to leverage religion to dominate others and that religions and nation-states should remain wary partners.[3]

This ambivalence is consistent with my reading of early Adventist history. In the mid-nineteenth century, US Adventist church administrators argued against the prevailing religious current that even if Christians then formed the country's demographic majority, they should *not* marshal state authority to transmute the nation from a secular democracy open to all into a theocracy of any sort. These church leaders taught this despite their theological beliefs about a God who operated materially, in the realms of history and politics, as well as in a distant, spiritual realm (see Daniel 2 and Romans 13).[4]

Because of this theology, early Adventists risked their limited social influence and courted the disapproval of more respected religious groups to advocate for their own liberties while seeking to secure conditions in which others might also flourish. They assumed that the church has one appropriate lane of authority, the state has another separate and distinct lane, and the church should watch these lanes carefully to prevent state interference in religious matters and religious tyranny's "improper influence" on individual conscience or minority populations.[5]

Adventist leaders joined public conversations about religious freedom issues on the denomination's behalf during the church's first century, and this engagement launched publications and independent associations to advocate for the separation of church from state and civil law. Some of the institutions they created to support their advocacy and public education, like the International Religious Liberty Association (1893) and *Liberty Magazine* (1906), are still active today.

In those early years, though, several state legislatures debated regulating labor, civic services, trading, and entertainment on Sundays, the day each week when

[3] Debbie Michel, "Religious Liberty Leaders Emphasize Connecting with the Marginalized," *Adventist Review*, October 24, 2019, https://adventistreview.org/news/religious-liberty-leaders-emphasize-connecting-with-the-marginalized/ (accessed December 19, 2025); see also Alana Crosby, "Reconstructing Religious Liberty in a Time of Religious and Secular Extremes," *Adventist Review*, November 14, 2023, https://adventistreview.org/news/reconstructing-religious-liberty-in-a-time-of-religious-and-secular-extremes/ (accessed December 19, 2025); Jason Hines, "Liberty Twice Removed," *Spectrum Magazine*, February 25, 2021, https://spectrummagazine.org/views/2021/liberty-twice-removed (accessed December 19, 2025); and Dwayne Leslie, "Why Uganda Should Consider the Greatest Commandment," *Huffington Post*, May 18, 2014, https://www.huffpost.com/entry/why-uganda-should-conside_b_4984262 (accessed December 19, 2025).

[4] Bible, Daniel 2:1–47; and Romans 13:1–10 (New International Version).

[5] Samuel London, Jr., *Seventh-day Adventists and the Civil Rights Movement* (Jackson: University of Mississippi Press, 2010).

many Christians conducted weekly worship services and/or rested from work.[6] By 1888, a US senator had introduced a federal bill "to secure to the People the enjoyment of the Lord's Day, commonly known as Sunday, as a Day of Rest, and to Protect its observance as a Day of Religious Worship." This being a time before the general adoption of the weekend, both Adventist leaders and secular advocates strongly opposed the sacralization of Sunday either as the "Christian Sabbath" or as the "civil Sabbath."[7]

Adventists like E.J. Waggoner and Alonzo T. Jones wrote and testified publicly against the Sunday Rest bill, using Adventists' concept of religious liberty to defend their own tradition's practices while also rallying with others against popular majorities or states straining toward coercion through the law. Jones's congressional testimony describes religious bigotry as stagnant, and cruel when entangled with civic authority: "No man can allow any legislation in [*sic*] behalf of the religion, or the religious observances, in which he himself believes, without forfeiting his own religious freedom," he wrote.[8]

Just twenty years later, though, another Adventist religious liberty leader encouraged the Louisiana state legislature to regulate alcohol statewide. As the Southern Union's secretary of temperance and religious liberty, S.B. Horton described the sale of alcohol as a "cancerous evil upon the body politic."[9] In the name of pure morals and civic order, he also endorsed "restrictive legislation" against sex or marriage between white and Black people and against gambling, as if these were morally equivalent vices. Horton's argument in the past century offers a cautionary tale about a kind of morality that aims to teach people to protect physical health, families, and social cohesion but allows for some exemption, some group to which protection need not apply. As Howard Thurman later argued, a common philosophy of exemptions in Horton's era, racism, threatens individual, home, and culture all at once.[10]

By the time I began working alongside religious and secular civil rights advocates in the mid-2000s, I noticed that the people most often invoking "religious liberty" in public debates frequently also advanced exclusive religious, political, or legal positions. By the early 2010s, largely because of Christian rhetoric dominating civil marriage referenda and legislative debates, equality advocates

[6] Bethany Rupert, "The Sunday Rest Bill and the Battle to Keep the Civil Sabbath," *Seton Hall Legislative Journal* 39, no. 2 (2015): 285–330, https://scholarship.shu.edu/cgi/viewcontent.cgi?article=1084&context=shlj (accessed May 15, 2023).

[7] Ellet Waggoner, *The Blair Sunday-Rest Bill* (Oakland, CA: Pacific Press, 1889).

[8] Ibid., v, 88.

[9] S.B. Horton, "To the Honorable Members of the Senate and House of Representatives of the General Assembly, Baton Rouge, La.," in *Official Journal of the Proceedings of the Senate of the State of Louisiana at the First Regular Session of the Third General Assembly under the Adoption of the Constitution of 1898; Begun and Held in the City of Baton Rouge, May 11, 1908* (Baton Rouge, LA: Daily State Publishing Company, State Printers, 1908), 101–104.

[10] Howard Thurman, *The Luminous Darkness* (Richmond, IN: Friends United Press, 1989/1965).

and lay people were souring on religious people who used religious or moral philosophy to justify restricting or stratifying access to marriage, medical care, education, commercial services, and public bathrooms. These religious appeals often rested on one kind of religion, usually evangelical or fundamentalist forms of Christianity.

The above examples from the Seventh-day Adventist tradition illustrate how oppositional politics and rhetorical frames can function in contemporary American culture. Our diverse society includes competing and sometimes incommensurable assumptions about whether or how to acknowledge or resolve civic differences. As several scholars have argued, the conflicts that result in our time echo conflicts present before the founding of the United States, when diverse peoples later described as Indigenous encountered European settlers empowered by kings, queens, and trading companies to colonize the Americas.[11] The United States' early era of overt genocide and open enslavement was also a period in which Christian denominations dispersed across the continent, establishing educational and medical institutions and shaping community life as they spread.[12] Religions' mixed legacies in colonial and post-colonial America are evidence that genuine religious devotion may not guard adherents against discriminatory beliefs or practices. Sincerity of conviction may not mitigate feelings of superiority or ulterior motives for service.

We live "in the wake" of these multiple heritages, our choices framed in advance by legal and social and moral choices already made.[13] Our discourses indicate the *in medias res* (in the middle of the story) character of a nation that's not-yet-finished and still-being-born. Langston Hughes spoke to this theme in 1935: "America—you've never been America to me, but I swear this oath: you will be!" And Vincent Harding added his voice to this refrain of becoming and unfolding in 2012:

> We are citizens of a country that we still have to create: a just country; a compassionate country; a forgiving country; a multi-racial, multi-religious country; a joyful country that cares about its children and about its elders; that cares about itself and about the Earth; that cares about what the earth needs as well as what individual people need. I am—you are—a citizen of a country that does not yet exist, and that badly needs to exist.[14]

[11] Sabrina Dent and Corey Walker, eds., *African Americans and Religious Freedom: New Perspectives for Congregations and Communities* (Washington, DC: Freedom Forum, 2021).

[12] Miroslav Volf, *Flourishing: Why We Need Religion in a Globalized World* (New Haven, CT: Yale University Press, 2016).

[13] Christina Sharpe, *In the Wake: On Blackness and Being* (Durham, NC: Duke University Press, 2016).

[14] Vincent Harding, "Vincent Harding: Creating America," YouTube video, Children's Defense Fund National Conference, October 19, 2012, 2:51, https://www.youtube.com/watch?v=T6W42KLpNgQ (accessed December 19, 2025).

Alternative Practices

I advocate for religion in public life primarily as a technology for cultural transformation in the direction of love, belonging, and flourishing.[15] As I do, I reckon with this dual truth: Religion *can* be wielded for power and domination, dividing communities rather than binding members to another for common health and service. At the same time, religious institutions, education, and community engagement structures from Sabbath and Sunday Schools to summer camps and seminaries can and do play a critical role in shaping civic culture. Religious and non-religious community groups offer members space for affinity, belonging, encouragement, and ethical formation. Through such communities, people gain relationships and frameworks to anchor themselves in a rapidly changing society, and practice in aligning with others like and unlike them in service of a story that transcends their individual lives.

In 2020, while serving at a multifaith seminary, I began collaborating with the staff at Columbia Law School's Law, Rights, and Religion Project to promote a new quality of discourse about religious freedom among people of faith and moral courage, both clergy and lay. Since then, through reports such as "All Faiths and None: A Guide to Protecting Religious Liberty for Everyone," public webinars, and workshops with activists and legislators, we have aimed that discourse toward pluralism and democracy, not toward sectarian protectionism or discrimination.

The "All Faiths and None" report, media guide, and conversation deck for the lay public each presents six principles for an inclusive, pluralistic expression of religious freedom.[16] The Law, Rights, and Religion Project identified these principles in 2019 by convening leaders from across the social and policy spectrum for the purpose of ensuring that free exercise of religion is accessible to people of all faiths, not only a favored few.

Per "All Faiths and None," religious liberty must be:

1. Neutral
2. Non-coercive
3. Non-discriminatory
4. Not absolute and so networked with other rights
5. Democratic
6. Pluralistic

[15] Keisha McKenzie, "A Tale of Two Briefs: How Current Adventist Legal Strategy Fails the Good Samaritan Test," *Adventist Today* 25, no. 2 (2017): 9–11.

[16] Elizabeth Platt, Katherine Franke, Keisha McKenzie, and Katharine Henderson, "All Faiths and None: A Guide to Protecting Religious Liberty for Everyone" (New York: Law, Rights, and Religion Project & Auburn Theological Seminary, 2020), https://lawrightsreligion.org/our-work/all-faiths-and-none (accessed December 19, 2025).

All of these principles derive from long-standing US legal and social traditions about equality, civic participation, and an expectation of neutral treatment from the government. They are also reflected in foundational civic "American's creed" texts like the US Constitution, texts that are constantly appealed to in contemporary sociopolitical debates and that frame conflicts and queries about identity, belonging, and exclusion in or from the nation-state.[17]

As we discuss these principles with lawyers, educators, faith leaders, and policy advocates forging civil society coalitions, we have encouraged them to recognize how our respective disciplinary, professional, religious, and civic training and varied contexts of work and service predispose us to prioritize one or a few principles over others. We order the principles, exploring through dialogue why our respective priorities make sense given our backgrounds, experiences, and beliefs, and why others might prioritize them differently based on their own. In these exercises, each participant realizes that we value all six principles to some degree, yet each of us also privileges one over others. Perhaps we privilege the rule of law, or the law neutrally applied; we tend to hear this more from attorneys and policy writers attempting to build legal protections out of the law's minimum standards of behavior. Or perhaps we instead elevate the aspiration of a pluralistic, democratic community in which many, diverse voices have a constructive contribution and must be considered as we work through conflicts and draft regulations; we tend to hear this line more from civic advocates and organizers.

In December 2021, for example, I and two colleagues from Auburn Theological Seminary were invited to facilitate a new coalition of business leaders, legislative attorneys, faith group liaisons, and LGBTQ+ equality leaders from state organizations across the United States. I used the "All Faiths and None" conversation deck to help these leaders root conversations about emerging national nondiscrimination legislation in their civic values, not just their political conclusions. I also designed the facilitation plan so we could surface participants' key questions and areas of consensus and support participants, their colleagues at home, and concerned observers in building common sense about the legislative proposals and their implications.

We and our host team acknowledged that our conversation was not a blank slate but began *in medias res*—in the context of nearly fifty years of efforts to balance nondiscrimination, religious expression, and freedom of association at the federal level; amidst broad fatigue with institutions, rigid nationalisms, and incremental compromises; and despite the strain of a global pandemic and mass bereaving and disabling event. We intentionally embedded discussions about

[17] See, for example, the Independence Hall Association's archive of classic civic texts from the Magna Carta (1215) to a selection of twentieth-century presidential speeches: USHistory.org, "Historic Documents," https://www.ushistory.org/DOCUMENTS/index.html (accessed December 19, 2025).

religious liberty and specific policy options in three days of structured and unstructured relationship building, meal sharing, storytelling, and learning from local community and faith leaders about their concerns for their city and their ideas about how the coalition's work could address those concerns, with respect for people of all faiths and none.

But the value of such facilitation exercises is not merely that participants pause to reflect. It's also that, as participants *practice* curious conversation about our deepest commitments, the ideals and principles that motivate us as we re-enter worlds of pragmatic negotiation and compromise, we collectively transform our meeting rooms into mini-democratic laboratories, places and spaces grounded in inclusive participation (who gathers), respectful listening and expression (how we gather), and shared concerns (to what common end we're gathered). We practice the form of relations that our daily work appeals to and legitimates itself in reference to. In these rooms and conversations, we're *rehearsing* the futures we intend to inhabit.[18]

In *Inclusion and Democracy* (2002), Iris Young explains the fundamentals underlying inclusive political decision making and how they work to legitimize the outcomes that emerge:

> Democracy entails political equality, that all members of the polity are included equally in the decision-making process and have an equal opportunity to influence the outcome. Inclusion increases the chances that those who make proposals will transform their positions from an initial self-regarding stance to a more objective appeal to justice, *because they must listen to others with differing positions to whom they are also answerable.* Even if they disagree with an outcome, political actors must accept the legitimacy of a decision if it was arrived at through an inclusive process of public discussion.[19]

Young rightly notes that groups and systems can flout this norm through external exclusion, which is keeping interested or impacted parties out of the conversation, or through internal exclusion, which is ostensibly including parties but negating, deprioritizing, or otherwise marginalizing them while they're present. American political history includes innumerable examples of both kinds of discursive and decision-making exclusion.

From states that refused to seat duly elected Black legislators during Reconstruction in the nineteenth century, that have constructed or arbitrarily

[18] Ruth Wilson Gilmore, "Where Life Is Precious, Life Is Precious," *On Being with Krista Tippett*, March 30, 2023, https://onbeing.org/programs/ruth-wilson-gilmore-where-life-is-precious-life-is-precious/ (accessed December 19, 2025).

[19] Iris Young, *Inclusion and Democracy* (Oxford: Oxford University Press, 2002), 52, emphasis added.

enforced rules that restricted voters in the twentieth or twenty-first centuries, and that inconsistently engage the still-here Indigenous peoples who preceded the United States as a nation to the school boards, city councils, and executive agencies that rush through public comment forums or dismiss lay feedback as inherently uninformed—both overt, external and implicit, internal forms of exclusion undermine the inclusive norms that are necessary for a healthy civic life and that the "All Faith and None" religious liberty principles promote.

However, these principles are not a checklist to tick off and lay aside. Rather they are a moral framework that can guide collective reflection and conversation about the nature, limits, and potentials of the social systems we steward. They prompt us to uncover perspectives from the people not yet accounted for as we acknowledge our varying social positions and negotiate shared solutions. Reflecting on the time-ground on which we all stand, Christina Sharpe points toward what yet lies ahead: work "to imagine and transform spaces for and practices of an ethics of care (as in repair, maintenance, attention), an ethics of seeing, and of being in the wake as consciousness."[20]

There are obstacles to that work in our minds and common narrative frames. The US public square is not yet 250 years old, but from its earliest years, it has inspired idealism *and* mistrust, hope *and* cynicism. Much of that mistrust is well earned and a logical waystation for those who We the People abandoned at the birth of the nation and who have been targeted ever since by laws crafted for private or sectarian benefit rather than for broad-based well-being.

In the past two decades, however, a sharper assessment than mere ambivalence has hovered over US politics like a methane cloud: the belief that US civic institutions are on the cusp of failing or have already failed, and cannot be repaired by changing out personnel, rules, or administrations or by expecting self-correction and waiting out the stink. Entropy, according to "brokenists" across the social, religious, and political landscape, has finally caught up with us and we can no longer avoid it. "The most vital debate in America today," Alana Newhouse writes, "is between those who believe there is something fundamentally broken in America, and that it's an emergency, and those who do not. . . . We aren't confused; we are having a fight—and it's one you might benefit from joining."[21]

This brings us back to a metaphor of conflict. I choose to respond with different metaphors as I join another social conversation *in medias res*. In 2001, some politicians and community leaders metabolized the 9/11 attacks by

[20] Sharpe, *In the Wake*, 130–131.

[21] Alana Newhouse, "Everything Is Broken: And How to Fix It," *Tablet Magazine*, January 2021, https://www.tabletmag.com/sections/news/articles/everything-is-broken (accessed December 19, 2025); and Alana Newhouse, "Brokenism," *Tablet Magazine*, November 2022, https://www.tabletmag.com/sections/news/articles/brokenism-alana-newhouse (accessed December 19, 2025).

blending jingoism, warmongering, and Christian crusade rhetoric into a foul civic smoothie for the nation to sip. They especially demonized Muslim freedom of worship—in one instance, blocking the construction of a Muslim community center and mosque in downtown Manhattan—and otherwise marginalized or excused violence against Muslims, Sikhs, and anyone else deemed visibly different, sufficiently other, and insufficiently patriotic.

That same year, Christian theologian Walter Brueggemann wrote that the prophet's work is, on one hand, to help shape "a new social community to match the vision of God's freedom," and, on the other, "to cut through the despair and to penetrate the dissatisfied coping that seems to have no end or resolution."[22] Divesting from the imperial call to domination—a kind of emergency surgery for social health—impels us to practice community in new ways, and to joyfully craft material, linguistic, and relational structures strong enough to support that emerging vision. This is an invitation to generate imagination, symbols, and narratives that sharpen our visions of a shared future that's not-yet, a future that might even be judged unlikely given precedents or given human nature.

But in this moment of challenge and potential for the United States and for the wider world of which it is but one part, what might it mean to acknowledge and grieve that we have not yet achieved the fullness of our social vision? "There is grief work to be done in the present," Brueggemann notes, "so that the future may come. There is mourning to be done for those who do not know of the deathliness of their situation. There is mourning to be done with those who know pain and suffering and lack the power or freedom to bring it to speech.... Those who have not cared enough to grieve will not know joy."[23]

Might we then transform ourselves, and our habits, concepts, and tools, not simply to recover or preserve a pre-existing civic order but to go beyond what has been—drawing out the "America that will be," and working with others across interest groups and demographic segments to approach or even achieve our collective promise?

I scan the landscape we are in now, of laws, cases, briefs, and rules about Indigenous sacred lands and government appropriation to extend oil production; about how to balance free association rights with public health protections; about whether some might access public accommodations and be free from discrimination; about the welfare of children and state regulations for fostering and adoption; and about how we negotiate freedom of speech, free religious exercise, and freedom from coercion in public spaces—and I practice imagining.

[22] Walter Brueggemann, *The Prophetic Imagination*, 2nd ed. (Minneapolis, MN: Fortress Press, 2001), 7, 63.
[23] Ibid., 119.

I imagine religions operating at their full, humanizing potential. I imagine them offering all who want them a sense of common collective identity with no reason to fear that their individual or affinity interests in society will be effaced. I imagine religions of more kinds than I can name teaching spiritual disciplines and grounding rhythms and practices that individuals, families, communities, and groups can use their whole lives to build deeper reflective capacities, greater empathy, and a stronger sense of dignity and belonging in the ecosystem called Earth.

I imagine religion that evolves beyond autocracy and threatening physical or social violence to enforce it; religion that doesn't substitute inspiration and moral exemplars with armed or suited strongmen; and religion that doesn't dilute religious liberty for all into religious regulation of difference or trade cooperation for control. I imagine spirituality so well rooted that it regularly transmutes our honed tendencies to outrage and mutual shouting; that it makes space for reflection and trauma recovery; and that it promotes hopeful, humble organizing for multigenerational transformation.

As I wrote in the foreword to "All Faiths and None," "[W]e are called to expand public understanding of a religious liberty that truly supports freedom for all people, and together we are committed to building legal structures and community networks strong enough to scaffold a world where all belong."

Let us imagine that world as possible.

Let us live as if it can be so.

And may religion and religious liberty be an asset to us as we work for good and on common ground.

6
Political Partisanship and Its Effect on the Future of Religious Liberty

Asma T. Uddin

"Religious liberty for some is religious liberty for none"—the mantra of many religious liberty advocates. The idea is that picking and choosing among the beliefs and practices one considers worth protecting ultimately dilute the right for everyone. If we cede power to the government to decide "right" beliefs from "wrong" ones, we have ceded far too much.

In many ways, "religious liberty for all" is a simple, straightforward concept. But it has been contested throughout American history and continues to be contentious today. Native Americans, Catholics, Mormons, Jews, Muslims, and others have faced exclusion.[1] And in recent years, religious liberty has become even more fractured and yet another victim (among many, many other victims) of our deeply polarized national condition.

This chapter explores key precipitating factors and solutions for polarization, including how it implicates religious groups. First, it explores key drivers of that polarization. Next, the discussion focuses on a specific case study: the current relationship between American Muslims and conservative white evangelicals in the United States. The case study considers how these groups are pitted against each other in national, political, and legal conversations and what that conflict means for the future of religious freedom in the United States. Finally, the chapter concludes by offering core principles and a few best practices for advancing religious freedom for all.

Polarization and Group Identity

Selective protection of rights is a function of polarization, which in turn is rooted in group identity.[2] The concept of selective protection of rights suggests that a

[1] *Employment Division* v. *Smith*, 494 U.S. 872 (1990); and *Stormans, Inc.* v. *Wiesman*, 579 U.S. 942 (2016).

[2] Henri Tajfel, "Experiments in Intergroup Discrimination," *Scientific American* 223, no. 5 (November 1970): 96–103, Experiments in Intergroup Discrimination on JSTOR.

Asma T. Uddin, *Political Partisanship and Its Effect on the Future of Religious Liberty* In: *Modeling Religious Pluralism*. Edited by: Simran Jeet Singh, Oxford University Press. © Oxford University Press 2026.
DOI: 10.1093/oso/9780197745809.003.0006

person belongs to a group, which is their "in-group." Those outside this group are the "out-group." A person's attachment to their group is so significant that loyalty to it boosts their self-esteem.[3] Studies have shown that when a person becomes isolated from their group, the stigma of that isolation triggers both a psychological and physical assault on their body.[4] It appears that on an evolutionary level, humans are programmed to signal their allegiance to their tribe as a way of avoiding the loneliness and stress that come with being cast out.

Yet, while it is natural and neutral for groups to favor their own, that favoritism becomes problematic when charged with strong emotions.[5] Oxford political scientists Miles Hewstone, Mark Rubin, and Hazel Willis write that "the constraints normally in place, which limit intergroup bias to in-group favoritism, are lifted when out-groups are associated with stronger emotions."[6] Stronger emotions include things like the feeling the out-group is moving against you: "an out-group seen as threatening may elicit fear and hostile actions."[7] "High-status" groups (groups that are a numerical majority and have power) do not feel threatened by minorities when the status gap is very wide, but they are more likely to feel threatened when the status gap is closing.

People's allegiance to their political tribes is no different. Elections are pure team rivalry. Studies have found that in the election context, winning is preeminent, and Americans are driven by what they oppose rather than what they support. For example, a 2016 Pew study found that a "deeper affection" for the Republican Party increased voting much less than "very unfavorable views" of the Democratic Party.[8] Among Americans who are highly engaged in politics, this disparity became even starker—the more they hated the other side, the more likely they were to donate money to their own party. This is why politicians focus so much of their messaging on generating fear and hatred of the other party.

In America's present political climate, group rivalries pose an escalating threat because of what one political scientist calls "mega-identities":[9]

> A single vote can now indicate a person's partisan preference *as well as* his or her religion, race, ethnicity, gender, neighborhood, and favorite grocery store. This is no longer a single social identity. Partisanship can now be thought of as

[3] Ibid.

[4] Lilliana Mason, *Uncivil Agreement: How Politics Became Our Identity* (Chicago: University of Chicago Press, 2018), 139.

[5] Miles Hewstone, Mark Rubin, and Hazel Willis, "Intergroup Bias," *Annual Review of Psychology*, 53, no. 1 (2002): 575–604.

[6] Ibid.

[7] Ibid.

[8] Pew Research Center, "Partisanship and Political Animosity in 2016," June 22, 2016, https://www.pewresearch.org/politics/2016/06/22/partisanship-and-political-animosity-in-2016/ (accessed December 19, 2025).

[9] Mason, *Uncivil Agreement*, 139.

> a mega-identity, with all the psychological and behavioral magnifications that implies. . . . If you told someone on the phone whom you had never met before that you are white, that single fact would not tell them much more about you. But if you told them that you are a Republican, they could reasonably assume that you are not black, lesbian, gay, transgender or bisexual, nonreligious or Jewish.[10]

Another way to think about mega-identities is as the difference between issue-based and identity-based polarization. In the first case, people cluster together based on their policy opinions. With identity-based polarization, people cluster together based on political identities. As writer Ezra Klein explains, "[O]ur political identities are polarizing our other identities, too," and issue conflicts are just one of many expressions of that hostility.[11]

What is more, the individual issues or identities reinforce mega-identities, and when one is activated, all of them are activated. An older, but apt illustration of this phenomenon is the 2004 ad by the Club for Growth, a conservative group that advocated for lower taxes and deregulation, against then-presidential candidate Howard Dean. The ad features someone asking an older white couple what they think of Dean's plan, and the man responds, "'I think Howard Dean should take his tax-hiking, government-expanding, latte-drinking, sushi-eating, Volvo-driving, *New York Times*-reading—.' His wife cuts in, 'Body-piercing, Hollywood-loving, left-wing freak show back to Vermont, where it belongs.'" All of these are traits of the single (in this case, liberal) mega-identity.[12]

Case Study: Muslim-Christian Relations in the United States

Applied in Muslim-Christian contexts, the foregoing dynamics play out in the following manner. Demographic shifts are precipitating the precise dynamics that lead to heightened intergroup prejudice. First, the white racial majority is declining. According to Pew, white people will become a minority by 2055; US Census data suggests that this shift may happen as soon as 2044.[13] Second, and also for the first time in US history, white Protestant Christians are a minority in America.[14] In 1976, eight in ten Americans were white Christians, and 55 percent

[10] Perry Bacon Jr., "Democrats Are Wrong About Republicans. Republicans Are Wrong About Democrats," *FiveThirtyEight*, June 26, 2018, https://fivethirtyeight.com/features/democrats-are-wrong-about-republicans-republicans-are-wrong-about-democrats/.

[11] Ezra Klein, *Why We're Polarized* (New York: Simon and Schuster, 2020), 68.

[12] Klein, *Why We're Polarized*, 68.

[13] Pew Research Center, *Importance of Religion and Religious Beliefs* (Washington, DC: Pew Research Center, 2015), https://www.pewresearch.org/religion/2015/11/03/chapter-1-importance-of-religion-and-religious-beliefs/ (accessed December 17, 2025).

[14] Robert P. Jones, *End of White Christian America* (New York: Simon & Schuster, 2016).

of all Americans were white Protestants. In 1996, white Christians still made up two thirds of the population.[15] Today, they hardly constitute a majority.[16] Third, the demise of white Protestant America has brought with it an end to "the cultural and institutional world built primarily by white Protestants that dominated American culture until the last decade."[17] Not only is Christianity declining, but so is religious affiliation writ large. More and more Americans are religiously unaffiliated (the so-called nones), and in 2019 the percentage of nones became roughly the same as the percentage of evangelicals or Catholics.[18] (By 2016, the nones already constituted the nation's largest religious voting bloc.)[19]

For conservative Christians, the cultural decline is reflected most clearly in the conflict between gay rights and traditional religious beliefs about sexuality and marriage.[20] In June 2023, the US Supreme Court in *303 Creative* v. *Elenis* ruled in favor of a Christian website designer who did not want to design wedding websites for gay couples.[21] In 2018, the Court heard *Masterpiece Cakeshop* v. *Colorado Civil Rights Commission*,[22] where a Christian baker declined to make a custom wedding cake for a gay couple.[23] These cases turn on a disagreement about the nature of marriage. While many Americans see marriage as a legal relationship, traditional religious believers see it as primarily a religious or sacramental relationship.[24] Culturally, those two conceptions of marriage are entangled, which in recent years has led to conflicts between LGBTQ+ individuals and Christian conservative marriage counselors, adoption agencies, and wedding vendors.[25]

In the political context, the cases represent dual narratives of vulnerability. For one set of Americans, the clash is between America's powerful Christian majority and a marginalized, oppressed sexual minority. A sampling of news headlines

[15] Pew Research Center, "In U.S., Decline of Christianity Continues at Rapid Pace," October 17, 2019, https://www.pewforum.org/2019/10/17/in-u-s-decline-of-christianity-continues-at-rapid-pace/ (accessed December 17, 2025).

[16] Jones, *End of White Christian America.*

[17] Robert P. Jones, "The Great Trump Hope," *New York Times*, July 11, 2016, https://www.nytimes.com/2016/07/11/opinion/campaign-stops/the-evangelicals-and-the-great-trump-hope.html?ref=opinion&_r=1 (accessed December 17, 2025).

[18] Samuel Smith, "Religious 'Nones' Now as Big as Evangelicals in the US, New Data Shows," *Christian Post*, March 20, 2019, https://www.christianpost.com/news/religious-nones-now-as-big-as-evangelicals-in-the-us-new-data-shows.html (accessed December 17, 2025).

[19] Christopher Ingraham, "The Non-Religious Are Now the Country's Largest Religious Voting Bloc," *Washington Post*, July 14, 2016, https://www.washingtonpost.com/news/wonk/wp/2016/07/14/the-non-religious-are-now-the-countrys-largest-religious-voting-bloc/ (accessed December 17, 2025).

[20] *Obergefell* v. *Hodges*, 576 U.S. 644 (2015).

[21] *303 Creative* v. *Elenis*, 143 S. Ct. 2298 (2023).

[22] *Masterpiece Cakeshop, Ltd.* v. *Colo. Civil Rights Comm'n*, 138 S. Ct. 1719 (2017).

[23] Ibid.

[24] Douglas Laycock, "Religious Liberty and the Culture Wars," *University of Illinois Law Review* 3 (June 2014): 839–880, https://illinoislawreview.org/wp-content/ilr-content/articles/2014/3/Laycock.pdf (accessed December 17, 2025).

[25] Ibid.

tells the story: "Let's Call 'Religious Freedom' by Its Real Name: Poisonous, Anti-LGBTQ+ Bigotry";[26] "303 Creative a 'Cynical Ploy' for Discrimination";[27] and "The New Faith-Based Discrimination."[28] About the conservative evangelicals who bring these claims, *Huffington Post* says, "Evangelicals Reaffirm Their LGBT Ignorance and Bigotry."[29] For these observers, religious claims in the LGTBQ+ context are not sincere; instead, they are pretexts for animus. As Professor Andrew Koppelman has summed up, "The toxic core of the conflict is the racism analogy—the idea that those who embrace traditional sexual morality are as bad as racists and deserve to be treated like racists."[30]

For another set of Americans, the narrative is entirely different. The clash represents a battle between traditional Christians struggling to live by their values in a society that insists on forcing them to conform to changing mores.[31] Multiple Christian groups have issued statements outlining their beliefs about sexuality and lamenting that these beliefs no longer hold sway in a "post-Christian" American society.[32] Their fears are borne out by numerous legal challenges to traditional religious practice; as evangelical attorney Luke Goodrich explains to his co-religionists, their religious practices also face legal threats from "laws requiring religious groups to pay for abortions . . . laws requiring doctors to help with assisted suicide, to restrictions on free speech on college campuses, to the elimination of long-standing tax exemptions for churches."[33] He then goes on to describe the extensive litigation in each of those contexts.[34]

[26] Tim Teeman, "Let's Call 'Religious Freedom' by Its Real Name: Poisonous, Anti-LGBTQ Bigotry," *Daily Beast*, November 5, 2019, https://www.thedailybeast.com/lets-call-religious-freedom-by-its-real-name-poisonous-anti-lgbtq-bigotry (accessed December 17, 2025).

[27] Jeff Dellinger, "303 Creative Case a 'Cynical Ploy' for Discrimination, CFI Tells SCOTUS," *Cfi*, August 19, 2022, https://centerforinquiry.org/press_releases/303-creative-case-a-cynical-ploy-for-discrimination-cfi-tells-scotus/ (accessed December 17, 2025).

[28] Louise Melling, "The New Faith-Based Discrimination," *Boston Review*, December 14, 2022, https://www.bostonreview.net/articles/the-new-faith-based-discrimination/ (accessed December 17, 2025).

[29] Tim Rymel, "Evangelicals Reaffirm Their LGBT Ignorance and Bigotry," *HuffPost*, August 31, 2017, https://www.huffpost.com/entry/evangelicals-reaffirm-their-lgbt-ignorance-and-bigotry_b_59a79affe4b096fd8876c0a0 (accessed December 17, 2025).

[30] Andrew M. Koppelman, *Gay Rights vs. Religious Liberty? The Unnecessary Conflict* (New York: Oxford University Press, 2020).

[31] See, for example, Sara Savat, "Cultural Backlash: Is LGBTQ Progress an Attack on Christianity?" *WashU*, August 26, 2021, https://source.wustl.edu/2021/08/cultural-backlash-is-lgbtq-progress-an-attack-on-christianity/ (accessed December 17, 2025): "Many Christians have come to see themselves as being on the losing side of the culture wars."

[32] See Council on Biblical Manhood and Womanhood, "The Nashville Statement," https://cbmw.org/nashville-statement/#preamble (accessed June 19, 2023); and Manhattan Declaration, "The Manhattan Declaration: A Call of Christian Conscience," https://www.manhattandeclaration.org (accessed June 19, 2023).

[33] Luke Goodrich, *Free to Believe: The Battle over Religious Liberty in America* (Colorado Springs, CO: WaterBrook, 2019), sneak peek excerpt, https://waterbrookmultnomah.com/wp-content/uploads/pdf/Sneak-Peek-Free-to-Believe-1.pdf (accessed December 17, 2025).

[34] Ibid.

The frustration and anger about a post-Christian America are manifested in hostility toward minorities, including religious minorities, and particularly American Muslims. The concept of mega-identities helps to explain the dynamic. Muslims often serve as a proxy for the political left.[35] Muslims—and especially liberal advocacy on behalf of Muslims—are traits of the liberal mega-identity, and opposition to Muslims is a trait of the conservative mega-identity. Of course, polarization alone is not to blame for this cold reception, but partisanship and political tribalism are also critical to the analysis, and often overlooked.[36]

The political component is vividly illustrated in variations of Obama's "Hope" poster with a woman in a hijab. The poster was used to protest the 2016 election of President Donald Trump and was ubiquitous in the January 2017 Women's March on Washington.[37] More generally, liberals have championed the hijab for years and featured women who wear headscarves in prominent outlets. The phenomenon seems peculiar, since the hijab, as a facet of a modest (or restrictive) dress code for women, is not ordinarily something that liberals would champion. But Muslims and hijab are part of the Left's mega-identity, and the Right—which is not normally associated with feminism—makes feminist arguments against the hijab. When the conservative tribe opposes everything in the liberal tribe, it opposes liberals' advocacy for Muslims and consequently positions itself against Muslims' rights.

Consider supporting empirical data: A 2016 study measured Americans' levels of unease with and willingness to sanction negative speech about different religious groups.[38] Researchers found that Democrats "express the greatest unease—and the greatest willingness to sanction those who make the disapproving comments—with statements about Jews and Muslims." It also found that Republicans exhibit "exceptionally low levels of discomfort with an unwillingness to sanction negative comments about Muslims." In a polarized culture, where mega-identities rule, if liberals sanction anti-Muslim speech, conservatives make sure not to. It is not that Republicans are above sanctioning speech; it is just that they do not do it for Muslims—because Democrats do that, and Republicans do not want to be like Democrats.

[35] Asma T. Uddin, *Politics of Vulnerability* (New York: Pegasus Books, 2021), xxiv.

[36] Allyson F. Shortie and Ronald Keith Gaddie, "Religious Nationalism and Perceptions of Muslims and Islam," *Politics and Religion* 8, no. 3 (2015): 435–457, https://doi.org/10.1017/S1755048315000322.

[37] Jesus Garay, "These Posters Protesting Trump Were Created by the Man Responsible for Obama's 'Hope' Artwork," *Guff*, 2016, https://guff.com/these-posters-protesting-trump-were-created-by-the-man-responsible-for-obamas-hope-artwork (accessed December 17, 2025).

[38] C. Karpowitz, J. Quinn Monson, and K. Patterson, "Who's In and Who's Out: The Politics of Religious Norms," *Politics and Religion* 9, no. 3 (2016): 508–536, https://www.politico.com/magazine/story/2016/07/measuring-the-backlash-against-the-muslim-backlash-214034 (accessed December 17, 2025).

In the opposing camp, Democrats express positive views of Muslims, in part, because it distinguishes them from Republicans. In 2015 and 2016, the University of Maryland conducted three national polls measuring Americans' views about Islam and Muslims.[39] The last survey was done just days after the June 2016 Pulse nightclub shooting in Orlando, Florida, where a Muslim attacker killed forty-nine people and wounded fifty-three others. The polls found that Americans' attitudes about Muslims improved between each of the three surveys, even after the Orlando shooting. But the positive upward movement depended on one's party affiliation. Republicans stayed relatively fixed across all three polls, whereas Democrats' views rose by twelve points.

Commenting in 2016, one political scientist explained it as follows: "It's less about Islam and Muslims, and more about taking political sides."[40]

Unfortunately, this political proxy-ism is not just a matter of how we respond to surveys or whether we are willing to engage in negative speech about others. The partisan divide can also drive active opposition to Muslims' human rights.[41] From nationwide protests to halt the construction of mosques and Muslim cemeteries to widespread surveillance of Muslim communities, the incursions on Muslims' religious freedom are blatant.[42] But among the Americans who have decried this human rights violation, the usual partisanship has prevailed—liberals on one side, and many conservatives decidedly on the other side.[43]

The epigraph for this chapter captures the broader implications of this religious freedom exclusion: Religious liberty for some is religious liberty for none. If liberty cedes to government the power to selectively protect religions that it likes (or views as politically expedient) and not protect the ones it does not like, it is granted power that it can exercise against any religion.

This very simple point can be hard to see when Americans are mired in tribalism. But it holds the key to moving forward.

[39] Shibley Telhami, "Measuring the Backlash against the Muslim Backlash," *Politico Magazine*, July 11, 2016, https://www.politico.com/magazine/story/2016/07/measuring-the-backlash-against-the-muslim-backlash-214034 (accessed December 17, 2025).

[40] Ibid.

[41] Asma T. Uddin, *When Islam Is Not a Religion: Inside America's Fight for Religious Freedom* (New York: Pegasus Books, 2019), https://www.simonandschuster.com/books/When-Islam-is-Not-a-Religion/Asma-T-Uddin/9781643136059 (accessed December 17, 2025).

[42] Laurie Goodstein, "Around Country, Mosque Projects Meet Opposition," *New York Times*, August 8, 2010, A1, https://www.nytimes.com/2010/08/08/us/08mosque.html (accessed December 17, 2025); and Josh Gerstein, "Court Mulls FBI Mosque Surveillance," *Politico Magazine*, December 8, 2015, https://www.politico.com/blogs/under-the-radar/2015/12/court-mulls-fbi-mosque-surveillance-216529 (accessed December 17, 2025).

[43] Karpowitz, Quinn Monson, and Patterson, "Who's In and Who's Out"; and Telhami, "Measuring the Backlash."

Best Practices for Advancing Religious Freedom for All

Understanding the social psychology involved in the Christian-Muslim divide makes clear that healing requires disrupting the mechanisms of out-group hostility. Out-group hostility results when the in-group feels threatened. To counteract that hostility, strategies for healing must focus principally on reducing perceptions of threat. Political scientists have various strategies to help us achieve that.

Superordinate Goals

One strategy is called "superordinate goals." Creating superordinate goals is a social science approach to reducing prejudice. The theory was first tested by husband-and-wife team Muzafer and Carolyn Wood Sherif, both social psychologists, when they brought a group of boys to a camp where they were split into two groups that would compete at first (producing intragroup solidarity and intergroup rivalry) and then given a common goal to increase intergroup solidarity.

In our present political climate, there is evidence that religious freedom might be the cross-cutting issue—the superordinate goal—that can help bring warring groups at least a little bit closer. The reason, again, is that religious liberty for some is religious liberty for all. A clear form of this is the use of precedent as a building block in judicial decision making—a case where a Christian won helps set precedent for a case in which Muslims or other religious minorities win, and vice versa. All religious claims are intrinsically connected, and a robust conception of religious liberty protects a wide variety of religious beliefs and practices from government incursion.[44]

Religious liberty is particularly suitable for this project because, for superordinate goals to work, it is important that groups are not made to feel like their identity is eroding. People should sense the freedom to hold onto their distinctiveness even as they let go of their prejudices.[45] Such authenticity is inherent to religious liberty.

[44] See *Burwell* v. *Hobby Lobby Stores*, 573 U.S. 682 (2014), https://supreme.justia.com/cases/federal/us/573/682/ (pro-Evangelical holding promulgated with help from case involving Muslim prisoner denied a halal diet) (accessed December 17, 2025).

[45] Asma T. Uddin, "Christian-Muslim Relations in a Tribalized America: Strategies for Healing," September 13 (Washington, DC: Aspen Institute, 2021), 8, https://www.aspeninstitute.org/publications/christian-muslim-relations-in-a-tribalized-america-strategies-for-healing/ (accessed December 17, 2025).

Tolerance and Empathy

Intolerance is about specific beliefs, practices, or ways of living that the in-group disapproves of. It can be group-based if the entire out-group endorses—or is perceived as endorsing—the disapproved belief or practice. But the focus is on specific actions, rather than hating a category of people as people. In the context of US debates about religious liberty and sexual freedom, liberals do not oppose conservatives as a group so much as they disapprove of conservatives' beliefs and practices related to gay marriage, contraception, abortion, and so on.[46]

Embracing tolerance can help bridge differences, but coexistence with people who have widely variant beliefs and practices often requires something more. Empathy is that essential ingredient. Whereas tolerance implies a "putting up with" dissenting beliefs and practices, empathy seeks to understand where the other person is coming from. As one expert describes it, empathy in our engagement with others means that "what is present before the listener is not merely an argument, but a person."[47] In a series of interviews with conflict resolution experts, the *New York Times* uncovered various methods these experts use to encourage tolerance.[48] One approach involved gathering people with socially strained beliefs and inducing them into peaceful dialogue (our alleged goal of listening) through an exercise in solidarity. The psychologist would begin by gathering the group and having them sit in a circle. As a prompt, each person was asked to share stories about their family, and as a rule, no interruptions were to be allowed. The participants grew keen to listen to each other, and when the conversation turned to polarizing topics, their respectful candor remained.[49] This result came because "the other side had heard [the other] and that they had become, in a fundamental way, equals." As one facilitator explained, they all expected it to be harder than it actually was. "I really learned that no matter how differently we think or vote, if we take a moment to see the other person for who they are, as somebody with a family and a story, that made the hard stuff easier." She characterized the process as "having a hard conversation in a soft place."

Similarly, Professor Brené Brown says that the people who overcome polarization are those who "lean into vulnerability" by staying "*zoomed in*."[50] They

[46] Arthur Brooks, "Political Polarization," *New York Times*, March 2, 2019, https://www.nytimes.com/2019/03/02/opinion/sunday/political-polarization.html (accessed December 17, 2025).

[47] Padmasiri De Silva, "Tolerance and Empathy," in *Religious Tolerance, Education and the Curriculum*, edited by Elizabeth Burns Coleman and Kevin White (Rotterdam: SensePublishers, 2011), 99–110, https://doi.org/10.1007/978-94-6091-412-6_8.

[48] Sabrina Tavernise, "A New Country for Conflict Resolution Experts," *New York Times*, February 4, 2019, https://www.nytimes.com/2019/02/04/us/conflicting-experts-peacebuilders.html (accessed December 17, 2025).

[49] Ibid.

[50] Brené Brown, *Braving the Wilderness: The Quest for True Belonging and the Courage to Stand Alone* (New York: Random House, 2019).

commit "to assessing their lives and forming their opinions of people based on their actual, in-person experiences." "Zooming in" means questioning what we hear on the news and from the mouths of politicians. Because when we see people close-up, it is a lot harder to hate them—a lot harder to recede into our "go-to emotions": pain and fear, anger and hate.

Importantly, leaning into vulnerability does not mean we have to stop fighting for what we believe in. But it does allow one to accept the essential humanity of one's opponents. In any conflict, the players are all humans, with shared human tendencies toward group identity, group loyalty, and perceptions of threat. Accepting—and building on—these human attributes is key to a path forward.

PART III
ADDRESSING HATE AND POLARIZATION

One of my greatest frustrations with hate violence—in addition to the hatred *and* the violence—is how hard it is to make real, meaningful culture change that would address the hatred and violence at their root. For instance, when I have worked on these issues, whether on the ground or at a national level, it has felt like people don't care about bigotry until someone commits an act of violence. Then, people react, shaking their heads and announcing their concern: "This is not who we are." And then we move on, with little commitment to identifying the causes and conditions of the violence, let alone addressing them. Wouldn't we be better off accepting that, in fact, this is exactly who we are and that it's our responsibility to do more than shake our heads?

I've watched communities around the country rehearse this script as if on repeat. I've also observed that, as hate has become normalized, these same communities have become desensitized, paying less and less attention to the hurt and suffering that people are enduring.

I've often wondered if the gestures of sympathy are more harmful than helpful. As I tell my daughters, there's no point in apologizing if you're not going to change your behavior.

What I've longed for is what so many people from the margins have requested. What if, instead of only reacting to hate when it produces violence, we were proactive in addressing bigotry at its core? What if, instead of responding to the symptoms, we focused on eradicating the disease itself?

To me and to so many others who work on these issues, this has long felt like a more effective strategy, one that would move us beyond our whack-a-mole approach to a plan of action that leads to a meaningful cultural shift. Of course, culture change is slow, and it requires patience and endurance. But what other option do we have?

To prescribe an effective remedy, we must first identify the illness. And when it comes to the disease of hate and polarization, the role of religion is often overlooked.

Religious actors can be perpetrators of hate violence, as we have seen in various forms, from the Ku Klux Klan to ISIS. We have countless examples of how people of faith can be victims of these hatreds, including Anne Frank and Uyghur Muslims. And we also see how religious leaders can be agents of change, including figures like Mother Teresa and Dr. Martin Luther King, Jr.

Each of these examples speaks to the difficulty, importance, and urgency of building religious pluralism. There is so much suffering that emerges from hatreds and polarization, and religion is directly and deeply implicated. Being aware of what this looks like and how it shows up in our world today is the first step toward developing an effective solution.

That is why this section features leaders who are at the forefront of shifting culture in our society, and who are doing so with an understanding that many overlook: To effectively address hate and polarization, we must account for religion.

In their chapter, Eboo Patel and Mary Ellen Geiss, who serve as president and chief programming officer for Interfaith America, respectively, make a strong case for the potential and promise of engaging religion in bridgebuilding work. They also share some strategies on how to do this effectively based on their years of experience leading Interfaith America.

Melissa Borja, assistant professor of American culture at the University of Michigan, looks at the rise of anti-Asian hate during the COVID-19 pandemic and places it in the context of anti-Asian racism in US history. She examines the role that religious leaders and communities played in perpetuating this hatred, as well as the ways in which religious leaders and communities addressed hatred.

And in her chapter, Uma Vishwanathan, who previously served as executive director for the New Pluralists, reflects on the challenges we face as a society and her own commitments to pluralism as a solution. She grounds this reflection in her own faith practice as a Hindu and also in her professional work as executive director of New Pluralists.

These chapters are written by nationally recognized leaders, each of whom has direct knowledge and experience of these issues through their work on the ground. It's a fascinating view into how they see the landscape in which they work, and how each of them is striving proactively to create a world in which all people can thrive.

7

Faith Is a Bridge

Why Engaging Religion Is Essential for Addressing Polarization

Eboo Patel and Mary Ellen Geiss

Introduction

In 2006, Madeleine Albright wrote a book called *The Mighty and the Almighty*, which lamented the absence of expertise on religion in the State Department during her tenure as secretary of state. In the book, she explores the various ways that a basic understanding of religion was missing from international diplomacy efforts. While the State Department had numerous economic or constitutional experts, only a single person at that time possessed expertise on interfaith relations. What was the result, in Albright's calculation? The United States was underprepared to navigate the many global issues in which religious diversity was highly implicated—Northern Ireland, the Middle East, the Balkans, and parts of Africa. Albright suggests that understanding religious diversity and religious communities may have led to reconciliation and peacebuilding opportunities in ways we hadn't previously imagined.

Albright is not alone in her perspective. Secretary of State John Kerry famously stated, "If I went back to college today, I think I would probably major in comparative religion, because that's how integrated it is in everything that we are working on and deciding and thinking about life today."[1] These two leaders are reflecting on the work of academic fields that study the integral role of religion in conflict *and* conflict resolution on a global scale. Including scholars such as R. Scott Appleby, Ashutosh Varshnay, and Douglas M. Johnston, the study of international peacebuilding in particular draws on fields of diplomacy, international relations, religious studies, conflict resolution, and more. Critical insights from this body of research illuminate and inform the potential for religiously diverse communities to mitigate conflict and promote cohesion in local, national, and international contexts across the globe.

[1] "John Kerry Would Study Religion," C-SPAN, August 7, 2013, https://www.c-span.org/video/?c4461670/user-clip-john-kerry-study-religion (accessed December 19, 2025).

Eboo Patel and Mary Ellen Geiss, *Faith Is a Bridge* In: *Modeling Religious Pluralism*.
Edited by: Simran Jeet Singh, Oxford University Press. © Oxford University Press 2026.
DOI: 10.1093/oso/9780197745809.003.0007

Scholars of international peacebuilding are not naïve about the role that religion plays in causing violence and division. From historical events like the Crusades and the European wars of religion to more modern events like the Partition of India, the Irish Troubles, and the ongoing difficulties in the Middle East—religion has been at the root of so many destructive and bloody events throughout world history. However, as R. Scott Appleby wrote in *The Ambivalence of the Sacred*, religion is just as equally a source of peacemaking and conflict resolution. Appleby writes, "The unique social location, institutional configuration, cultural power, and remarkable persistence of religions commend the cultivation of elements within them that foster harmonious and just relations between peoples and nurture the seeds of reconciliation when conflict threatens or after it occurs."[2] Indeed, only focusing on the potential for religion to cause conflict and violence undercuts our ability to utilize the assets within religious traditions and communities to mitigate conflict and promote cohesion.

As polarization becomes an ever more dangerous force in the US context, it is paramount that we apply these key learnings to the domestic context. While US-focused efforts to strengthen social cohesion have expanded dramatically over the past decade, religious diversity remains an underleveraged component of a comprehensive and impactful bridgebuilding approach. Just as international leaders have recognized, belatedly, that religious identities and diversity play powerful roles in global affairs, so too domestic leaders must understand and engage the power and potential for religious diversity to bridge divides at home.

This chapter will highlight the value of proactively engaging diverse religious identities, communities, and traditions in such domestic bridgebuilding efforts. Our point is not only that religious identity is an equally important and often under-attended form of identity; in our view, leaving religion out of conversations about identity is similar to excluding race, gender identity, sexual orientation, or ideology. The larger opportunity, which we will emphasize here, is that religious identities and religious traditions also bring unique *assets* to bridgebuilding work, assets that effective bridgebuilders leave aside to the detriment of their work. At its best, religion can provide powerful tools that facilitate bridging in addition to expanding the American imagination to believe that bridging is possible. In the interest of constructing a strong, effective, and comprehensive approach to national bridgebuilding efforts, engaging religious identity and religious diversity proactively is an essential and underutilized tool.

[2] R. Scott Appleby, *The Ambivalence of the Sacred: Religion, Violence, and Reconciliation* (Lanham, MD: Rowman & Littlefield, 2000), 8.

The Promise and Purpose of Bridgebuilding Work

Among the greatest challenges we face in contemporary American domestic life is the problem of polarization. However, as Bill Clinton recognized about the brilliance of American civic life, for every problem in America, there's someone out there working on the solution.[3] Americans' negative feelings toward the opposing political party have increased dramatically[4] over the past decade. About three in four Americans think[5] that their fellow citizens have too little confidence in each other, and trust in national institutions is on the decline.[6] Most Americans[7] believe that the nation is deeply divided over its most important values.

True to Clinton's view, American civil society has offered up a myriad of solutions to these intractable challenges in the form of a vibrant sector of civic bridgebuilding, which has grown dramatically in just the past several years. Understanding the significance of America's deepening polarization, civic leaders across the country have taken on the challenge of strengthening our civic fabric both nationally and at the grassroots level. Alongside the civic organizations responding to this challenge, scholars and journalists are studying this topic with intensity, resulting in a research base that informs the work in evidence-backed ways. Philanthropic and field-building collaboratives[8] have emerged as well, providing essential resourcing and infrastructure to connect, coordinate, and sustain efforts over time. Notably, Mackenzie Scott named bridging[9] as an explicit priority in her game-changing philanthropic investments over the past several years, shining a particular spotlight on the significance of this work. President Biden identified himself as something of a bridgebuilder in

[3] Bill Clinton, "State of the Union Address," January 23, 1996, Archives.gov, https://clintonwhitehouse4.archives.gov/WH/New/other/sotu.html (accessed October 19, 2023).

[4] "U.S. Is Polarizing Faster than Other Democracies, Study Finds," Brown University, January 21, 2020, https://www.brown.edu/news/2020-01-21/polarization (accessed December 19, 2025).

[5] Stacy Rosenberg, "Americans' Trust in Other Americans," Pew Research Center—U.S. Politics & Policy, May 30, 2020, https://www.pewresearch.org/politics/2019/07/22/the-state-of-personal-trust/ (accessed December 19, 2025).

[6] Dan Vallone, et al. "Two Stories of Distrust in America," More in Common, 2021, https://www.moreincommon.com/media/yfcbfmmp/mic_two-stories-of-distrust.pdf (accessed December 19, 2025).

[7] "Most Americans Say Nation Is Deeply Divided over Values, Poll Says," *PBS NewsHour*, October 16, 2020, https://www.pbs.org/newshour/nation/most-americans-say-nation-is-deeply-divided-over-values-poll-says (accessed December 19, 2025).

[8] Alex Daniels, "Grant Maker Bolsters Human Connection as a Way to Take on Polarization," *The Chronicle of Philanthropy*, May 4, 2021, https://www.philanthropy.com/?s=rant+Maker+Bolsters+Human+Connection+as+a+Way+to+Take+on+Polarization (accessed December 19, 2025).

[9] Belinda Luscombe, "MacKenzie Scott Gave away $6 Billion Last Year. It's Not as Easy as It Sounds," *Time*, May 25, 2021, https://time.com/6050873/mackenzie-scott-profile/ (accessed December 19, 2025).

chief, naming national unity[10] as a top priority in his inaugural address. Taking these various dynamics collectively, the field is poised to make a significant national impact.

It is worth noting that diversity is the necessary precondition for bridgebuilding. If we lived in a more homogeneous society with little ethnic, racial, or religious diversity, there would be fewer differences that required bridging.[11] The fact of our diversity creates the context in which bridging is necessary, and it also makes bridgebuilding more challenging—differences in identity contribute to our sense that we are divided, as well as to the social conditions of inequality and marginalization, all of which exacerbate and perpetuate divisions. However, research also shows[12] that diversity, productively harnessed, can make an even stronger civic whole by generating "bridging" social capital, which is stronger than in-group connections. With this research in mind, our diversity is a key strength—but one that we must effectively leverage to generate a stronger whole. Intentional bridgebuilding efforts are precisely the mechanism we need to leverage that strength.

However, in typical approaches to engaging diversity in the US context, religious diversity is engaged less frequently than other forms of identity. A variety of historical factors led early leaders of the multicultural movement to underemphasize religious identity as an element of diversity engagement, including a wrongful assumption[13] that the nation would "secularize" and religion would diminish in social importance over time, as well as a cultural construction of religion as an inherently private phenomenon.[14] As our understandings of religious identity and the role of religion in society have evolved, the larger diversity movement has adapted to include proactive engagement of religious diversity as an element of diversity efforts—albeit with persistently less attention than other forms of identity. We have argued elsewhere[15] that the larger diversity, equity, and inclusion movement must be more proactive in engaging religious identity and diversity given the profound impacts that religion has in American lives, history, society, and culture. We believe that underappreciating religious identity

[10] The White House, "By the President of the United States of America: A Proclamation," January 20, 2021, https://www.federalregister.gov/documents/2021/01/25/2021-01748/a-national-day-of-unity (accessed December 19, 2025).

[11] Robert Putnam, "E Pluribus Unum: Diversity and Community in the Twenty-First Century, The 2006 Johan Skytte Prize Lecture," *Scandinavian Political Studies* 30 (2007): 137–174.

[12] Ibid.

[13] "O Come All Ye Faithful," *The Economist*, November 3, 2007, https://www.economist.com/special-report/2007/11/03/o-come-all-ye-faithful (accessed December 19, 2025).

[14] Douglas Jacobsen and Rhonda Hustedt Jacobsen, *No Longer Invisible: Religion in University Education* (New York: Oxford University Press, 2012), 20–26.

[15] Eboo Patel, "The New Identity Politics of Religion," *The Interfaith Observer*, February 1, 2017, https://www.theinterfaithobserver.org/journal-articles/2016/6/6/the-new-identity-politics-of-religion.html (accessed December 19, 2025).

leaves lingering dynamics that pervade the emerging field of bridgebuilding in the same way the challenge persists within the broader diversity, equity, and inclusion movement.

We close this section with a thought experiment: Imagine you are launching a bridging initiative. Maybe it's a local council; maybe it's a national conference. In either case, you will have taken care to create a space where people from diverse identities and divergent perspectives can find common ground. There are people from a variety of races, ethnicities, gender identities, and sexual orientations present. There are people who voted differently. There are people who live in cities and people who live in small towns, day laborers and corporate CEOs, people whose ancestors were on the *Mayflower*, people whose ancestors came in chains, and people who are undocumented. As you scan the list of the attendees, you feel a flush of pride. Then one of your colleagues asks you: I'm curious what our religious diversity looks like. Do we have evangelicals and atheists coming? Buddhists and Baha'is? Muslims and Mormons? Honestly, you have no idea, and you can't help but wonder: If you have not been as proactive about religious diversity as you have been about other dimensions of identity and ideology, can you really be said to be doing effective bridgebuilding work? And what opportunities are you leaving behind?

The rest of this chapter will focus on these key questions. What are the distinctive assets that religious identity and religious diversity bring to bridging efforts in the US context? Why does it matter, and how does our unique American history serve as a strength in this work? What opportunities or tools do we lose when the bridgebuilding field does not engage religion proactively? We contend that religious identity, diversity, and traditions are powerful tools in the essential work of combatting American polarization.

Religious Identity Matters Because Representation Matters

G.K. Chesterton wrote that the United States is a nation with the soul of a church.[16] That statement underscores the deep religiosity of the United States, a fact that is not always fully engaged in typical diversity and inclusion efforts. In bridgebuilding efforts, we must respect and prioritize the variety of ways that Americans identify, and that includes reflecting the deep commitment that many Americans hold to their religious identities.

While it is true that the numbers of the faithful have declined in recent years, Americans are still far more religious than our counterparts in most other industrialized nations. In terms of both self-identification and religious practices,

[16] G.K. Chesterton, *What I Saw in America* (London: Hodder and Stoughton, 1923).

Americans are far more likely[17] to report the priority of religious identity in their lives (through frequency of prayer, attending religious services, belief in God or a higher power, etc.). Among 102 countries, the United States is the only country[18] with both an above-average GDP per capita and an above-average frequency of prayer.

Our remarkable religious diversity is a distinctive element of America's religiosity. The United States is perhaps the most religiously diverse nation in human history, from the indigenous spiritualities that predate European arrival, to our very founding as a place for religious liberty, to the massive influx of religiously diverse immigrants arriving through the Immigration Act of 1965. American religiosity reflects religious identities from nearly every corner of the globe.

Notably, American religiosity holds true across our religiously diverse communities. Seventy-two percent of all Americans say that religion is important to them[19] personally, and even those who do not find religion as personally relevant report[20] that religion is still important within their family. Chesterton may have written that we are a nation with the soul of a church, but the research shows that we are also a nation with the soul of a temple, a synagogue, a mosque, a ward, a gurdwara, and a meditation circle.

What's our point here? Religion matters to Americans, and religious diversity is our powerful reality. Race, gender, sexuality, geography, level of education, and class—these are all important identities to people, inspirations to cooperate and reasons for conflict and division. So is religion. Given the value that Americans place on their religious identity, bridgebuilders should similarly prioritize it.

The Special Role of Religion in American History

Navigating religious identity and diversity in a productive new way was an essential priority for the nation's Founders. Part of America's founding ideals as a land of liberty emerges from the number of colonists who settled in America escaping religious oppression in their originating countries. Indeed, many of the

[17] George Gao, "How Do Americans Stand Out from the Rest of the World?" Pew Research Center, March 25, 2015, https://www.pewresearch.org/short-reads/2015/03/12/how-do-americans-stand-out-from-the-rest-of-the-world/ (accessed December 19, 2025).

[18] Dalia Fahmy, "Americans Are Far More Religious than Adults in Other Wealthy Nations," Pew Research Center, July 31, 2018, https://www.pewresearch.org/short-reads/2018/07/31/americans-are-far-more-religious-than-adults-in-other-wealthy-nations/ (accessed December 19, 2025).

[19] Megan Brenan, "Religion Considered Important to 72% of Americans," *Gallup News*, December 14, 2018, https://news.gallup.com/poll/245651/religion-considered-important-americans.aspx (accessed December 19, 2025).

[20] AP-NORC Center for Public Affairs Research, "How Important Is Religion to Americans?" December 2021, https://apnorc.org/projects/how-important-is-religion-to-americans/ (accessed December 19, 2025).

European settlers had personal experiences or recent family histories of religious persecution or religious wars, experiences that formed early commitments to religious liberty in the American experiment.

While America is often conceptualized as a Christian or Judeo-Christian nation, in fact the Founders were deeply committed to the principle of religious pluralism. These (generally) wealthy, (loosely) Christian, (presumably) straight, (most assuredly) white male slaveholders prioritized and created a constitutional system that protected the freedom of religion, barred the federal government from establishing a single church, prevented religious tests for those running for office, and beautifully articulated the principle of religious pluralism within a religiously diverse democracy.

Jewish leader Moses Seixas wrote to George Washington inquiring about the place for Jews in the newly formed country, to which Washington replied, "It is now no more that toleration is spoken of, as if it was by the indulgence of one class of people that another enjoyed the exercise of their inherent natural rights . . . [the US government] gives to bigotry no sanction, to persecution no assistance."[21] Benjamin Franklin made a personal financial contribution to each of the religiously diverse communities in Philadelphia and, furthermore, raised money for a new hall that was, in his words, "expressly for the use of any preacher of any religious persuasion," explicitly stating that this space would be open to Muslim preachers. President John Adams utilized this ethic in his international affairs, signing a treaty with Tripoli in 1791 that stated:

> As the government of the United States of America is not in any sense founded on the Christian Religion,—as it has in itself no character of enmity against the laws, religion or tranquility of Mussulmen,— and as the said States never have entered into any war or act of hostility against any Mahometan nation, it is declared by the parties that no pretext arising from religious opinions shall ever produce an interruption of the harmony existing between the countries.[22]

Pages of history have been and will be written about the role of religion and religious diversity in the founding of our nation, but the Founders' commitment to religious liberty and the flourishing of religiously diverse communities is clear. The north star set by the Founders, at least in the case of religion, is clearly articulated and worth achieving. The foundational bedrock of our history in engaging religious diversity gives us firm ground from which to build.

[21] Mark A. Mastromarino, *The Papers of George Washington: Presidential Series*, vol. 6, July–November 1790 (Charlottesville: University Press of Virginia, 1996).

[22] Denise Spellberg, *Thomas Jefferson's Qur'an: Islam and the Founders* (New York: Vintage Books, 2013).

Religious Traditions Have Wisdom and Practices for Peacemaking

As noted throughout this chapter, religion is widely acknowledged to be a source of profound conflict—and, from the perspectives of many scholars and activists across the globe, just as equally a source of peacemaking and conflict resolution. What, then, are the distinctive assets that religiously diverse traditions hold for purposes of reconciliation and bridgebuilding?

A vision for the way the world ought to be: Religious traditions frequently offer aspirational ideas for the possibilities of a more just, kind, loving, and relational world, and thus encourage believers to work toward that vision of how the world ought to be. Within Judaism, the concept of *tikkun olam* (often translated as "repair the world") envisions an ideal world and articulates how Jewish people can constructively build a more just and peaceful world. In Christianity, the figure of Jesus Christ illustrates a path of reconciliation and peace, and Christians are encouraged to follow in his footsteps (John 2:6, "Whoever says he abides in [Christ] ought to walk in the same way he walked"). The first Sikh guru, Guru Nanak, lived a path of selfless service and humility, and emphasized how engaging in such service could change the world to a more just and compassionate place. These examples demonstrate the inspirational potential that religious traditions offer believers, both painting a picture of the possibility of a better world and instructing believers to pursue that path.

Stories/models to emulate: While we frequently tell the stories of how religion divides us, we less frequently explore the remarkable stories and models of bridgebuilding that emerge from within religious communities. Learning the stories and histories of interfaith relationships provides powerful models that can appeal to diverse constituencies as values-based paths to follow in our own time. Saint Francis embarked on an international peacemaking expedition and befriended[23] Sultan al-Malik al-Kamil, a relationship that may have influenced contemporary practices of Christianity. Akbar the Great was considered a pioneer of interfaith dialogue,[24] corresponding with European monarchs on the value of religious tolerance, hosting interfaith dialogues in his court, and making intentional efforts to integrate non-Muslims in his empire. Interfaith bridgebuilding was at the heart of the US civil rights movements of the 1960s and 1970s, from the relationship[25] between Rabbi Abraham Joshua

[23] Thomas Cahill, "The Peaceful Crusader," *New York Times*, December 25, 2006, https://www.nytimes.com/2006/12/25/opinion/25Cahill.html (accessed December 19, 2025).

[24] Craig Considine, "Finding Tolerance in Akbar, the Philosopher-King," *Huffpost*, April 10, 2013, https://www.huffpost.com/entry/finding-tolerance-in-akba_b_3031746 (accessed December 19, 2025).

[25] "Abraham Joshua Heschel, *The Martin Luther King, Jr. Research and Education Institute*, https://kinginstitute.stanford.edu/heschel-abraham-joshua (accessed October 19, 2023).

Heschel and Martin Luther King, Jr., to the engagement between Coretta Scott King and Malcolm X,[26] to the key leadership role[27] Bayard Rustin played in the 1963 March on Washington, to the inspiring role that Gandhi played for the entire movement.[28] Our traditions are replete with powerful, inspiring models for bridgebuilding deeply embedded in religious and ethical values systems, as meaningful today as they were at the time.

Prayer or meditation practices: The Greater Good Science Center's *Bridging Differences Playbook* emphasizes[29] the essential interior or "intrapersonal" work that bridgebuilders must do to develop strong skills and dispositions to effectively bridge divides. Religious traditions offer prayer and meditation practices that support the inner or spiritual capacities to engage in this work productively. For example, the Buddhist metta[30] (lovingkindness) prayer focuses on cultivating unconditional goodwill for all, and intentionally extends that goodwill to friends, family, and even enemies. The Prayer of St. Francis of Assisi begins, "Lord, make me an instrument of your peace," seeking for God to grant that the person praying "not so much seek . . . to be understood as to understand," among other illuminations to the world. Secular meditation practices can focus on seeing the humanity of others and cultivating good intentions toward others.

Theology/wisdom of cooperating with others: Alongside prayers that cultivate the skills and dispositions for bridgebuilding, religious communities also offer theological and ethical wisdom to ground our relational work in deep traditions. The story of the Good Samaritan in the New Testament underscores not only the value of selfless service, but also the importance of caring for individuals and communities with whom we disagree. The prophet Muhammad set an example for prioritizing peace in the Treaty of Hudaybiyah, laying down arms and accepting humiliating negotiating terms to achieve reconciliation. The Hindu concept of *ahimsa* is understood as one of the highest virtues, which focuses on nonviolence and non-injury toward all other living beings. Deep within a variety of religious and ethical traditions, religious traditions underscore the depths that

[26] Coretta Scott King, interview by Blackside Inc., Washington University Libraries, Film and Media Archive, Henry Hampton Collection, November 21, 1988, http://digital.wustl.edu/e/eii/eiiweb/kin5427.0224.089corettascottking.html (accessed December 19, 2025).

[27] Cheryl Corley, "Bayard Rustin: The Man Who Organized the March on Washington," *NPR All Things Considered* (broadcast), August 15, 2013.

[28] Erin Blakemore, "How Mahatma Gandhi Changed the Face of Political Protest," National Geographic Culture, May 4, 2021, https://www.nationalgeographic.com/culture/article/mahatma-gandhi-changed-political-protest (accessed December 19, 2025).

[29] Greater Good Science Center, *Bridging Differences Playbook* (Berkeley: University of California, 2021), https://greatergood.berkeley.edu/images/uploads/Bridging_Differences_Playbook-Final.pdf (accessed December 19, 2025).

[30] Melvin Escobar, "Loving-Kindness: May All Beings Be Happy," *Lion's Roar*, September 20, 2022, https://www.lionsroar.com/loving-kindness-may-all-beings-be-happy/ (accessed December 19, 2025).

practitioners should find within themselves to maintain right relationships and positive engagements with one another.

Deeply sourced values and virtues: Fundamentally, bridging deep divides calls on practitioners to embody profound values and virtues such as humility, compassion, generosity, and forgiveness. These are shared values that span many religious and ethical traditions, but the rich religious sources that inspire these values make their embodiment a higher calling and more robust necessity. Rather than relying on a thin or generic commitment to the idea of forgiveness, drawing on the religious and ethical inspiration for these values adds both a deeper level of obligation and a higher aspiration to the full extent of living out the idea. Evoking the model of Jesus Christ, or the Buddha, or Guru Nanak evokes an entirely different mode of engagement in the religious imagination. Humility is an especially critical value in the context of bridgebuilding.

Bridging deep divides requires a recognition that we may not have all the answers and our own opinions and assumptions may be incomplete. We have to truly believe that our perspectives will be enriched by hearing from and engaging with individuals who understand the world differently. An ancient Jewish rabbinical tale conveys the story of a rabbi who comes to the synagogue with a slip of paper in each pocket. In one pocket, the paper reads, "You are nothing but dust and ashes." In the other pocket, the paper reads, "The world was created for you."

While many interpret this story to understand the importance of balancing perspectives, it is also at its core about the importance of humility—the humility to know which pocket to draw into more deeply to recall whatever message might be most important in a given moment. Both slips of paper are true, and true at the same time. Balancing these truths is an ongoing and profound act of humility, and similarly in bridging divides, we must be constantly holding multiple truths alongside one another and maintaining the humility not to let one truth overshadow another. This story is just one example of how deeply sourced values and virtues from religious and ethical traditions can motivate the most powerful dispositions to engage differences productively and positively.

An Essential Skillset in Bridgebuilding and Reconciliation

Cultivating, developing, and utilizing the peacebuilding assets within religious communities are no simple tasks—we call this *interfaith leadership*, and it takes training, education, and experience to do it well. When interfaith leadership is intentionally honed, the potential for transformative engagement is powerful. Here is one of these situations.

As horrific news of a hostage situation in Coleyville, Texas, emerged, Imam Omar Suleiman was already in the car with his family. Checking the local social media feed, Imam Suleiman and his wife realized that their friend, Rabbi Charlie Cytron-Walker, was being held hostage in his local synagogue. Imam Suleiman immediately called fellow religious leaders in the area, then drove over to see if he could help.

Imam Suleiman later wrote that the hostage taker's ramblings and clothing made it clear that he was a Muslim. Suleiman knew that he had a distinctive skillset as an imam to help in this situation—perhaps to calm down the hostage taker, perhaps to offer spiritual support. He offered that help to local law enforcement.

While he waited, though, a different skillset came into use. He walked across the street to the local Catholic church, where he found Rabbi Cytron-Walker's wife and daughter waiting. As he later wrote,[31] "[T]here was nothing political in our discussions . . . [it] was all pastoral, which was enough: what do you say to a wife and daughter who are wondering if they'll ever see their husband and father again?"

Two Muslim women joined the small group at the church sometime later, bringing Rabbi Cytron-Walker's favorite samosas in the hope he would soon be freed. They were soon joined by other religious leaders in the area, Jewish, Muslims, and Christians gathered together in solidarity and prayer and, most of all, community.

Imam Suleiman is a powerful example of a bridgebuilder of two kinds—someone with a deep knowledge of Muslim communities who could serve as a powerful expert and partner to law enforcement dealing with a highly tense situation. Simultaneously, his first phone call is also revealing: not to law enforcement to offer his help, but rather to religiously diverse leaders to rally the community in support and solidarity in the midst of fear and animosity. In a moment that could have deepened divisions between communities in the United States, Suleiman and others instead demonstrated the power of religion to bring people together. In his words, "We will continue to insist on the humanity of our neighbors and be human ourselves. We will continue to live our faith and contribute through it."

As the bridgebuilding movement expands in the United States, may we all so powerfully leverage the potential of religious diversity to cut through our divides and showcase a sacred alternate path forward.

[31] Omar Suleiman, "11 Hours of Prayer and Solidarity at the Colleyville Synagogue Standoff," *Religion News*, January 18, 2022.

8
Religious Communities and Anti-Asian Racism during the COVID-19 Pandemic

Melissa May Borja

In April 2021, on one of the holiest days of the Christian year, over 120 families at a predominantly Asian American church in New Jersey gathered for their Good Friday service to pray, sing, and commemorate the crucifixion of Christ. But the peaceful online service was interrupted by Zoom-bombers, who blasted pornographic images across the screen and assailed listeners with ear-splitting screams and racist slurs, including cries of "I hate Asians!" and "Chinks!" A member of the congregation described the incident to the online news magazine *AsianFeed*:

> I saw children crying and covering their ears, moms rushing to grab and shield their kids. Over thirty families left the call fearing for their safety, with the rest sitting in shock and horror, shaking with rage and fear. . . . I am devastated that the perpetrators orchestrated the attack to threaten a community in their own homes, violating them and their deeply held commitments. After the attack, I did not feel safe in my own dining room where I had been watching the service with my husband. This incident goes to show how Anti-Asian hate does not stop when we come home from the streets and close the door behind us. It follows us, finding its way into our most vulnerable and sacred places.[1]

The Good Friday Zoom-bombing was one of thousands of attacks against people of Asian descent across America and around the world during the first two years of the COVID-19 pandemic. Between March 2020 and March 2022, Stop AAPI Hate received over eleven thousand reports of anti-Asian hate incidents.[2] And many of these incidents occurred in "vulnerable and sacred spaces," such as the Asian American church in New Jersey.

[1] Michael Lai, "Asian American Church Zoom-Bombed with Racial Slurs and Pornographic Images during Good Friday Service," *AsianFeed*, April 3, 2021, https://www.asianfeed.com/article/michaellai//2021/04/asian-american-church-zoom-bombed-good-friday (accessed December 19, 2025).

[2] Stop AAPI Hate, "Two Years and Thousands of Voices," July 2022, https://stopaapihate.org/2022/07/20/year-2-report/ (accessed December 19, 2025).

Melissa May Borja, *Religious Communities and Anti-Asian Racism during the COVID-19 Pandemic*
In: *Modeling Religious Pluralism*. Edited by: Simran Jeet Singh, Oxford University Press. © Oxford University Press 2026. DOI: 10.1093/oso/9780197745809.003.0008

Focusing on the specific case of anti-Asian racism and violence during the COVID-19 pandemic, this chapter explores the relationship between religion, racism, and community mobilization against racism in the United States. How did religious communities experience pandemic-related racism? In what ways, if any, did religious identities, institutions, beliefs, and practices contribute to racist attacks and scapegoating during the pandemic? And how did diverse Americans draw on religious identities, institutions, beliefs, and practices as an antidote to racism?

I argue that religious institutions are central to understanding the acts of anti-Asian racism that surged during the pandemic. On one hand, they were important sites where anti-Asian racism was enacted, endorsed, and encouraged. Churches and temples are often highly visible places where Asian American communities gather, and their significance and visibility were perhaps one reason why they were targeted in attacks. Religious institutions were also places that explicitly fostered anti-Asian rhetoric and beliefs, particularly the scapegoating of Asian and Asian American people for the COVID-19 pandemic. But while religious institutions were part of the problem of anti-Asian racism, they also showed potential to be part of the solution. Churches and temples served as sites of support, education, intra-community and interfaith mobilization, and affirmation of the pluralist commitment to create a society where people of different racial and religious backgrounds can live peaceably with one another.

In making this argument, I aim to make one basic intervention: to highlight that religion is a critical, often overlooked aspect of racially targeted acts of harassment, violence, and discrimination. The issue of COVID-related anti-Asian racism has received significant attention in both scholarly literature and mainstream news media.[3] However, in contrast to themes of race and gender, the religious dimensions of anti-Asian racism have received comparatively little engagement, despite the fact that a growing body of scholarship has illuminated how religious difference has contributed to the racialization of Asian people as "heathens" and a "yellow peril" that threaten the prosperity, safety, morality, and well-being of the American nation.[4]

Similarly, in discussions about responses to anti-Asian racism, the work of religious individuals and institutions involved in mobilizing against racism and targeted violence has received relatively little recognition. This religious antiracism activism has taken many forms. Some activists have focused on change

[3] See, for example, the October 2020 issue of *Journal of Asian American Studies*, which focused on anti-Asian racism during the COVID-19 pandemic.

[4] Kathryn Gin Lum, *Heathen: Religion and Race in American History* (Cambridge, MA: Harvard University Press, 2022); Khyati Joshi, *White Christian Privilege: The Illusion of Religious Equality in America* (New York: New York University Press, 2020); and John Kuo Wei Tchen and Dylan Yeats, eds., *Yellow Peril! An Archive of Anti-Asian Fear* (London: Verso, 2014).

within their own religious communities, while others have drawn on their faith to call for government accountability and policy change at the local, state, and national levels. These efforts are part of a longer history of religiously rooted racial justice activism within Asian American communities that has had far-reaching—if underappreciated—impact, and that has drawn serious scholarly attention only recently.[5]

That religion receives such limited consideration in scholarly and public conversations about anti-Asian racism is unfortunate because, as this chapter will show, religious beliefs, practices, identities, and institutions have shaped the trajectory of the social and political problem of anti-Asian racism in several critical (and often competing) ways. The tendency, though, has been to view only one aspect: either how religion has aided anti-racism endeavors, or alternatively how religion has bolstered white supremacy and Christian nationalism. However, both have been true, and it is instructive to hold these multiple realities of contemporary American religious life together. Religion is neither an inherently positive force that fosters harmonious relations in a multiracial society, nor is it an inherently harmful weapon of those who defend religious and racial hierarchies. Ultimately, religion is a resource used by diverse people and deployed for a wide variety of ends.

Religious Communities as Sites of Hate

As highly visible centers of Asian American life, Asian American religious institutions have often been targets of racist attacks. The Good Friday Zoombombing of the Asian American church in New Jersey was just one of several attacks on Asian American churches during the COVID-19 pandemic. For example, in Scottsdale, Arizona, an Asian American church was vandalized by people who destroyed the church's wiring, pipes, and doors. Jeff Liou, national director of theological formation for InterVarsity Christian Fellowship, told Religion News Service that vandals had painted racist graffiti near his church.[6] There have also been several attacks on Buddhist temples. Vandals smashed windows, destroyed lanterns, and set fire to property at Higashi Honganji Buddhist

[5] For examples of histories of religious communities engaged in racial justice work, see Jane Hong, "The Asian American Movement and the Church," *Journal of Asian American Studies* 25, no. 1 (February 2022): 63–94, https://doi.org/10.1353/jaas.2022.0002; and Stephanie Hinnershitz, *Race, Religion, and Civil Rights: Asian Students on the West Coast, 1900–1968* (New Brunswick, NJ: Rutgers University Press, 2015).

[6] Emily McFarlan Miller, "Asian American Christians Denounce Anti-Asian Racism amid Coronavirus," *Religion News*, April 2, 2020, https://religionnews.com/2020/04/02/asian-american-christians-release-statement-against-anti-asian-racism-amid-coronavirus/ (accessed December 18, 2025).

Temple in Little Tokyo in Los Angeles.[7] In Austin, Texas, vandals ruined statues and furniture at the Thien Hau Temple. And in Montreal, vandals shattered religious objects at two Buddhist temples.[8] In many of these attacks, the precise motive behind the attack was not clear. However, Louis Le, a volunteer at the Chua Quan Am Temple, one of the temples vandalized in Montreal, linked the destruction in his community to rising anti-Asian sentiment during the COVID-19 pandemic. "My theory is that it's because of the coronavirus at the moment," Le told Radio Canada International. "People associate it with the Asian community. They're prejudice[d] and unjust."[9]

Looking beyond the COVID-19 pandemic, attacks on Asian American religious institutions have been part of the long history of racism and violence against Asian Americans in the United States. For example, while Japanese Americans were incarcerated during the Second World War, Japanese American Buddhist temples were vandalized. As Duncan Williams chronicled in *American Sutra*, the vandalism at Nichiren Buddhist Temple in Los Angeles in 1944 was so severe that the US government allowed for one member of the temple to leave Amache camp in Colorado to return to California, where she found the temple had been utterly destroyed: "Nothing was untouched, sewing machines were ruined, furniture broken, mirrors smashed to smithereens, broken glass from breakable articles, household goods scattered helter-skelter, trunks broken beyond repair," she said.[10] Attacks on Asian American Buddhists occurred again later in the twentieth century, when in the 1970s, 1980s, and 1990s, Southeast Asian refugees experienced intense racist backlash as they were resettled in the United States.[11] In Portland, Maine, for example, local opponents of Southeast Asian refugees worked to prevent the building of a Cambodian American Buddhist temple. With the aid of some allies, including a local Quaker group, the Cambodian American community in Portland eventually succeeded in establishing the Watt Samaki Buddhist Center. However, in 1993, vandals stole

[7] Andrew Campa, "Fire, Vandalism Rock Buddhist Temple in Little Tokyo," *Los Angeles Times*, February 26, 2021, sec. California, https://www.latimes.com/california/story/2021-02-26/higashi-honganji-fire (accessed December 18, 2025).

[8] Katie Hall, "Police Investigating Vandalism at Buddhist Temple in North Austin," *Austin American-Statesman*, April 29, 2020, https://www.statesman.com/news/20200429/police-investigating-vandalism-at-buddhist-temple-in-north-austin (accessed December 18, 2025); and CBC News, "Montreal Police Suspect Hate-Crimes after Vandals Hit Buddhist Temples, Chinatown," *CBC News*, March 4, 2020, https://www.cbc.ca/news/canada/montreal/vandalism-temples-1.5485151 (accessed December 18, 2025).

[9] Terry Haig, "Buddhists Sites and Temples Are Vandalized in Montreal," *Radio Canada International*, March 5, 2020, https://www.rcinet.ca/en/2020/03/05/buddhists-sites-and-temples-are-vandalized-in-montreal/ (accessed December 18, 2025).

[10] Quoted in Duncan Ryūken Williams, *American Sutra: A Story of Faith and Freedom in the Second World War* (Cambridge, MA: Harvard University Press, 2019) 232.

[11] United States Commission on Civil Rights, "Recent Activities against Citizens and Residents of Asian Descent" (Washington, DC: US Commission on Civil Rights, 1986).

the Buddhist center's electronic equipment and graffitied its wall with a hateful message: "Dirty Asian, Chink, Go Home."[12]

During the War on Terror in the opening decades of the twenty-first century, Asian Americans who are Muslim or assumed to be Muslim have been the target of Islamophobic attacks. Mosques all across America have been vandalized, burned, and bombed. So many mosque attacks have occurred in the past two decades that the ACLU keeps an updated map of incidents of violence and discrimination targeting mosques in every state.[13] Sikh Americans, also impacted by Islamophobia, have found that their religious institutions have also been subjected to vicious acts of hate and violence. In 2012, for example, a white supremacist man gunned down six people and injured four others at a Sikh gurdwara in Oak Creek, Wisconsin.[14]

Religious Communities as Sources of Hate

Religious communities have not only been sites of hateful attacks; they have also been places that support and sanctify racism and religious bigotry. Numerous scholars have chronicled the long history of how Christian churches have fostered white supremacy and religious hatred in the United States.[15] The role of some white Christian leaders in the rise of anti-Asian racism during the COVID-19 pandemic was no exception. In May 2020, for example, Keith Kilgore, a pastor at Oxbow Presbyterian Church in Antwerp, New York, took to Facebook to blame Chinese people for the COVID-19 pandemic. "We wouldn't be in this mess if the Chinks would have kept Kosher," he declared. Elsewhere on Facebook, he called COVID-19 "kung flu," a term widely regarded as stigmatizing and harmful to Asian and Asian American people. In addition to using derogatory terms for Chinese people, Kilgore had previously given a sermon in which he described slavery as an institution that had benefited Black people and had declared on social media that "Allah sucks."[16]

[12] Pirun Sen, "Watt Samaki Temple," Pluralism Project Archive, Harvard University, https://hwpi.harvard.edu/pluralismarchive/watt-samaki-temple (accessed July 20, 2023).

[13] American Civil Liberties Union, "Nationwide Anti-Mosque Activity," https://www.aclu.org/other/nationwide-anti-mosque-activity (accessed July 20, 2023).

[14] Steven Yaccino, Michael Schwirtz, and Marc Santora, "Gunman Kills 6 at a Sikh Temple near Milwaukee," *New York Times*, August 5, 2012, sec. U.S., https://www.nytimes.com/2012/08/06/us/shooting-reported-at-temple-in-wisconsin.html (accessed December 18, 2025).

[15] For examples of this scholarship, see Bradley Onishi, *Preparing for War: The Extremist History of White Christian Nationalism—and What Comes Next* (Minneapolis, MN: Broadleaf Books, 2023); Robert P. Jones, *White Too Long: The Legacy of White Supremacy in American Christianity* (New York: Simon & Schuster, 2020); and Jemar Tisby, *The Color of Compromise: The Truth about the American Church's Complicity in Racism* (Grand Rapids, MI: Zondervan, 2019).

[16] Ben Muir, "Oxbow Pastor's Comments, Behavior Raise Concerns," *Watertown Daily News*, June 27, 2020, https://www.nny360.com/communitynews/faithperspectives/oxbow-pastor-s-comments-behavior-raise-concerns/article_767b2476-d820-5a89-8b69-06644565c0d2.html (accessed

Even if white Christian leaders do not explicitly use anti-Asian, anti-Black, or Islamophobic rhetoric themselves, they have often refused to condemn the words and actions of others and, in the eyes of their critics, have been complicit in reinforcing white supremacy and Christian privilege. The professor and activist Lucas Kwong, for example, condemned Christian nationalism's impact on anti-Asian hate, the silence of white Christian pastors in the rise of anti-Asian attacks during the pandemic, and the role of Christian leaders and churches in condoning racism, which he described as "Sanctified Sinophobia."[17] Most notably, through his online project *Against Christian Xenophobia*, Kwong shared a list of American politicians who identified as Christian, who used or advanced rhetoric and policies that were xenophobic and racist, and who, as Kwong put it, "use a nationalistic version of the Christian faith to launder their disregard for Asian lives." In addition, Kwong identified the churches to which these politicians belonged, and he urged the pastors of these churches to hold the politicians accountable. Kwong asked church leaders to "meet with the offending members, urging them to repent of the sin of racism and consequent endangerment of Asian lives." He called for churches to "institute disciplinary measures, up to and including stripping the offending members of membership." Most importantly, he invited churches to reflect on the health of their institutions and "offer an accounting of how such racism could be allowed to flourish in their churches." He urged congregations to create "plans to combat anti-Asian racism at their churches and even materially contribute to the struggling Asian populations in their vicinity." In the absence of these actions, Kwong urged both denominations and members of these churches to take action. These measures are necessary, Kwong argued, because "while anti-Asian racism runs rampant throughout America today, it particularly flows from Christian nationalists in positions of power." Ultimately, he said, "[A]nti-Chinese malevolence lurks where the flag meets the cross."[18]

December 18, 2025). For a discussion on the danger of stigmatizing rhetoric, see Sean Darling-Hammond, Eli K. Michaels, Rucker C. Johnson, et al., "After 'The China Virus' Went Viral: Racially Charged Coronavirus Coverage and Trends in Bias against Asian Americans," *Health Education & Behavior*, September 10, 2020, 109019812095794, https://doi.org/10.1177/1090198120957949.

[17] Lucas Kwong, "Lamenting Sanctified Sinophobia, Demanding Transformation," *ISAAC* (blog), December 24, 2020, https://isaacweb.org/lamenting-sanctified-sinophobia-demanding-transformation/ (accessed December 18, 2025); and Lucas Kwong, "'God Bless Mr. Truman': Christian Nationalism's Impact on Anti-Asian Hate," *ISAAC* (blog), January 7, 2021, https://isaacweb-org.fhs00040.managedword.com/2021/01/07/god-bless-mr-truman-christian-nationalisms-impact-on-anti-asian-hate/ (accessed December 18, 2025).

[18] Lucas Kwong, "An Open Letter on Anti-Asian Racism & Christian Nationalism," *Against Christian Xenophobia*, accessed July 20, 2023, https://www.againstchristianxenophobia.com/against-christian-xenophobia (accessed December 18, 2025).

Religious Communities as Solutions to Hate

Kwong focused his efforts on churches because he recognized that religious institutions have the potential to be more than places that produce racist harm. Instead, they can be sites of healing and hope where people can gather to find comfort, community, and the courage to resist. For Asian Americans and many other groups, churches, temples, and mosques have long served as community institutions that are centers of power and mobilization, and amid the rise of COVID-related racist attacks, they were more than a setting and a source of hate—they were also a solution to it.

In the immediate aftermath of an event, religious institutions have served as a site of first response for people in urgent need of safety and support. For example, after the FedEx shooting in Indianapolis in April 2021—an attack that targeted a location with a large Sikh workforce and resulted in the death of four Sikh employees, and that Sikh activists considered a possible hate crime—community members gathered at the gurdwara, the Sikh place of worship, to grieve the victims. Especially in places like Indiana, which has a relatively undeveloped infrastructure for addressing anti-Asian racism, religious congregations like Sikh Satsang of Indianapolis have played an important role in convening and comforting community members in the wake of an attack.[19]

Religious communities and networks have also emerged as a site of long-term movement building. Early in the COVID-19 pandemic, for instance, the Asian American Christian Collaborative (AACC) issued a statement about anti-Asian racism that spoke directly to Asian Americans and acknowledged their pain and their needs, while also urging Christian leaders to "speak without ambiguity against racism of every kind."[20] The AACC organized an array of responses to anti-Asian racism during the pandemic, most notably a nationwide series of prayer rallies after a mass shooting in Atlanta claimed the lives of six Asian and Asian American women in March 2021.[21] The AACC was one of many Christian churches and organizations that condemned anti-Asian racism and called for change.[22] Christians were not the only people who drew on their

[19] Cate Charron, "Sikh Prayer Service Emphasizes Community, Inclusion One Year after the Fedex Shooting," *The Indianapolis Star*, April 10, 2022, https://www.indystar.com/story/news/local/2022/04/10/fedex-shooting-sikh-community-remembers-through-prayer-inclusion/9514774002/ (accessed December 18, 2025).

[20] Asian American Christian Collaborative, "Statement on Anti-Asian Racism in the Time of Covid-19," March 2020, https://www.asianamericanchristiancollaborative.com/read-statement (accessed December 18, 2025).

[21] Asian American Christian Collaborative, "National Rally: Stand for AAPI Lives and Dignity 3/28/21," https://www.asianamericanchristiancollaborative.com/rally (accessed July 20, 2023).

[22] Melissa Borja and Kayla Zhang, "'Please Love Our Asian American Neighbors': Christian Responses to Anti-Asian Racism during the COVID-19 Pandemic," *Theology Today* 79, no. 4 (2023): 370–389.

religious convictions to take action, decry racism, and express their support for Asian Americans. Muslims, calling attention to the long-standing problem of Orientalism, issued statements denouncing anti-Asian prejudice.[23] Buddhist activists organized May We Gather, which planned pilgrimages and other projects of "mourning, mending, and renewal" to remember the victims of anti-Asian violence and to "heal America's racial trauma."[24] Representatives from over 180 Jewish American organizations issued a collective statement calling for "kindness and solidarity," not scapegoating. The statement highlighted the importance of showing love, compassion, and empathy to neighbors, and the importance of learning the lessons of Jewish history. Noting that "Jews as a people have a long history of being singled out and stigmatized during times of societal crisis, including being blamed without basis for the spread of disease," the statement called "all people and particularly all leaders to reject conspiracy theories and the singling out of Asian Americans, foreigners, immigrants, Jews, or any other communities in this moment."[25]

Faith-based efforts to address anti-Asian racism developed not only within religious communities, but also across religious and racial groups. In these efforts, groups leaned into specific beliefs, practices, and histories while identifying shared values, theological commitments, and experiences. Collaborations between Asian Americans and Jewish Americans offer an instructive example. For example, in March 2020, less than a week after the World Health Organization declared COVID-19 a global pandemic, Anti-Defamation League CEO Jonathan Greenblatt and presidential candidate Andrew Yang co-authored an opinion essay in *USA Today* in which they warned America of "another serious contagion"—"the scapegoating and blaming of Asian, Jewish and other minorities for this public health crisis." Alarmed by how COVID-19 had spurred an uptick in stigmatizing rhetoric and racist attacks against Jews and Asian Americans, Yang and Greenblatt spoke frankly about the ugly history of Sinophobia and antisemitism in the United States and its dangerous resurgence in 2020. They urged "all Americans to come together and stand against the anti-Asian and anti-Jewish blame game." In doing so, they wrote as individuals who, despite their different racial and religious backgrounds, shared a commitment to addressing hate in all its forms.[26]

[23] Zeba Khan, "When Racism Goes Viral: The Coronavirus and Modern Muslim Orientalism," *MuslimMatters.org* (blog), February 1, 2020, https://muslimmatters.org/2020/02/01/coronavirus-racism-china/ (accessed December 18, 2025).

[24] Duncan Ryūken Williams et al., "May We Gather," May We Gather, https://www.maywegather.org (accessed July 20, 2023).

[25] Anti-Defamation League, "Joint Statement of Solidarity by Jewish Communal Organizations," April 1, 2020, https://www.adl.org/news/article/joint-statement-of-solidarity-by-jewish-communal-organizations (accessed December 18, 2025).

[26] Andrew Yang and Jonathan Greenblatt, "Yang and Anti-Defamation League CEO: Avoid Coronavirus Racism," *USA Today*, March 20, 2020, https://www.usatoday.com/story/opinion/2020/

Greenblatt and Yang's joint opinion essay was a prime example of pluralist ideals in action.[27] Yang and Greenblatt and the leaders of the Jewish organizations acknowledged their distinctive identities and experiences. They also used these differences as a foundation to unite across racial and religious boundaries, condemn the hateful backlash, and advance the common cause of creating a safe and inclusive America. Their op-ed reflected how they both aimed to honor particularity—in this case, specific experiences of hate on the basis of specific racial and religious backgrounds—and also use those differences as a source of solidarity and mutual support.

To be sure, there are limitations to faith-based efforts to address anti-Asian racism and other forms of white supremacy and hate. For example, how do they engage people who are not religious? This question is especially important for Asian Americans engaged in contemporary anti-racism activism, given the fact that an increasing proportion of the American population has no religious affiliation, and the percentage of "religious nones" is particularly high among Asian Americans.[28] Moreover, many Asian Americans practice traditions that are centered in the home rather than in congregations or other types of formal religious institutions. The efforts described above favor those groups that fit the congregation-centric model that is the norm in a predominantly Christian country like the United States. They run the risk of failing to engage groups that organize spiritual life differently and that might not be readily recognized as religious in the first place. Despite these factors, however, religion remains a powerful force in the United States, and whether religious groups choose to wield their power to uphold white supremacy or to create a more inclusive, just, and pluralistic country remains to be seen.

03/20/yang-anti-defamation-league-ceo-avoid-coronavirus-scapegoating-racism-column/2877976001/?fbclid=IwAR2cVVeepwUZHrkpYBltzDbsTvKGk-giWQtIiczwmrDWSA3Z4D4KQM1ugSk (accessed December 18, 2025).

[27] For definitions of "pluralism," see Courtney Bender and Pamela Klassen, eds., *After Pluralism: Reimagining Religious Engagement* (New York: Columbia University Press, 2010); and Diana Eck, *A New Religious America: How a "Christian Country" Has Now Become the World's Most Religiously Diverse Nation* (New York: HarperSanFrancisco, 2001).

[28] Pew Research Center, "Asian Americans: A Mosaic of Faiths," August (Washington, DC: Pew Research Center, 2012).

9

Hinduism, America, and the Making of a New Pluralism

Uma Viswanathan

From our founding, American democracy promised the opportunity to coexist and govern across our traditions, values, beliefs, and worldviews. But this promise holds within it a paradox. The enactment of American democracy often rests upon the concept of compromise. Yet we cannot always find a neat compromise that falls in between two positions, particularly when sacred values are in direct opposition.

We see this paradox play out as we grapple with the importance of protecting free speech and free expression—cornerstones of our liberty—in a context where hatred, rage, and fear are spreading through public consciousness. In the pursuit of justice for historic and current harm, we can find ourselves trapped by dangerously reductive stories of identity, sorting ourselves into victims and oppressors, with little room for healing, redemption, compassion, and growth. While we protect the enterprising spirit that drives individual economic mobility and national prosperity, we must also protect our shared natural resources and our collective mental health and well-being.

The Paradox Is Tearing Us Apart

We live within rapidly shifting demographic, technological, environmental, and social change, while forces actively exploit our differences, stoking anxiety and polarizing communities. The stress of these tensions fuels our worst impulses—to fear or reject those who are different, to value some lives more than others, or to win at all costs. These impulses undermine our ability to tackle challenges, reduce our ability to self-govern, and enable hate, extremism, and violence to take root. The scale and nature of the challenges we face require us to learn to navigate across our differences.

Uma Viswanathan, *Hinduism, America, and the Making of a New Pluralism* In: *Modeling Religious Pluralism*. Edited by: Simran Jeet Singh, Oxford University Press. © Oxford University Press 2026.
DOI: 10.1093/oso/9780197745809.003.0009

This Is Where Pluralism Comes In

Pluralism is the belief that the coexistence of diverse opinions, ways of life, and value systems enriches all members of a society. I serve as the executive director of New Pluralists, a collaborative of philanthropists, storytellers, researchers, and practitioners advancing pluralism in American culture. We believe pluralism can come to life through the choices we make, encounters we have, and stories we tell as citizens, colleagues, community members, and neighbors.

At New Pluralists, we have come to describe and express pluralism as five guiding principles:

- Honor Human Dignity: We listen from a place of mutual respect, and uphold the individual dignity, worth, and potential of every person.
- Take Responsibility for Repair: We confront our past and reckon with our present in order to heal and strengthen our communities.
- Widen the Circle: We expand our sense of who belongs and embrace our common humanity.
- Find Strength in Difference: We design better solutions through our differences, not in spite of them.
- Strive for a Greater Sum: We challenge the zero-sum view that one group's gain is another's loss, and instead look to create win-win situations through curiosity, collaboration, and creativity.

A Hindu Perspective on the Project of Pluralism

My orientation to advancing pluralism in American culture is infused with a dharmic way of seeing and being in the world. I notice that contemporary notions of pluralism are rooted in Western political philosophy, and what Hinduism and other dharmic traditions can offer to the universal project of pluralism are not often sought, valued, or recognized.

I was born into a Hindu family and have been practicing and teaching meditation and yogic philosophy for nearly twenty years. I am also a social change leader and funder who has worked within and supported a myriad of communities and movements. Based on both sets of experiences, I see pluralism as pivotal to our futures as democracies. I see the places where we can get tripped up on pluralism when we only see it through a Western mindset. I offer some Hindu perspectives that enrich my understanding and expression of pluralism.

Advaita as pluralism. The *Advaita* tradition of Hinduism upholds the concept of non-duality as distinct from dualism, which separates divinity from its creation. According to Advaita, there is only one ultimate Divine consciousness,

Brahman—a singular reality, the cause of all causes, which encompasses all that is both manifest and unmanifest in creation. At the same time, there is an apparent reality of infinitely diverse and multifold expressions, the illusion called *maya* that makes us believe and behave as if we are distinct from each other. While gold is still gold no matter what form it takes, a gold bangle is distinct from a gold ring; in the same way, our unity and our diversity coexist. The purpose of human evolution is to awaken from the dream of maya to the reality that we are Brahman, to see ourselves as non-different from Divinity.

To live in a pluralistic society, we must be willing to make choices for the greater good. If we see the world from a dualistic frame, we believe we are separate from each other and all of life and nature. Making choices for the sake of others, choices that don't serve us or even go against our self-interest, requires an act of benevolence, of altruism. In times of peace and abundance, this type of action is more possible. In times of uncertainty or scarcity, it becomes a lot harder to overcome the instinct to hoard resources and protect ourselves from those we see as the "other."

Hinduism complicates the very notion that there is an other. Every living thing exists in relation to one another—humans, plants, animals, mountains, and oceans. All of nature. Every choice I make has an impact on everything around me; if I harm another, I am harming myself. The more I recognize the reality of total interdependence with all of creation, the more my choices can benefit the whole of a community or society, and not just what I understand to be myself. Interdependence is not something I choose to believe in when the conditions are right. It is simply a fact of life. While the right hand is distinct from the left hand, they belong to the same body.

The Self beyond identity. In the work of pluralism, it's important to acknowledge that identity categories like race, class, and political affiliation are historical and shape people's realities in critical ways. At the same time, we exist in relationship to one another, and our identities are complex and fluid. While a convenient proxy, sorting ourselves into identity categories as shorthand for diversity can cause us to miss important nuances about people's beliefs and experiences. It can reinforce stereotypes. The Sanskrit greeting "namaste" means this: The Divine in me recognizes the Divine in you. This view of Self is not about erasing our distinct qualities and traits. In fact, it allows for a full expression of our diverse identities. For Hindus, there are seven layers to our existence, all of which work in concert with each other. These layers are (from most gross to most subtle) body, breath, mind, intellect, memory, ego, and the Self. We could say that our identity forms around the six outermost layers of our existence, and that these layers are what make us apparently distinct from each other. Think about how discourses on diversity have asked us to think of ourselves and others only in terms of our physical form, senses and perceptions, judgment of experiences, memories, and relationships or comparisons to others (who are similar or different). Hinduism takes us a step deeper, to a deeper layer that is witnessing those faculties. This is the Self, which recognizes itself as one with all forms of Divinity. It is from this place of the Self, which is not limited by identity, that pluralism can flourish.

Truth is multidimensional. Pluralism requires a worldview that allows multiple concepts of being and doing in the world to coexist. This isn't about "both-sidesism," nor is it about having moral certitude. Pluralism asks us to skillfully navigate moral dilemmas. As a Hindu, I see Truth not in binaries, but as multidimensional. My understanding of the teachings is that we do not hold fixed rules about right and wrong, good and evil. The answer to "What is right?" is usually, "It depends." *Vairagya* (dispassion) enables us to observe and be curious, to be fluid and flexible in our frames of reference as we navigate ethical and moral dilemmas. The more clear and present we are, the better we are at perceiving options. Sometimes, the right action is to reduce conflict, to create ease among people so they can hear others. Other times, the right action is to turn the heat up, so we can see things in a new light. Contradictions and moral dilemmas live not just among us but within us. Within our layers of existence and varied life experiences, we contain paradoxes. Yet we are still whole and unified.

The wisdom and practices that form my Hindu worldview aren't the only views. Within Hinduism, there are multitudes of scriptures and teachings and traditions—a plurality of perspectives about our relationship to Divinity, nature, and ourselves. I hold my perspective as my perspective. And I'm also not trying to convert you to my Hindu perspective—that would be counter to the dharmic way of life. I simply invite practitioners and scholars of pluralism to step beyond the Western academy, to consider what's possible if we incorporate Hindu and other dharmic worldviews into how we shape, understand, and practice pluralism.

PART IV
RELIGION AND RACIAL JUSTICE

In 2009, three renowned raagis—Sikh religious musicians—were removed from a US Airways flight at the Sacramento International Airport. The reason? The pilot refused to fly with them onboard because "passengers expressed baseless concerns about the musicians' appearance."[1]

I had grown up loving these raagis and their kirtan, and I was outraged. Maybe they didn't speak much English, but these were our community elders. And this was racism, pure and simple. It also felt absurd. The musicians hadn't done anything wrong. If passengers felt uncomfortable, they could have gotten off the plane. Why did the musicians have to bow to the discomfort of racists? I told myself then that, if I was ever in a similar situation, no matter how uncomfortable, I would respond calmly, *I'm sorry you feel uncomfortable in my presence. Feel free to go back to where* you *came from.*

I haven't had the occasion to say this, and I don't even know if I'd be bold enough to say it if the opportunity presented itself. But I've thought about it a lot since then. It carries an echo of something I realized in the racist backlash that followed the terrorist attacks of September 11, 2001. Back then, people would ask why I continued to practice Sikhi when wearing a turban caused me so much pain. The backward logic was clear to me then, as it is now: *Looking different is not the source of my suffering. Racism is.*

Many people view race and racism as being disconnected from religion and religious identity. We tend to talk about these as discrete categories, as if they don't overlap in any way, and as if people don't experience them together. But a closer look tells us that the two are more closely interlinked than we might think—in their origins, in how people experience them, and more. A clearer understanding of how the two are connected creates a clearer vision for a collective path forward.

[1] American Civil Liberties Union, "Sikh Religious Musicians Settle with US Airways after Wrongful Removal from Flight," 2009, https://www.aclu.org/press-releases/sikh-religious-musicians-settle-us-airways-after-wrongful-removal-flight (accessed December 16, 2025).

Recognizing that any sincere effort to build religious pluralism must take seriously and attend to racism, this section includes chapters that help clarify the close relationship between racism and religion.

Kaitlin B. Curtice, an Indigenous writer and storyteller, surfaces ways in which Christianity has colonized and oppressed Indigenous peoples, and she shares stories of resistance from her Potawatomi tradition. She then proceeds to offer a vision for religious pluralism that draws from Indigenous spiritualities, including her own.

Randal Jelks, a professor of African American and African Diaspora Studies, offers a brief historiographical view of Black American religion, making the case that we can improve our understanding of the Black religious experience by viewing it from a lens of plurality rather than homogeneity.

In my chapter, I try to clarify the relationship between religion and racism, particularly in the United States. I make three key points through historical evidence: that religion gave birth to American racism, that religion has been leveraged to perpetuate and uphold racism, and that religious communities have been racialized.

Each of our chapters shares unique perspectives and experiences, and yet, there is a common thread that binds them together: a willingness to acknowledge the ugly reality of racism and a commitment to bending the arc of history toward justice. We each believe the two go hand-in-hand, and that achieving justice necessitates that we all work together toward it.

10

Staying in the Spiritual Fire of Equity and Kinship

Kaitlin B. Curtice

To begin a conversation on the intersection of religion and racial justice, I want to take us back to 1978, when the American Indian Religious Freedom Act was passed by President Jimmy Carter. As stated by the National Library of Medicine, a report was released that "found that Indians were often prevented from visiting their sacred sites, denied the use of religious sacraments, and kept from performing services in their traditional manner. The report recommended that Congress take measures to protect Indian religious practices from unnecessary government interference."[1] I am a citizen of the Potawatomi nation and write on the complex intersection of identity and spirituality. Indigenous religious freedoms are still limited and penalized today, from police brutality toward Indigenous protestors on sacred land to high school students being punished for wearing their regalia to graduation.

The genocide and oppression Indigenous people have faced not just here on Turtle Island but around the world have taken away our civil liberties time and again, and as we know, colonization is an ongoing, systemic problem that we are constantly trying to navigate—and it doesn't just affect Indigenous peoples.

Our very relationship to the lands and waters around us as Indigenous people is a direct threat to the status quo of capitalism and colonization, and the intergenerational suffering of Indigenous people affects our spiritual lives as well. President Jimmy Carter may have recognized this problem in 1978, but we know that the foundations of the United States were never meant to hold care or respect for its Indigenous nations and peoples. Realizing this has helped me recognize the deep significance of religious pluralism.

It is important to remember that there is great diversity within Indigenous tribes and peoples within the United States, and it is imperative that we do not assume that our religious backgrounds are monolithic. Indigenous peoples

[1] National Library of Medicine, "1978: American Indian Freedom of Religion Legalized," Native Voices: Native Peoples' Concepts of Health and Illness, US National Institutes of Health, https://www.nlm.nih.gov/nativevoices/timeline/545.html (accessed June 28, 2025).

Kaitlin B. Curtice, *Staying in the Spiritual Fire of Equity and Kinship* In: *Modeling Religious Pluralism*.
Edited by: Simran Jeet Singh, Oxford University Press. © Oxford University Press 2026.
DOI: 10.1093/oso/9780197745809.003.0010

follow a number of different religions and spiritual paths, and some do not consider themselves religious at all. Our spiritual backgrounds are often reflected in our cultures and stories, and we carry them in our bodies and languages, which means ongoing colonization affects every aspect of our lives.

Coloniality and Indigeneity: Solidarity and Kinship

As someone who grew up Indigenous and heavily involved in the Southern Baptist church, I know firsthand the complexities of navigating colonialism within American Christianity. Because we live in a nation whose backdrop has been colonized Christianity, it is confusing for Indigenous peoples, as many of our ancestors had (and continue to have) Christianity weaponized against them even as many of us grew up in Christian spaces.

In our Potawatomi culture, the word for America is *chemokmankik*, referring to the Europeans who brought weapons against Indigenous peoples on this land. *Chemokmankik* loosely translates to "land of the long butchering knives." The imagery speaks to the very background, both spiritual and political, that this nation was founded on.

Even in the face of colonization, within our traditions is a culture of resistance. Many Indigenous people today, no matter their religious background, are fighting for human rights and the rights of Mother Earth against brutality perpetrated by the police and government institutions. Because these movements are rooted in kinship and solidarity, we understand that we cannot do this work alone. Our spiritual lives do not exist in a vacuum, meaning that however our spiritual lives are policed by the institutions and governments around us, we are connected by that oppression across the world as others' spiritual lives are controlled and suppressed. When I notice what my own people are going through, I naturally begin to ask questions about what other groups might be experiencing. My hope is that this leads us to conversations and collaborations toward a better future.

Religious pluralism is an incredibly important part of fighting for a better future in a world fraught with oppression. Religious pluralism allows us to examine what resistance means in our own cultures and religions, both individually and as a collective. No matter what religion or spiritual background we have, we belong to one another, so the work of religious equity cannot happen in a vacuum; it happens through the work of paying attention and practicing solidarity with one another.

How do we resist hate and fight for racial and religious equity in a world such as ours?

The power of solidarity and kinship is that we remember what role resistance plays in our daily lives, and we have conversations about how to resist the status quo of hate, white supremacy, and colonization around us by choosing care for ourselves, one another, and Mother Earth.[2]

As we face systemic colonialism and white supremacy in our world today, the possibility of our gathering in solidarity with others to resist these systems of hate and oppression means our interfaith conversations are gifts of intervention. They give us language to understand the depth of the violence and oppression that have gathered us together, reminding us that stories and dialogue bring solidarity, and solidarity gives us the courage to move toward change.

A Five-Step Antidote

I offer here five principles and practices for advancing racial justice through the lens of religious pluralism. As an author and poet, I believe that words hold meaning, and embodying those words can change the world we live in. First, we must reckon with our nation's foundational history. Second, we must examine and begin to heal our relationship to the land. Third, we must pay attention to the work of storytelling. Fourth, we must invest in collective care, and fifth, we must intentionally support grassroots organizations who are doing the work of racial equity and religious pluralism.

In order to advance racial justice through the lens of religious pluralism, we must first reckon with the backdrop of the nation we currently live in. As a storyteller, it is important to me to ask how a story came to be, where it came from, and who it benefits. When talking about equity, we must also talk about colonialism. Researching settler colonialism on this land is important for us to understand how the status quo of racism and white supremacy has been upheld. This will involve unlearning and grief for many of us, as we have been taught a history upheld by mostly powerful, wealthy white men in America. Telling the truth about history means uncovering pain and trauma, yet staying committed to the conversations we need to be having about that truth.

Second, we must understand our connection to the land. This may seem like an arbitrary aspect of justice work, but it is at the core of much of the oppression we witness today. The Doctrine of Discovery, a document created in the 1400s, gave European Christian men permission to invade and take over any lands they deemed "unchristian" or "savage," and kill anyone that got in their way.[3] This resulted in Indigenous peoples being separated from their homelands, and generations of spiritual separation from the land followed, a tragic suffering that

[2] Kaitlin B. Curtice, *Living Resistance: An Indigenous Vision for Seeking Wholeness Every Day* (Grand Rapids, MI: Brazos Press, 2023).

[3] See Sarah Augustine, *The Land Is Not Empty: Following Jesus in Dismantling the Doctrine of Discovery* (Nashville, TN: APG Sales and Distribution, 2021).

took place across the globe in many nations. When we begin to repair our relationship to the lands around us, we begin to create pathways toward healing and religious pluralism. All of us working individually and collectively toward this repair with the land are essential in our equity work.

Third, we must pay attention to the stories told to us *and about us*. I've noticed two distinct camps within interfaith conversations: One is interested in jumping directly into action; the other asks for a slower movement of learning one another's stories before we jump into action. While both camps are necessary, it poses a dilemma. We need action now to create a better world and more just society; yet when we slow down and listen to one another's stories, we become better equipped to know what that action should look like. Religious pluralism is an important space to examine our own stories and others', and it often takes time. The dance between action and story-sharing cannot be ignored and helps us know how to approach this work in a society that does not value true healing. In this process, we also need to notice where our stories are and aren't being told in mainstream media and hold those reporting entities accountable to telling the truth about history.

Fourth, to advance racial justice through the lens of pluralism, we need to invest in our collective care so that we can sustain this work for future generations. For folks from communities whose religious and cultural rights have been suppressed, it is difficult to practice cycles of rest and care that will help us continue the work. For instance, communities suffering from the climate crisis are already marginalized on multiple levels, and in order to support those communities, networks of care are necessary. True solidarity means coming together, pooling resources, and recognizing that those with privilege have the opportunity to support resistance on every level.

And lastly, we must support organizations who are doing the grassroots work of religious equity. The Sikh Coalition, Dayenu, NDN Collective, Shoulder to Shoulder Campaign, and Interfaith America are all organizations advocating for racial equity and care for different populations in America as well as equity in climate conversations. The collaboration of organizations centered around Sikh, Jewish, Indigenous, Muslim, and other faiths creates powerful networks of justice and activism when they partner together to challenge the status quo around us. When we support their work, we support future generations by giving them a chance to build on what we have started.

Conclusion

It took centuries to build the nations and societies we live in today, which means change will not come quickly. Being dedicated to the lifelong work of equity and belonging must be a goal; we must pass on what we have learned to future generations so that they can continue the work we only hope to begin in our lifetime.

Arundhati Roy writes about this time we are in—as we reckon with the effects of a worldwide pandemic and exist in a time in which we continue to fight for a better and more equitable world. She says, "We can choose to walk through it, dragging the carcasses of our prejudice and hatred, our avarice, our data banks and dead ideas, our dead rivers and smoky skies behind us. Or we can walk through lightly, with little luggage, ready to imagine another world. And ready to fight for it."[4]

In our Potawatomi culture, we believe in the seven fires prophecy and the idea of seven generations. The prophecy helps us ask what kind of world we are creating today—how we are practicing equity and care when the status quo of colonization, white supremacy, racism, and hate is all around us. But we also ask ourselves how we are living in a way that gives the most love to those who will come seven generations after us. What kind of world are we leaving for them, and how can we leverage our lives today to fight for that better world?

Rumi once wrote, "Stay in the spiritual fire. Let it cook you." Today the spiritual fire we are staying in is the fight for human rights and the rights of Mother Earth. The two are connected, as are our stories and the ways they overlap in this world. Remaining dedicated to the work of advancing racial justice through religious pluralism means we are staying in the fire and letting it cook us. We are doing the work in our generation so that future generations have a better chance of knowing what justice is. We hope for a better world, and in the process, we become a crucial and connected part of creating that better world together.

[4] Arundhati Roy, "The Pandemic Is a Portal," *Financial Times*, April 3, 2020, https://www.ft.com/content/10d8f5e8-74eb-11ea-95fe-fcd274e920ca (accessed December 15, 2025).

11

Black American Religious Pluralism

Rethinking a Historiography

Randal Maurice Jelks

Introduction: Religious Repression and the Life and Death of African Gods

It is time to rethink Black American historiography from the vantage point of religious pluralism. The ways we reflect on histories of religion are sometimes overdetermined by socioeconomics and not often considered from the perspectives of faith(s) and religion(s). This absence is especially notable when we think about multivariant experiences of Black peoples in the Americas, where the transatlantic slave trade forcibly migrated 10 to 15 million Africans.

Beginning roughly in 1533, Europeans venturing into this "new world" brought enslaved people from West and West Central Africa to the Americas via the slave trade until slavery was abolished in Brazil in 1888. In other words, from beginning to end, enslavement lasted 350 years in the Americas.

The global transformation wrought by the transatlantic slave trade in the mid-1500s was enabled by the theological justification of the Portuguese using similar language that explained the Roman Catholic crusades, the series of invasive anti-Muslim wars from 1096 to 1291 justifying Portuguese invasive actions as Portuguese sailors slowly explored the various people along the African continent's western coastline. The papal bull was issued in 1452 and was titled "Dum Diversas." Portugal's great headway was followed by its Spanish cousins. Spain also sought theological incursion into its forays in the Americas, first through the papal bull of 1493 "Inter Caetera," known as the Doctrine of Discovery, followed by the 1494 Treaty of Tordesillas, settling disputes between Portugal and Spain. Entering into competition with Portugal and Spain for global hegemony was the English monarchy, led by the Tudor King Henry VIII, who established the Anglican Church as the king's Protestant theological arm.[1]

[1] See Ana Lucia Araujo, *Humans in Shackles: An Atlantic History of Slavery* (Chicago: University of Chicago Press, 2024); Hebert Klein, *The Atlantic Slave Trade*, 2nd ed. (Cambridge: Cambridge University Press, 1999/2010); Peter E. Russell, *Prince Henry "the Navigator": A Life* (New Haven, CT: Yale University Press, 2000); and Paul Gottschalk, *The Earliest Diplomatic Documents*

Randal Maurice Jelks, *Black American Religious Pluralism* In: *Modeling Religious Pluralism*.
Edited by: Simran Jeet Singh, Oxford University Press.
DOI: 10.1093/oso/9780197745809.003.0011

Theology, philosophy, and political theory supported imperial claims about the superiority of Western civilization, in part by denigrating the diverse religious communities they encountered. This included colonial studies on Africa—what the philosopher V.Y. Mudimbe calls the invention of Africa—which reduced to a monolith the continents' diverse peoples, faiths, and cultures.[2] This monolithic rendering made indigenous religions of Africa pejoratively "heathenish" or "Black Magic."

The fact is, before the transatlantic slave trade commenced, and while it occurred, the African continent was ripe with religious diversity. People living within walking distance of one another had different worldviews and traditions. When the Atlantic slave trade began shipping people to the Americas, those captives were already religiously diverse, and some, perhaps, were quietly nonreligious or anti-religious.

My argument here is limited and specific, and it is based on my perspective from Black America. Here I want to outline what I think is a way of reading the dimensions of both Africa's journey and Black America's symbiotic relationship with the continent's multiple histories through a lens of religious pluralism. Religious pluralism has been a cornerstone of Black religious liberal thinking and is arguably an under-explored element of African and African American religious thought. The African Gods were never completely wiped out by the catastrophe of transatlantic enslavement. Historian James H. Sweet pointed this out in his 2013 article, "Defying Social Death: The Multiple Configurations of African Slave Family in the Atlantic World." If the family managed to reconfigure itself under the harshness of a slave system, African diversity of religious expressions remained both on the African continent and throughout the Americas, even though they were suppressed by religious agents such as the Spanish Inquisition and Protestant doctrine. It must be added that this suppression of religious faith(s) was true within European monarchies themselves in their attempts to create ordered uniformity.[3] While African religious expressions were changed given the social conditions and setting of enslavement, they found ways of creative adaptation. They did not die but found new ways of living and serving the needs of people traumatized by historical forces beyond their control. This is what the political theorist Hannah Arendt calls "natality."

on America: The Papal Bulls of 1493 and the Treaty of Tordesillas Reproduced and Translated (Berlin: Paul Gottschalk, 1927).

[2] V.Y. Mudimbe, *The Invention of Africa: Gnosis, Philosophy, and the Order of Knowledge*. Bloomington: Indiana University Press, 1988.

[3] R.I. Moore, *The War on Heresy* (Cambridge, MA: Belknap Press of Harvard University Press, 2012).

Arendt defines natality as a precondition of politics as a new beginning or politics arising out of traumatic circumstances. One way of understanding Arendt's natality is to see it as a kind of resurrection from the dead; communities reframe and rebuild themselves even after being shattered.[4] In contradistinction, the historical sociologist Orlando Patterson recognizes that in human history, particular those enslaved faced "natal alienation," the loss of all their birth rights or the properties natural to personhood.[5] Patterson describes natal freedoms such as one's choice of names and rituals of worship are stolen at birth by systems of enslavement and oppression for the benefit of the owner class and the imperial nation. Natal alienation is a defining feature of all historical slaveholding societies; they seek to maintain political and economic dominance and limit pluralistic communities that challenge hierarchical uniformity and enslavement itself. New beginnings, however, were found in diverse religious expressions throughout the Americas as seen in Candomblé, Catholicism, Hoodoo, Obeah, Islam, Protestant denominationalism, Pentecostalism, Santeria, Umbanda, and Voodoo. All these expressions of faith(s) created new ways of knowing and building community. As such all these religious expressions were heavily surveilled and seen as threats to the dominate imperial order, which began being established in and outside Europe in the seventeenth century.

War, Religious Repression, and Resistance in Europe

In 1452, some eighty-one years before the Portuguese began forcibly migrating Africans to the Americas, Pope Nicholas V issued a papal bull titled "Dum Diversas," justifying Portuguese enslavement of Africans into the Americas, by stating the following:

> As we indeed understand from your pious and Christian desire, you intend to subjugate the enemies of Christ, namely the Saracens, and bring [them] back, with powerful arm, to the faith of Christ, if the authority of Apostolic See supported you in this.... Apostolic authority by this edict, to invade, conquer, fight, subjugate the Saracens and pagans, and other infidels and other enemies of Christ, and wherever established their Kingdoms, Duchies, Royal Palaces, Principalities and other dominions, lands, places, estates, camps and any other possessions, mobile and immobile goods found in all these places and held in whatever name, and held and possessed by the same Saracens, Pagans, infidels,

[4] Hannah Arendt, *The Human Condition* (Chicago: University of Chicago Press, 1958), 7, 98–99.

[5] Orlando Patterson, *Slavery and Social Death* (Cambridge, MA: Harvard University Press, 1982), chap. 2.

> and the enemies of Christ, also realms, duchies, royal palaces, principalities and other dominions, lands, places, estates, camps, possessions of the king or prince or of the kings or princes, and to lead their persons in perpetual servitude, and to apply and appropriate realms, duchies, royal palaces, principalities and other dominions, possessions and goods of this kind to you and your use and your successors the Kings of Portugal.[6]

This edict from Nicholas V gave the Portuguese kingdom religious justification to perceive Africans as "pagans" and enslave them. In this instance, European imperialism used its Roman Catholicism as a justification for how Portugal would negotiate with various polities on the African continent.[7]

As Constantinople fell to the Muslim-led Ottoman Empire, Spain consolidated. The kingdoms of Aragon and Castile merged as one kingdom through the marriage of Isabella I of Castile and Ferdinand II of Aragon. While Columbus landed on the island of Cuba and traveled to another island—what the lost sea captain called Hispaniola (today the countries of Haiti and the Dominican Republic)—Spain's first couple instituted an Inquisition, a Catholic judicial tribunal to make Spain Catholic by prosecuting Jews, Muslims, and pagans. Religious repression has been a staple in the making of the modern world and our contemporary history.

Spain would not let its smaller neighboring sibling—Portugal—outpace them economically in imperial wealth. The competition between these two countries resulted in the introduction of sugar cane into current-day Brazil and throughout the Caribbean region. The competition became so worrisome to Pope Alexander VI that it played a major role in his issuing the Treaty of Tordesillas in 1494, which essentially divided South America into two, half for Spain, and half for Portugal, a portending of how European powers would divide Africa at the 1884 Berlin Conference.[8] The Portuguese brought Africans into Brazil by the millions, and Spain followed its lead soon after, bringing its inquisitional powers to repress African religions—both traditional religions and Islam—just as Pope Nicholas V had instructed.[9]

[6] Pope Nicholas V, "Dum Diversas," F/CA, 2020, https://www.facechangealliance.com/dumdiversas.

[7] Herman L. Bennett, *African Kings and Black Slaves: Sovereignty and Dispossession in the Early Modern Atlantic* (Philadelphia: University of Pennsylvania Press, 2019).

[8] Éric Schnakenberg, "Treaty of Tordesillas, June 7, 1494," *Encyclopédie d'histoire numérique de l'Europe*, https://ehne.fr/en/encyclopedia/themes/international-relations/europe-and-legal-regulation-international-relations/treaty-tordesillas-june-7-144 (accessed October 27, 2024).

[9] One of the best reconstructions of this history is found in James H. Sweet, *Domingos Álvares, African Healing, and the Intellectual History of the Atlantic World* (Chapel Hill: University of North Carolina Press, 2011).

Spiritual Holocaust

Africans were religiously diverse before arriving in the Americas. Their religious experiences would continue to be diverse, with each groups' composition dependent upon the imperial authority under whom they wound up laboring and living—British and Dutch Protestants, French, Portuguese, or Spanish Catholics. In Brazil and throughout the Caribbean, especially Barbados and Jamaica, African traditional religious practices faced a death-dealing labor regime that historian Vincent Brown referred to as *The Reaper's Garden*.[10] This violence became too much for the consciences of some Western Europeans, many of whom fought a bloody civil war in France. Religious toleration as established by the 1598 Edict of Nantes between Catholics and Huguenots came as a result of a war at a standstill, not a democratic framing of religious diversity as a good in and of itself.[11] And although the Huguenots fought for religious toleration in France, upon arrival in South Carolina, they would inflict both religious intolerance and labor violence on Africans and African-descended people.[12] It would be only one set of English Protestants who widened their spiritual understandings to agree that enslavement was abominable, though notably, they only announced their views *after* they were wealthy enough to let some enslaved people free.

As the historian Jon Butler once argued, the transatlantic slave trade did not come with a practice of religious toleration, but instead a brutal suppression resulting in "a spiritual holocaust."[13] Butler built on Albert Raboteau's 1978 *Slave Religion*, where Raboteau calls slavery in the United States "the death of African Gods."[14] Yet none of these historians took full enough account of their own Anglo-American perspective. Though E. Franklin Frazier argues that slavery really killed African culture in the Caribbean as it had done in North America,[15] Zora Neale Hurston's anthropological fieldwork in the Caribbean in the 1930s recorded the ways in which Obeah and Voodoo continued to be practiced alongside Christianity in the Caribbean and regions of the United States.[16]

[10] Vince Brown, *The Reaper's Garden: Death and Power in the World of Atlantic Slavery* (Cambridge, MA: Harvard University Press, 2008).

[11] Mack P. Holt, *The French Wars of Religion, 1562-1629* (Cambridge: Cambridge University Press, 1995).

[12] Owen Stanwood, *The Global Refuge: Huguenots in an Age of Empire* (New York: Oxford University Press, 2020).

[13] Jon Butler, *Awash in a Sea of Faith: Christianizing the American People* (Cambridge, MA: Harvard University Press, 1990), chap. 5.

[14] Albert J. Raboteau, *Slave Religion: The "Invisible Institution" in the Antebellum South* (New York: Oxford University Press, 1980), chap. 2.

[15] See the important new discussion on the different objectives of Melville Herskovitz and E. Franklin Frazier in Livio Sansone, *Field Station Bahia: Brazil in the Work of Lorenzo Dow Turner, E. Franklin Frazier and Frances and Melville Herskovits, 1935-1967* (Leiden: Brill, 2023).

[16] Zora Neale Hurston, *Tell My Horse* (Philadelphia: J.B. Lippincott, 1938); and Will Coleman, *Tribal Talk: Black Theology, Hermeneutics, and African/American Ways of "Telling the Story"* (University Park: Pennsylvania State University Press, 2000).

And as historian Katharine Gerbner has documented, there were reasons why some enslaved persons in the English-speaking Caribbean chose to become Protestant Christians, from literacy to manumissions. Other enslaved persons resisted enslavement by practicing traditions outside the monitoring of fearful slave owners.[17]

It's important to understand these ways in which Butler and Raboteau's arguments were limited; they did not fully account for the fact that the United States was only one part of Black people's religious history and encounters in the Americas. Neither Butler nor Raboteau considered in their writings that religious suppression, wherever it occurs, drives religious practice and ritual underground. We can also see that lived religious experiences are much more malleable than these scholars accounted for or theoretically explored. They did not account for the communities that had what Sean Redding calls, "invisible institutions," including those that were deemed witchcraft and Black Magic.[18] Nor did they consider the religion in Maroon communities throughout the Caribbean or Catholicism and Vodun in Haiti, or religious exchanges across urban, enslaved communities, which cultural anthropologist J. Lorand Matory convincingly demonstrated in his 2005 book *Black Atlantic Religion: Tradition, Transnationalism, and Matriarchy in the Afro-Brazilian Candomblé*.[19]

Patterson brings evidence to show how slave owners wished and steadily attempted to totalize the lives of enslaved persons from the ancient world to the modern one. He held that those enslaved in Jamaica were completely and utterly stripped of their African identities. This is what he meant by "social death," leaving those enslaved by the British resentful and resistant without purpose. His theory of natal alienation accounts for what master classes have done, by ascertaining the power to possess the birth rights and the freedoms of those enslaved, including their intellectual gifts.

In 1807, the young United States joined Great Britain in suppressing slave trading directly from Africa. This alongside the 1803 Louisiana Purchase created the conditions for internal slave trade from the upper South to the lower South, bringing enslaved persons into Alabama, Louisiana, and Mississippi from Kentucky, Maryland, and Virginia.[20] The internalization of the slave trade

[17] Katharine Gerbner, *Christian Slavery: Conversion and Race in the Protestant Atlantic World* (Philadelphia, University of Pennsylvania Press, 2018).

[18] Sean Redding, "Witchcraft in Africa: Political Power and Spiritual Insecurity from the Precolonial Era to the Present," *Oxford Research Encyclopedia of African History*, March 26, 2019, https://oxfordre-com.proxyiub.uits.iu.edu/africanhistory/view/10.1093/acrefore/9780190277734.001.0001/acrefore-9780190277734-e-441 (accessed October 28, 2024).

[19] James Lorand Matory, *Black Atlantic Religion: Tradition, Transnationalism, and Matriarchy in the Afro-Brazilian Candomblé* (Princeton, NJ: Princeton University Press, 2005).

[20] Steven Deyle, *Carry Me Back: The Domestic Slave Trade in American Life* (New York: Oxford University Press, 2005); and Walter Johnson, *Soul by Soul: Life inside the Antebellum Slave Market* (Cambridge, MA: Harvard University Press, 1999).

transformed Black American identity religiously and politically, a shift that historian Michael Gomez powerfully demonstrated in his 1998 study of slavery titled *Exchanging Our Country Marks*.[21] Gomez argues that African Americans were deeply tied to Africa—that, in essence, the continuous slave trade bonded and renewed enslaved communities with various ethnicities with communal ties from West and West Central Africa. The ending of the transatlantic slavery created the conditions for the evolution of an American ethnic identity.

Persons born on the African continent were now outnumbered by those born in the United States, and we can begin to see the formation of an African American identity. This is where Gomez's view on natality proves useful. That is, given the circumstances the enslaved found themselves under, they chose within their ability to act creatively, using Evangelical Christianity and other religious means—which would often be attacked as Black magic, heathen, and witchcraft—in ways that kept the slave-owning classes constantly worried about power they did not control.[22] Those enslaved found enough freedom to be spontaneous and create anew in their own invisible and visible institutions, such as the African Methodist Episcopal (AME) denomination, and spaces within larger white denominations such as in the Episcopal, Methodist, and Presbyterian Churches.[23]

Between 1788 and 1820, we see something revolutionary: the formation of Black urban organizations under the rubric of Africa. The 1st African Baptist Church, Free African Society, the African Meeting House, the Abyssinia Baptist Church, 1st African Presbyterian, the AME denomination, the African Methodist Episcopal Zion in New York City, and the rural countryside camp meetings and praise houses where the Ring Shout lived.[24]

This type of natality is often overlooked as not being revolutionary, perhaps because renaming is not as radical or attention-grabbing as slave revolts or violent political revolutions such as in France, Haiti, Moscow, and the United States. However, these fraternal, religious, and rural associations kept democratic discourse alive, facilitated Black communities' networks among one another, and created the conditions and foundation for a social revolution. This methodical approach feels especially significant under the conditions of enslavement. Within these natal spaces, Black abolitionists as diverse as Mary Ann

[21] Michael A. Gomez, *Exchanging Our Country Marks: The Transformation of African Identities in the Colonial and Antebellum South* (Chapel Hill: University of North Carolina Press, 1998).

[22] Yvonne Patricia Chireau, *Black Magic: Religion and the African American Conjuring Tradition* (Berkeley: University of California Press, 2006); and Kathryn Gin Lum, *Heathen: Religion and Race in American History* (Cambridge, MA: Harvard University Press, 2022).

[23] Gary B. Nash, *Forging Freedom: The Formation of Philadelphia's Black Community, 1720-1840*, paperback ed. (Cambridge, MA: Harvard University Press, 1991).

[24] David W. Wills and Richard Newman, *Black Apostles at Home and Abroad: Afro-Americans and the Christian Mission from the Revolution to Reconstruction* (Boston: G.K. Hall, 1982).

Shadd Cary, Frederick Douglass, Martin R. Delaney, Henry Highland Garnett, Sojourner Truth, and Harriet Tubman debated the future of their communities politically and spiritually.[25]

Post-Emancipation Denominationalism, Racial Segregation, and Black Pluralism

The American Civil War was not the idyllic biblical year of Jubilee, the proscription from the Torah in the book of Leviticus that stated every fifty years slaves would be manumitted, debts relieved, and the land lay fallow. However, it was the closest thing to Jubilee possible for people who had lived in a slaveholding society for nearly 250 years. This Jubilee had a high sticker price. It cost roughly 600,000 lives. But there was reward in it, too: the abolition of slavery, access to citizenship for those born in the United States, and a new provision enabling all males to vote regardless of color and previous condition of servitude. These constitutional amendments were monumental, albeit limited. They freed a whole class of people and set the stage for those who would follow as immigrants to become naturalized citizens.

After emancipation, Black people had more autonomy and agency to make choices for themselves. In the South, one of the first choices Black people made was to separate themselves from white Southern congregations.[26] Why did so many among them abandon biracial settings for worship? Because Black congregants had been policed in slave-owning towns and cities. Because Many white Baptist and Methodist congregations feared Black independent theology as insurrectionary, especially since Nat Turner's 1831 rebellion.[27] Because they wanted to create their own institutions that suited where they lived, their families, and their own interiority. Black religionists, whether in urban or rural spaces, believed they could manage their own congregational and spiritual affairs without white management. They were free to argue, to join institutions of their own making, and to exchange religious conversation in Africa, the Caribbean, and elsewhere in the United States. Denominationalism, as it has been termed by scholars, sowed the seeds of Black religious pluralism.[28]

25 Vincent Harding, *There Is a River: The Black Struggle for Freedom in America* (New York: Harcourt Brace Jovanovich, 1981).

26 Katharine L. Dvorak, *An African-American Exodus: The Segregation of the Southern Churches* (Brooklyn, NY: Carlson Pub., 1991).

27 Kenneth S. Greenberg, ed., *Nat Turner: A Slave Rebellion in History and Memory* (Oxford: Oxford University Press, 2003); and Vanessa M. Holden, *Surviving Southampton: African American Women and Resistance in Nat Turner's Community* (Urbana: University of Illinois Press, 2021).

28 Nathan O. Hatch, *The Democratization of American Christianity* (New Haven, CT: Yale University Press, 1989); and H. Richard Niebuhr, *The Social Sources of Denominationalism* (New York: World Publishing, 1972).

Denominationalism began in the diversity of theological doctrines and expressions that independent congregations and denominations entertained at the time. Between 1870 and 1900, Black communities were a hotbed of denominationalism, creating and re-creating denominations throughout the South—Colored Methodist Episcopal, National Baptist Convention, and the Church of God in Christ.[29] Amid the anti-democratic state laws being passed throughout the South commonly referred to as Jim Crow, Black Protestantism was the democratic marketplace where Christian and non-Christian thought came to freely operate in Black communities. Alongside the growth of Black denominationalism was an intellectual discourse that occurred in the post-emancipation religious print culture.[30] Black men and women opened up new avenues for religious pluralism as they vociferously argued about religion, bourgeois behavior, and the interconnectedness of Africa and Black America.[31]

Alongside these denominational debates, new questions of theology and spirituality arose through encounters with East Asia and South Asia. Much of this had to do with British imperialism in India, beginning with the East India Company, the corporate entity that helped to colonize India in the eighteenth century. The British links to India, Iran, and other parts of the Near East brought new interfaith interactions and conversations, especially among the upper class.[32] Soon, converts such as Robert Turner would encounter the Baha'i faith among Black domestic servants.[33] The doors would slowly open to faith traditions outside the Western orbit, creating new opportunities to consider and accept religious diversity.

Yet, while formerly enslaved people were expressing more agency in their religious lives, state segregation laws were passed in state houses throughout the South. With *Plessey* v. *Ferguson* in 1896, the Supreme Court rendered a doctrine that states could create separate spheres as long as they were equal ones

[29] Anthea Butler, *Women in the Church of God in Christ: Making a Sanctified Word* (Chapel Hill: University of North Carolina Press, 2007); C. H. Phillips, *The History of the Colored Methodist Episcopal Church in America* (New York: Arno Press, 1972); James Melvin Washington, *Frustrated Fellowship: The Black Baptist Quest for Social Power* (Macon, GA: Mercer University Press, 1986); Calvin White, *The Rise to Respectability: Race, Religion, and the Church of God in Christ* (Fayetteville: University of Arkansas Press, 2012); and John Hope Franklin, *George Washington Williams, a Biography* (Chicago: University of Chicago Press, 1985).

[30] Eric Gardner, *Black Print Unbound: The Christian Recorder, African American Literature, and Periodical Culture* (New York: Oxford University Press, 2015).

[31] Edward Wilmot Blyden, *Christianity, Islam and the Negro Race* (Edinburgh: Edinburgh University Press, 1967); Alexander Crummell, *Africa and America: Addresses and Discourses* (Springfield, MA: Willey & Co., 1891); and Henry McNeal Turner, *Respect Black: The Writings and Speeches of Henry McNeal Turner* (New York: Arno Press, 1971).

[32] Robert H. Stockman, *The Bahá'í Faith in America.* vol. I. (Wilmette: Bahá'í Pub. Trust, 1985).

[33] Paul Teed, "Interfaith Encounter and Religious Pluralism: J. T. Underland's Mission to Brahmo Samajes of India, 1895–96," *American Studies* 50, no. 1/2 (2009): 51–69, https://journals.ku.edu/amsj/article/view/4109.

for blacks and whites, a laughable proposition given the US government's role in preserving and upholding racism. The emerging segregation laws deeply affected Black life in the South. They unleashed further repression, empowering the US military to promote racism in its ranks and into territories, including Guam, Haiti, the Hawaiian Islands, and Puerto Rico.

This discriminatory practice violated religious strictures that emphasized unity among believers. Black churches were designed to support small communities and families by building morale and keeping them morally and spiritually intact. Abolitionism and Jim Crow laws forced many decentralized Black congregations as houses of worship—with the notable exception of the AME Church—to collectively confront state laws and power. It was out of need for protection that Black congregants in both rural and urban contexts were forced to create a more unified block—which W.E.B. DuBois framed as "The Negro's Church"—to combat the deleterious effects of racial apartheid, murderous white mob violence, assailment of voting rights, and limitations on economic mobility. In the face of these great structural barriers, Black congregations at every level and setting were compelled to sustain natality and moral discourse by creating institutional networks through the holiness movement and through the rise of Black Pentecostalism.

The Great Migration

As legal impediments hardened in the South, migration out of the rural South slowly rose. New urban Black dwellers first came to Southern cities from rural plantations in the aftermath of the Civil War and continued branching out to the upper Southeast, the lower Midwest, and the West, bringing and creating new ritual, social, and spiritual spaces for themselves. They became Catholics, Episcopalians, part of the Holiness Movement, Methodist Episcopalians, Presbyterians, and Universalists or Unitarians, and they also affiliated with non-Christian traditions, becoming Jewish, Muslim, and Baha'i. Some also continued to engage secretively in suppressed forms of religion, such as Conjurin', Hoodoo, and worship of Vodun.[34] Finally the great migration, especially in port cities such as Baltimore, New Orleans, New York, and Philadelphia, would join with Anglophone and Hispanic Caribbean migration to make a Black religious cosmopolitanism.

[34] Jeffrey E. Anderson, *Conjure in African American Society* (Baton Rouge: Louisiana State University Press, 2005); Katrina Hazzard-Donald, *Mojo Workin': The Old African American Hoodoo System* (Urbana: University of Illinois Press, 2013); and, Hurston *Tell My Horse.*

Migration from the American South was never just a fact of Black life. Southern whites too fled the American South as the cotton economy began to fail upon meeting global competition.

White upland Southerners—meaning those from poor agricultural regions such as Appalachia within the South—fled North for new opportunities, too. This migration, which some scholars refer to as "The Hillbilly Exodus," led many white southerners to cities such as Benton Harbor, Chicago, Cleveland, Detroit, and Los Angeles. These migrants brought their cultures with them, including their Southern racism. They created racial divides within and across religious communities, including the Azusa Street Revival, a globally significant Pentecostalism revival led by Black clergyman William J. Seymour from Saint Mary's Parish, Louisiana. While this spiritual renewal movement began as an interracial one, it was quickly broken down by race into denominations such as the Assemblies of God serving whites and the Church of God in Christ and Pentecostal World Assembly serving Blacks.[35] What might have become of the Azusa Street daring spiritual revival was dimmed in the United States by the wages of whiteness, as W.E.B. DuBois so biblically framed the disputes between black and white laborers in his 1935 book *Black Reconstruction*.[36]

The Great Migration transformed the United States religiously. The spiritual marketplace widened with Caribbean immigrants bringing more fundamentalist churches that endorsed strict biblical literalist standards.[37] More importantly, the Universal Negro Improvement Association (UNIA), founded by Marcus Mosiah Garvey, substantially widened the discussion of what kinds of religion were good for Black people. Garvey, a Jamaican immigrant, observed in Costa Rica, Panama, and London that, in a white supremacist world, Black people were at the bottom of the hierarchy. Garvey began a religiously grounded populist campaign in Harlem, calling people back to Africa as a spiritual homeland and destiny. There is a direct line from Edward Wilmot Blyden to Garvey's mantra, "Africa for the Africans," that reverberated through his public speeches.[38] The UNIA was also fueled by its newspaper, *The Negro World*. Many Black leaders

[35] Iain MacRobert, *The Black Roots and White Racism of Early Pentecostalism in the USA* (New York: St. Martin's Press, 1988).

[36] W.E.B. Du Bois, *Black Reconstruction* (Millwood, NY: Kraus-Thomson Organization, 1976).

[37] Daniel R. Bare, *Black Fundamentalists: Conservative Christianity and Racial Identity in the Segregation Era* (New York: New York University Press, 2021); and Mary Beth Swetnam Mathews, *Doctrine and Race: African American Evangelicals and Fundamentalism between the Wars* (Tuscaloosa: University of Alabama Press, 2017).

[38] In 1887, Edward Blyden, a religious and political expatriate to Liberia and Sierra Leone, published *Christianity, Islam and the Negro Race*, which indicted Christianity and Christian missionaries for imperial arrogance. Blyden resigned his position as Presbyterian clergy and argued that Islam was better politically and spiritually for Black people in Africa. Blyden's argument anticipated the emergence of Marcus Garvey and the Nation of Islam in the United States. It was Blyden who coined the phrase "Africa for the Africans" in 1872 as he witnessed European encroachment and its spreading violence on the African continent.

(e.g., W.E.B. DuBois) and Black organizations (e.g., the NAACP leadership) did not like Garvey and considered him a charlatan. And yet, Garvey's message resonated. The UNIA chapters extended into major cities such as Detroit, New Orleans, and Omaha, and supporters gave enthusiastically to build the organization. The UNIA was as much a part of the Harlem Renaissance as were the young Black Bohemian artists and writers who flocked to the city to pursue their creative visions.[39] Garvey's entrepreneurialism would provide a template for new evangelists, including the great American preacher Father Divine,[40] and Elijah Muhammad, the Messenger of the Nation of Islam.[41]

Spiritual alternatives were porous in the context of a more cosmopolitan urban environment in ways that felt innovative. In the new and more anonymous urban environment, Black enclaves in larger cities were freer to show a diversity of spiritual and religious understandings.[42]

Civil Rights Movement and Beyond

The civil rights movement is one of the great revivalist and ecumenical moments in world history. Some people of faith refer to it as a Fourth Great Awakening. In the twentieth century, the Fourth Great Awakening became a revival movement that was more globally pluralistic, opening up conversations with Buddhists, Sikhs, Hindus, and more. And yet, race continues to be a dominant aspect of religious marginalization.

At the end of the nineteenth century, W.E.B. DuBois astutely predicted that "the problem of the twentieth century is the problem of the color line—the relation of the darker to the lighter races of men in Asia and Africa, in America and the islands of the sea."[43] This is precisely what we witnessed in the 1900s. Following the negotiation of the Treaty of Versailles at the end of the First World War, it remained clear to the darker races that their inferiority would be upheld by the United States and its European allies. For the darker races, the pursuit

[39] Randall K. Burkett, *Garveyism as a Religious Movement: The Institutionalization of a Black Civil Religion* (Metuchen, NY: Scarecrow Press, 1978).

[40] Robert Weisbrot, *Father Divine and the Struggle for Racial Equality* (Urbana: University of Illinois Press, 1983).

[41] Claude A. Clegg, *The Life and Times of Elijah Muhammad* (Chapel Hill: University of North Carolina Press, 2014); and Karl Evanzz, *The Messenger: The Rise and Fall of Elijah Muhammad* (New York: Pantheon Books, 1999).

[42] Milton C. Sernett, *Bound for the Promised Land: African American Religion and the Great Migration* (Durham, NC: Duke University Press, 1997); Judith Weisenfeld, *New World A-Coming: Black Religion and Racial Identity during the Great Migration* (New York: New York University Press, 2016); and Gayraud S. Wilmore, *Black Religion and Black Radicalism* (Garden City, NY: Anchor Press, 1973).

[43] W.E.B. Du Bois, "Of Dawn of Freedom," in *The Souls of Black Folk*, Project Gutenberg, January 1996, https://www.gutenberg.org/files/408/408-h/.

of self-governance and self-respect would be a protracted political and religious struggle, whether in India, South Africa, or the United States.

This period saw the rise of two contrasting Evangelicals. One was Billy Graham as America's newest, nationally televised anti-communist evangelist, who with the assistance of the media mogul William Randolph Hearst became a transformative American evangelist. The other was Dr. Martin Luther King, Jr., whose Montgomery Bus Boycott galvanized faith leaders globally to talk to one another across lines of religion, race, and militarism.

King's religious and political views were not fully original; there were exchanges that preceded his ascent to becoming a national and global voice for freedom and justice.[44] By 1957, as King became a global religious figure, the conversations were ripened with India's Independence, and the rise of African and Asian independence movements. These movements seeded conversations that crisscrossed everywhere—Atlanta, Bandung, Boston, Gethsemane Abbey in Kentucky, Geneva, Johannesburg, Manhattan, London, Montgomery, Mumbai, Paris, and Washington, DC. These conversations spread like wildfire, in protest marches in Selma, on the campuses of religious colleges and secular universities, and in newspaper columns and books.

The civil rights movement, in conjunction with the struggle against apartheid in South Africa in the 1970s and 1980s, created a global stir over racism as enshrined into state and national laws, and it opened doors for religious leaders to think with much more care about questions of exclusion, inclusion, and belonging in community.[45] King's expansive Christian liberalism became a model for how to connect with people across religious lines.[46] His religious openness followed the pattern of his two major mentors, Benjamin Mays and Howard Thurman, both of whom were transformed theologically through their encounters with Indians.[47] Malcolm X, too, would come to see and argue that the conversation within theological communities and outside the framework of Orientalism was necessary to create conditions of understanding and justice globally.[48]

[44] Dennis C. Dickerson, "Gandhi's," *Journal of African American History* 104, no. 1 (2019): 59–83; D.C. Dickerson, "William Stuart Nelson and the Interfaith Origins of the Civil Rights Movement," in *Churches, Blackness, and Contested Multiculturalism*, edited by R.D. Smith, W. Ackah, and A.G. Reddie (New York: Palgrave Macmillan, 2014), https://doi.org/10.1057/9781137386380_5; and Sudarshan Kapur, *Raising Up a Prophet: The African American Encounter with Gandhi* (Boston, 1992).

[45] Harold Kasimow, *Interfaith Activism: Abraham Joshua Heschel and Religious Diversity* (Eugene, OR: Wipf & Stock, 2015).

[46] Marc Andrus, *Brothers in the Beloved Community: The Friendship of Thich Nacht Hanh and Martin Luther Kling, Jr.* (Berkeley, CA: Parallax Press, 2021).

[47] Howard Thurman, *Jesus and the Disinherited* (Nashville, TN: Abingdon-Cokesbury Press, 1949).

[48] Zareena Grewal, "1965 and the Global Afterlife of Malcolm X," *American Studies* 54, no. 2 (2015): 9–20.

Standard US narratives on Black liberation are still dominated by the trope of the "Negro's Church." However, a closer reading demands that we think critically about this religious historiography as inherent to Black communities' internal religious pluralism, the idea that faith(s) have a right to coexist side-by-side, protected by civil liberties. Religious diversity is a feature of nearly all Black American communities, particularly those in urban metropolitan areas, which are religiously pluralistic and must find democratic conversations as a means to discuss differences of ritual and theological expressions. Taking a more expansive view is more likely to create more just conditions for all people to live and thrive and belong freely without imposition of state actors.[49] Finally, while so-called world religions such as Buddhism, Christianity, Hinduism, Islam, and Shintoism continue to receive attention and legitimacy, African-informed religions are still considered unworthy of recognition, both socially and legally.[50] This reminds us that Africa used as a term of being abject and disreputable continues to be the legacy of the transatlantic slave trade, especially in the minds of Christian theologians and publics.[51] Sadly, Africa's diverse religious traditions continue to exist without respectful engagement from conversation partners in the Americas.[52] Viewing Black religious historiography through the lens of pluralism helps clergy, religious scholars, and advocates to see religious pluralism, not as a threat to faith(s), but as a better form of democratic engagement with faith communities who share the same neighborhoods and planet.

[49] Randal Maurice Jelks, *Faith and Struggle in the Lives of Four African Americans* (London: Bloomsbury Academic, 2019).

[50] Daniel N. Boaz, *Banning Black Gods: Law and Religions of the Africa Diaspora* (University Park: Pennsylvania University Press, 2021).

[51] For Africa as abject, see Ira Berlin, "From Creole to African: Atlantic Creoles and the Origins of African-American Society in Mainland North America," *The William and Mary Quarterly* 53, no. 2 (April 1996): 251–288.

[52] USCIRF, *Religious Freedom Concerns for Followers of African Traditional and Indigenous Religions* (Washington, DC: United States Commission on International Religious Freedom, 2023).

12

To Fight Racism, We Need to Confront Religion's Racist Past

Simran Jeet Singh

Over Fourth of July weekend in 2020, President Donald Trump stoked racial tensions yet again when he held an Independence Day rally in South Dakota. Native leaders called for Trump to cancel the rally, and more than a dozen Indigenous activists and allies were arrested for blocking a highway leading to the event.[1]

And yet, Trump came, uninvited, to unceded Lakota territory. He arrived at the Six Grandfathers, known also as the sacred Black Hills, where he paid homage to Mount Rushmore, a national monument carved into the hills by a man with ties to the Ku Klux Klan.[2]

Among the detained activists was Nick Tilsen, president of the NDN Collective and a citizen of the Oglala Lakota nation. In explaining the religious significance of the Mount Rushmore site for Native communities, Tilsen said that "more than 50 different Indigenous nations actually have origin stories or ties or spiritual connections to the Black Hills" and that US law has recognized the Lakota nation as the rightful caretakers of that land.

As an observer, I felt outraged, not just because of Trump's presumptuous jaunt into land that was not his own and where he was not wanted, but also because the news story revealed to me my own ignorance. Growing up in the United States, I considered Mount Rushmore as nothing other than a symbol of American patriotism. What I had never learned, though, is that this site—and Trump's foray into it—signaled another meaning of what it means to be American: It fit right into the long history of racist abuse and violence that European colonists wrought in the "New World."

[1] This chapter is adapted from remarks I first delivered for the Council on Foreign Relations and then a column I published with Religion News Service: Simran Jeet Singh, "To Fight Racism, We Need to Confront Religion's Racist Past," *Religion News*, July 9, 2020, https://religionnews.com/2020/07/09/how-americas-religious-colonizers-brought-racism-with-them (accessed December 16, 2025).

[2] Diane Bernard, "The Creator of Mount Rushmore's Forgotten Ties to White Supremacy," *Washington Post*, July 2, 2020, https://www.washingtonpost.com/history/2020/07/03/mount-rushmore-gutzon-borglum-klan-stone-mountain/ (accessed December 15, 2025).

Simran Jeet Singh, *To Fight Racism, We Need to Confront Religion's Racist Past* In: *Modeling Religious Pluralism*. Edited by: Simran Jeet Singh, Oxford University Press. © Oxford University Press 2026.
DOI: 10.1093/oso/9780197745809.003.0012

A surface-level reading of this story might lead us to see Western imperialism and the displacement of Indigenous peoples as an assault against minoritized religious communities—which is not wrong. But if we understand the history behind it, we can also see the role that religion and theology played in creating the conditions for American racism.

Forming Racism, Then and Now

Consider this: On May 4, 1493, just a year after Christopher Columbus arrived in this new world, Pope Alexander VI issued the Papal Bull "Inter Caetera," which announced that any land not inhabited by Christians was open to be "discovered" by Christian rulers and that "the Catholic faith and Christian religion be exalted and be everywhere increased and spread, that the health of souls be cared for and that the barbarous nations be overthrown and brought to faith itself."[3]

This document, which would come to be known as the "Doctrine of Discovery," was foundational to the European colonization of the Americas and their presumptive claims of Western expansion, a vision also couched in religious language as "Manifest Destiny."

While some today ask what religion has to do with American racism, attending to the conquest and colonization of what would become the United States compels us to ask a different question: *Is it even possible to decouple religion from American racism?*

If we understand racism as "a marriage of racist policies and racist ideas that produces and normalizes racial inequities," the Doctrine of Discovery provides a prime example of how racism works, and how religion served to create those ideas and to act on them.[4] Religious authorities presented racist ideas of supremacy over Indigenous peoples, and these ideas were used to justify and sanctify the seizure of occupied lands, the physical removal of communities to undesirable reservations, and systematic violence of genocidal proportions.

Religion's role in producing American racism is undeniable.

Accepting this reality seems to be hard for people, in part because it is not part of the story that we tell ourselves, and in part because it feels uncomfortable. Is a predominantly Christian nation ready to accept that the Church was complicit in the colonial project and all the violence and suffering that came with it?

[3] Pope Alexander VI, "The Doctrine of Discovery, 1493," Gilder Lehrman Institute of American History, https://www.gilderlehrman.org/history-resources/spotlight-primary-source/doctrine-discovery-1493 (accessed December 15, 2025).

[4] Ibram X. Kendi, *How to Be an Antiracist* (New York: Penguin Random House, 2019), 17–18.

People handle this information in different ways, and even those who accept these realities tend to locate racist policies and racist ideas as quaint misconceptions of a distant past. *That was a long time ago*, they say. *We're far beyond that now*, they say.

And yet, a quick glance at recent history demonstrates otherwise. In 1823, the US Supreme Court upheld the Doctrine of Discovery in *Johnson* v. *M'Intosh*, which stands as a basis of international law to this day, and of US Indian law: In 2005, this was cited in the case of *City of Sherrill* v. *Oneida Indian Nation of New York*, which concerned the Oneidas' ability to reacquire reservation land that had been sold under coercion in the early nineteenth century.[5]

It is true that the Doctrine of Discovery is a historical document that was written and enacted more than five hundred years ago. It is also true that it has shaped American racism as we have known it, and it remains an active force in our world today.

Upholding Racism

The Doctrine of Discovery created the conditions for American racism, and it laid the groundwork for white supremacy, an ideology of racial hierarchy that would become entrenched within the United States. Settler colonialists honed the idea of race on this continent to justify the enslavement and eradication of nonwhite Christians. This is the underpinning of American racism—and Christianity is at the center of it.

We know, for example, that early Christian slaveholders used the Bible to justify the enslavement of darker-skinned people. The Curse of Ham is perhaps the best-known example. It draws from Genesis, and as scholars have shown repeatedly over the years, Ham has come to be understood as Black and his descendants have come to be understood as Africans.[6] The other popularly cited biblical passage is attributed to Paul in Ephesians 6:5–8:

> Servants, be obedient to them that are your masters according to the flesh, with fear and trembling, in singleness of your heart, as unto Christ; not with eye-service, as men-pleasers; but as the servants of Christ, doing the will of God from the heart; with good will doing service, as to the Lord, and not to men: knowing that whatsoever good thing any man doeth, the same shall he receive of the Lord, whether he be bond or free.

[5] *City of Sherrill* v. *Oneida Indian Nation of New York*, 544 U.S. 197 (2005), https://www.supremecourt.gov/pdfs/transcripts/2004/03-855.pdf (accessed December 15, 2025).

[6] Stephen R. Haynes, *Noah's Curse: The Biblical Justification of American Slavery* (New York: Oxford University Press, 2007).

Proponents of slavery cited these biblical references, among others, to justify and uphold anti-Black racism. Noel Rae's work on American slavery shows how white supremacists—including many early American religious leaders—would couple these excerpts with racist ideas to advocate for racial hierarchies and inequities. For instance, Rae gives us the example of Bishop Stephen Elliot of Georgia, who said that critics of slavery should:

> consider whether, by their interference with this institution, they may not be checking and impeding a work which is manifestly Providential. For nearly a hundred years the English and American Churches have been striving to civilize and Christianize Western Africa, and with what result? Around Sierra Leone, and in the neighborhood of Cape Palmas, a few natives have been made Christians, and some nations have been partially civilized; but what a small number in comparison with the thousands, nay, I may say millions, who have learned the way to Heaven and who have been made to know their Savior through the means of African slavery! At this very moment there are from three to four millions of Africans, educating for earth and for Heaven in the so vilified Southern States—learning the very best lessons for a semi-barbarous people—lessons of self-control, of obedience, of perseverance, of adaptation of means to ends; learning, above all, where their weakness lies, and how they may acquire strength for the battle of life. These considerations satisfy me with their condition, and assure me that it is the best relation they can, for the present, be made to occupy.[7]

Elliot's words echo the Doctrine of Discovery, announcing that the delivery of Christianity to peoples who had not received it was not just the right but also the "mission" of the modern West. The civilizing impulse, which is the firmament of the colonial project, was God-given and God-driven.

The formation and implementation of American racism come early in US history, but again, the ideologies of white supremacy are not limited to a distant past. Yes, early Christian slaveholders leveraged the Bible to uphold slavery, but so did vigilante groups in the early twentieth century who rode around in white hoods with a Bible in hand.[8] And into the twenty-first century, prominent evangelical pastors have held their bibles, too, as they spew racist hate against America's first Black president, and as they advocate for white supremacy and Christian Nationalism.[9]

[7] Noel Rae, *The Great Stain: Witnessing American Slavery* (New York: The Overlook Press, 2018).

[8] Kelly J. Baker, *Gospel According to the Klan: The KKK's Appeal to Protestant America, 1915–1930* (Lawrence: Kansas University Press, 2017).

[9] Bradley Onishi, *Preparing for War: The Extremist History of White Christian Nationalism—And What Comes Next* (Minneapolis, MN: Broadleaf Books, 2024).

White supremacy is a part of America's history, and white supremacy is part of its present, too.

Until very recently, we Americans have seemed to think similarly about all our racist structures: as part of a past that no longer pertained. We had ended slavery. We had ended Jim Crow. We had no further need for the Voting Rights Act.

Yet there's nothing "past" about American racism—and it will be our future unless we take radical action to break the cycle of exploitation, violence, and lies.

Religion and Racialization

There is another aspect of how race and religion intersect that I know intimately: the racialization of religion. The way I've experienced this as a Sikh man in the United States is that many people see my turban and beard and brown skin and read me as a Muslim. Coupling their presumptions with Islamophobic outlooks, Sikh Americans have been racialized as Muslims and have been treated (and mistreated) accordingly.[10]

I frequently encounter a question from people that helps clarify the relationship between race and religion: "Islam is not a race. It's a religion. So how can Islamophobia be racism?"

It's a fair question, especially in a society where we typically detach racial and religious identities from one another. It's also an important question, because it compels us to explore what Islamophobia is and how it manifests in our societies. I often answer the question of how we can understand Islamophobia as a form of racism by sharing simple examples of people who are not Muslim that have been targeted in anti-Muslim racism: Balbir Singh Sodhi, a Sikh American who was murdered after 9/11 by an Arizona man who spewed anti-Muslim hate.[11] Khalid Jabara, a Lebanese-American Christian killed in Oklahoma in 2016 by someone who presumed him to be Muslim.[12] Srinivas Kuchibhotla, an Indian national, who was called a terrorist before being fatally shot by Adam Purinton.[13]

[10] For more on the racialization of Muslims, begin with Sahar Aziz, *The Racial Muslim: When Racism Quashes Religious Freedom* (Berkeley: University of California Press, 2021). For more on the racialization of Sikhs, see my chapter, Simran Jeet Singh, "Muslimophobia, Racialization, and Mistaken Identity," in *Muhammad in the Post-9/11 Digital Age*, ed. Ruqqayya Khan (Austin: University of Texas Press, 2015).

[11] Ibid.

[12] Steve Almasy and Konstantin Toropin, "Oklahoma Man Found Guilty of Hate Crime in His Neighbor's Death," CNN, https://www.cnn.com/2018/02/07/us/oklahoma-stanley-vernon-majors-trial/index.htm (accessed December 15, 2025).

[13] US Department of Justice, "Kansas Man Sentenced to Life in Prison without Parole for Racially Motivated Shooting at Olathe Bar," https://www.justice.gov/opa/pr/kansas-man-sentenced-life-prison-without-parole-racially-motivated-shooting-olathe-bar (accessed December 15, 2025).

These examples scratch the surface of what Islamophobia has to do with racism. For people who are trying to understand the relationship between the two, they offer a good starting point.[14]

Addressing Racism through Understanding and Action

In understanding the close relationship between religion and racism, and understanding its stakes, an urgent question emerges: What might we do to correct for racism?

The answer is not as intuitive as it might seem. Most of us have presumed the solution to be non-racism. By not being actively racist, we figured that we were doing our part to end racism.

What we have learned collectively, though, is that when we sit by silently and allow racist ideas and policies to function, we enable racism's flourishing. Neutrality is neither the opposite of racism nor its solution. Making racial justice a reality requires sustained action.

We live in a world today where seeking racial justice has been politicized and made partisan. Here is how I understand it: To advance racial justice is to proactively fight against racism in all its pernicious forms, from the individual level to the systemic. This includes racist ideas that are formulated through theologies, disseminated through religious institutions, and enacted by religious communities.

Racial justice and religious pluralism are massive, global issues. Even when one makes a commitment to address them, it can be hard to know where to begin. How might we develop practices to help identify the ways we engage and uphold racism? And what steps can we take toward eradicating it?

We can begin by identifying and challenging the racist ideas and racist policies that we have normalized and rendered invisible—including those that religious ideas and religious institutions have helped to produce and promulgate. We must make apparent the relationship between racism and religion, because clearly diagnosing the disease is the first step toward prescribing an antidote.

To put it differently, because these racist ideas are so entrenched within us, becoming aware of racism and religion's role in upholding it is an ongoing process that entails a constant commitment. It is the exercise of searching for weeds daily and pulling them out by their root. For instance, studying the Church's arguments for colonization has helped me better understand the logic and shape

[14] For more resources on this particular form of racialized religion, see Islamophobia Is Racism, "Resource for Teaching and Learning about Anti-Muslim Racism in the United States," https://islamophobiaisracism.wordpress.com (accessed December 15, 2025).

of American racism. The exercise of introspection has also helped me to understand how white supremacist ideas have been instilled within me, a reminder that no individual is immune to these ideologies, and that each of us must work intentionally and actively to extricate them from within us.

Understanding is an important first step, but as many wise people have pointed out, scholarly study alone will not save us. Action is also necessary if we seek to create real, transformational change. This is why advancing racial justice necessitates active engagement.

For instance, upon learning of Christianity's central role in birthing American racism, someone committed to racial justice will be moved to action. What might we *do* upon learning that religious ideologies have motivated people to seize sacred sites and land from indigenous communities? How do we *respond* when becoming aware that our leaders have purposefully broken a treaty that honored those lands and that they are seeking to advance a mission of white Christian nationalism? Ultimately, this approach calls on us to go beyond cataloging the injustice and inhumanity, and to be moved to action—for the sake of justice and humanity.

As a historian, as a scholar of religion, and also as a person of faith who is trying to address these challenges in our lives, here is what I have come to understand about the commitment to racial justice: To live into racial justice is to strive toward challenging white supremacy and American exceptionalism in all its forms and toward humanizing people of different groups rather than creating hierarchies of power and dominance.

Sincerely cultivating racial justice would be a seismic shift from anything we have ever seen in American history before because, up until now, we have been so subsumed by the false binary of racism and non-racism. That we are beginning to broach the topic of racial justice more seriously gives me heart. This is a path toward a better, more humane, and more sustainable way forward.

PART V
RELIGION AND MEDIA

Growing up in the 1990s, I was thrilled when *Aladdin* came out. *Finally, a Disney character with a turban!* I dressed as Aladdin for Halloween for years, in part because it was my favorite movie, and in part because it was easy. *Throw on some traditional Punjabi clothes, tie a white turban, and go get that candy!*

It wasn't until graduate school that I read Edward Said's *Orientalism* and Jack Shaheen's *Reel Bad Arabs*. Both of those books broke my heart and helped me see another dimension of the story. Yes, Aladdin might feel like representation for a Sikh boy in Texas, but what does that say about the state of our cultural storytelling? And how do we get to a place where we insist on authenticity, where the media we consume helps us better see one another and helps us feel more seen?

This question has become central to my work, and it has also figured into our model for religious pluralism. Media is powerful and influential, and it shapes how we understand one another and our world. So, it should come as no surprise that we see media as a critical component of religious pluralism.

A 2024 global study found that 69 percent of American entertainment consumers—and 63 percent globally—say that TV and movies perpetuate religious stereotypes. Eighty percent of the respondents agreed that it is important that the entertainment industry improves portrayals of faith to make them more accurate.[1] Another study, in 2022, found that representations of Muslims in film and television perpetuated stereotypes of perpetual foreignness and violence: Nearly two thirds of Muslim characters were non-native speakers of English, over 30 percent were perpetrators of violence, and nearly 40 percent were targets of violence.[2]

These perspectives affirm my own observations and feelings—that while media is a powerful tool for humanizing, or dehumanizing, there is so much we

[1] Faith & Media Initiative, *The Global Faith & Entertainment Study*, HarrisX, February 13, 2024, https://www.faithandmedia.com/research/harrisxentertainment (accessed June 28, 2025).

[2] Al-Baab Khan, Katherine Pieper, Stacy L. Smith, Ariana Case, and Sam Wheeler, "Erased or Extremists: The Stereotypical View of Muslims in Popular Episodic Series," USC Getty Annenberg Inclusion Initiative, September 2022, https://assets.uscannenberg.org/docs/aii-study-muslim-erased-or-extremists-20220901.pdf (accessed December 18, 2025).

can and must do to ensure that we are using this tool to help us see the humanity in one another, including people we have not met before.

In this section, as with others, we hear from diverse leaders and thinkers on the challenges religious communities face pertaining to media, as well as suggestions on how we might improve these issues. Each speaks from their own unique vantage point, positionality, and expertise in the field.

We learn from Dr. Hussein Rashid, who previously served as assistant dean at Harvard Divinity School. He writes about the depictions of Muslims within American media. Rashid describes shifts from long-standing tropes and caricatures toward "more complex representations of Muslims in film and television," and he examines how these shifts reframe religion and religious communities in a way that advances religious pluralism.

Culture writer Esther D. Kustanowitz reflects on antisemitism in media, including common stereotypes about Jews and their place within the media landscape. She also takes on the notion of representation as the end goal, noting that careless and inauthentic storytelling can do more harm than good. Esther also offers best practices for how storytellers can share with more authenticity, accuracy, and depth.

The third chapter in this section, written by filmmaker and documentarian Jody Hassett Sanchez, considers the challenge of enhancing authenticity in how religion and religious communities are represented in film and television. Having interviewed a number of thought leaders with a diverse range of expertise, she offers perspectives, insights, and suggestions for how to bring these ideas to fruition.

Each of these chapters recognizes what so many of us already know: Media has a great deal of power to shape public understanding, and it can help us move toward pluralism or away from it. The analysis of our contributors, as well as their constructive suggestions, help us go beyond standard talking points and consider new ideas and approaches for enhanced representation, authenticity, and progress.

13
Representing the Muslim

Hussein Rashid

Broadly speaking, religion on screen can be divided into two main categories: confessional and representational. Confessional religion is not just the Sunday morning televangelists, but also shows like *Davey and Goliath*, which ran in the 1960s and 1970s; *VeggieTales*, which ran from the 1990s to the 2010s; and movies like the *Left Behind* and *The Chronicles of Narnia* series. These examples are intentionally chosen because of their US-based production. By locating a place, one can see the religious biases of that location, in this instance Christianity, as the default understanding of religion.

Representational media is about showing people who are living their lives, which may include their religious affiliations. These shows must demonstrate nuanced lived religion and be legible to audiences that may be socialized to reading religion as Christianity or a Christianity analogue.

Historian of religion Tomoko Masuzawa outlines the origin of the study of religion in comparative theology. In this intellectual genealogy, Christianity becomes the standard that defines the idea of religion, and thus how other religions are interpreted and explained.[1] This normalization of understanding religion through a Christian lens impacts popular culture as well as academic understandings of religion.

This chapter starts with a focus on representations of Muslims on screen, both film and television, and the arc of adding nuance to Muslim stories over several decades. By using ideas from parasocial contact theory and religious literacy to analyze this transformation, I set the basis for considering how other religious traditions are depicted on screen.

Representing the Muslim

While on-screen representations of Muslims have improved over the past several decades, these representations remain uneven, and still trade in Orientalist and

[1] Tomoko Masuzawa, *The Invention of World Religions: Or, How European Universalism Was Preserved in the Language of Pluralism* (Chicago: University of Chicago Press, 2005).

Hussein Rashid, *Representing the Muslim* In: *Modeling Religious Pluralism*. Edited by: Simran Jeet Singh, Oxford University Press. © Oxford University Press 2026. DOI: 10.1093/oso/9780197745809.003.0013

Islamophobic tropes. In early portrayals, the "Arab" and the "Muslim" are often indistinguishable. The antisemitic caricatures and themes that permeate US culture transform into signature anti-Arab representations. The constructed Arabo-Muslim starts by fitting into four broad categories: villains, shaykhs, maidens, and cameos. A recurring cultural trope is that pure American women are in constant danger from these male characters. The racial overtones of US anxiety around miscegenation are impossible to miss. This trope reflects and reinforces the deep cultural concern about preserving the whiteness that is at the core of what it means to belong in the United States. This fascination around purity casts non-white Christians both outside and inside the United States as equally threatening, foreign bodies that must be disciplined, fought, and expelled.

This concern of invasion of the Other is not just a physical concern, but an existential one. If there is an Other, the Self that rejects the Other is defined in relation to the Other. Thus, creating and defining the Other are acts of the construction of the Self. When screen depictions of Muslims show Muslims as violent, uncultured, dirty, misogynistic, and superstitious, it is a construction of the US Self that is pacifist, cultured, clean, equitable, and logical, and that representation for both Self and Other is immune to evidence to the contrary. These depictions are not factual constructs, but narrative constructs. The way to alter narrative constructs is with other narrative constructs.[2]

Narrative constructs are a way of approaching the depth of what representation means in the context of screens. It is not just about showing viewers people who are Muslim, but also about the stories that are told about them. The screen presence represents who Muslims are to the audience, and media is an important way that social cohesion and understanding of groups function.[3] Therefore,

[2] For further discussion of these ideas, see Rubina Ramji, "From Navy seals to *The Siege*: Getting to Know the Muslim Terrorist, Hollywood Style," *Journal of Religion and Film* 9, no. 2 (2005): 1–15, art. 6; Jack G. Shaheen, *Guilty: Hollywood's Verdict on Arabs after 9/11* (Northampton, MA: Olive Branch Press, 2008); Jack G. Shaheen, *Reel Bad Arabs: How Hollywood Vilifies a People* (New York: Olive Branch Press, 2001); Tim Jon Semmerling, *"Evil" Arabs in American Popular Film: Orientalist Fear* (Austin: University of Texas Press, 2006); Tim Jon Semmerling, "Those 'Evil' Muslims! Orientalist Fears in the Narratives of the War on Terror," *Journal of Muslim Minority Affairs* 28, no. 2 (2008): 207–223; Hussein Rashid, "Muslims in Film and Muslim Filmmaking in the United States," in *The Oxford Handbook of American Islam*, edited by Yvonne Yazbeck Haddad and Jane I. Smith (Oxford: Oxford University Press, 2014), 459–473; Stuart Hall, "Ethnicity: Identity and Difference," *Radical America* 23, no. 4 (1991): 9–13; Evelyn Alsultany, "Arabs, Muslims, and Arab Americans: Constructing an Evil Other," in *The Routledge Companion to Media and Race*, edited by Christopher Campbell (New York: Routledge, 2016), 241–249; Evelyn Alsultany, "Representations of Arabs and Muslims in Post-9/11 Television Dramas," in *The Colorblind Screen*, edited by Sarah Nilsen and Sarah E. Turner (New York: New York University Press, 2020), 140–166; Peter Gottschalk and Gabriel Greenberg, *Islamophobia and Anti-Muslim Sentiment: Picturing the Enemy* (Lanham, MD: Rowman & Littlefield, 2018); Brigitte Lebens Nacos and Oscar Torres-Reyna, *Fueling Our Fears: Stereotyping, Media Coverage, and Public Opinion of Muslim Americans* (Lanham, MD: Rowman & Littlefield, 2007); and Evelyn Alsultany, *Arabs and Muslims in the Media: Race and Representation after 9/11* (New York: New York University Press, 2012).

[3] Christopher Campbell, "Representation: Stuart Hall and the 'Politics of Signification,'" in *The Routledge Companion to Media and Race*, edited by Christopher Campbell (New York: Routledge,

showing "good" and "bad" Muslims is not sufficient enough to break the strength of stereotypes. The power of stereotypes comes not from any position of truth, but as a way to make sense of power dynamics in society. They are about representing the Other. Their strength comes from being part of a narrative web. We can counter those exclusionary narrative webs by helping new narratives to emerge that challenge the hegemony of harmful framings. In doing so, we enable individuals to make sense of the world in new ways.

More recent representations of Muslims attempt to offer more complex representations of Muslims in both film and television. The crime procedural show *Bones* (2009–2017) featured Pej Vahdat (b. 1982) playing the character of Arastoo Vaziri. The character is introduced in season four as an immigrant from Iran, and frequently observed performing Muslim liturgical prayers. Eventually the character reveals that he is a US citizen who served in the US military, and it is implied that he grew up in the United States and perhaps was even born in the United States. He initially keeps this hidden from the team he works with because he believed that they could not reconcile his religious commitments with the fact that he was a forensic anthropologist. His fear is well founded, as several members of his team question what they perceive as an inherent conflict between religion and science. While his colleagues' initial confusion is about religion in general rather than Islam specifically, the Vaziri character uses his understanding of his religion to argue for a different logic than they are used to, and a different understanding of how religion and science function. Thus, Vaziri is able to destabilize a narrative of a conflict between religion and science, using Islam as an example.

Tala Ashe (b. 1984) plays the character Zara Tomaz on the speculative fiction show *The Legends of Tomorrow* (2016–2022). She is introduced as a Muslim character from an alternate history near future Earth, who is persecuted for her religion. While the loss of her family is an important recurring plot point in the series, the depiction of her religious observance is not framed through trauma. It is more casual and organic in how it appears throughout the series. She refuses alcohol and pork, and talks about the struggle of fasting during Ramadan when someone asks her about her mood. These references are quick, and no one dwells on them as she introduces these aspects of her religious commitments. The lack of emphasis on her religious practice normalizes what it means to be Muslim. She is not presented as different; she simply is.

2016), 11–18; Evelyn Alsultany, "Challenging Stereotypes," in *How to Watch Television*, 2nd ed., edited by Ethan Thompson and Jason Mittell (New York: New York University Press, 2020), 91–98; and Dina Ibrahim, "Maybe Brown People Aren't So Scary if They're Funny: Audience Readings of Arabs and Muslims on Cable Television Comedies," in *The Colorblind Screen*, edited by Sarah Nilsen and Sarah E. Turner (New York: New York University Press, 2014), 167–188.

Movies are more complicated in their depictions of Muslims. In part, the complexity is due to the long development cycles of film; while movies can be more culturally impactful than television, they often trail cultural conversations around religion. Films like *X* (1992) and *Ali* (2001), about Malcolm X and Muhammad Ali, respectively, were both culturally and commercially significant, dealt with the religious understanding of the two men, and were based on historical figures. For fiction, many films in the twenty-first century were in the context of the War on Terror, such as *The Valley of Elah* (2007), focusing on the cost of war in the United States, and *Rendition* (2007), about "extraordinary rendition," the euphemism for US torture programs. While many of these films attempted to offer nuanced perspectives of Muslims, they accepted narrative representations that Muslims should be understood through the interests of national security.

There are several speculative fiction films that attempt to give a different representation to Muslims. *Pitch Black* (2000), about a spaceship that crashed on a hostile planet, introduces us to the character of Imam Abu al-Walid, who is referred to by his title, Imam, throughout the movie. He is a supporting character to the protagonist of the film, Riddick. Imam is visibly marked as being connected to Islam, and he is leading a contingent to a pilgrimage to New Mecca. Imam's religion is a defining characteristic for him, and while he does not spend any extended period talking about his religion—as it seems to be widely taken for granted that characters in the movie universe are familiar with it—he has many discussions of how it guides his actions. He is portrayed as honorable and a character that a viewer would want to empathize with, especially as a pacifist put into a combat situation. His narrative challenges the assumption that Muslims are inherently violent.

The 2013 film *Ender's Game*, which is premised on a perceived impending space alien invasion, introduces the character Alai (pronounced "ally" in the film). He is an integral part of the main character's development and part of the team that forms around that character. We only know Alai is Muslim through a brief exchange where he utters the greeting "as-salam alaykum." He does not discuss or embody his religion in any other way in the film, and other characters do not remark upon it. Alai offers a narrative of a Muslim who believes but is not defined by his religion, his compatriots accept him for who he is, and his religion is normalized in the future presented in the film.[4]

[4] For more detailed discussion of representation in these films and others, see Hussein Rashid, "The Incidental Muslim: The Characters We Overlook," in *Muslims in the Movies: A Global Anthology*, edited by Kristian Petersen (Boston: Ilex Foundation, 2021), 45–57.

Nuance and Religious Literacy

These examples illustrate how Muslim representation is changing. The narrative shifts position Muslims as less threatening, and less the Other against which the audience may be defining itself. Another mechanism by which these representations work is through the parasocial contact hypothesis (PCH). This hypothesis is based on the idea that media can create dissonance in the mind of a viewer; narrative shifts help drive changes of attitude.

Narrative shifts can also occur through how viewers identify with the protagonists in the narrative. For instance, identification does not have to be with the Muslim character(s), but can also happen with other characters who have positive interactions with the Muslim character(s). PCH posits that the narrative shift is only one part of the equation of creating nuance. Because of the weight of old narratives and stereotypes, the identification of the viewer with a character is instrumental in creating durable changes in perceptions.[5]

These durable changes in perceptions are tied to the narrative reframing. The four examples mentioned above—*Bones, The Legends of Tomorrow, Pitch Black*, and *Ender's Game*—incorporate elements of religious literacy into their narrative by reframing and inserting a critical apparatus for viewers to alter how they think about religion. The principles of religious literacy that are relevant for this conversation are that religions are internally diverse, understanding religion happens in context (social, cultural, historical, economic, etc.), religion and culture are not neatly separable, and religious communities are not defined solely by religion.[6]

The Vaziri character in *Bones*, introduced in 2009, is situated in a premier forensic anthropology lab, where the scientific method is meant to define the work that people do. Vaziri is correctly concerned that in the space of this establishment, and in the cultural context of the United States where the narrative frame is that religion and science are in conflict, his religious commitments would not

[5] Carole V. Bell, "Talking Racial Politics Online," in *Parasocial Politics: Audiences, Pop Culture, and Politics*, edited by Jason Zenor (Lanham, MD: Lexington Books, 2014), 133–152; S. Brent Rodriguez-Plate, "Seeing the Other in Cinema: Interreligious Connections through the Senses," *Journal of Beliefs & Values* 38, no. 3 (2017): 296–304; bell hooks, *Black Looks: Race and Representation* (New York: Routledge, 2015); bell hooks, *Reel to Real: Race, Class and Sex at the Movies* (New York: Routledge, 2009); Edward Schiappa, Peter B. Gregg, and Dean E. Hewes, "The Parasocial Contact Hypothesis," *Communication Monographs* 72, no. 1 (2005): 92–115; Donald Horton and R. Richard Wohl, "Mass Communication and Para-Social Interaction: Observations on Intimacy at a Distance," *Psychiatry* 19, no. 3 (1956): 215–229; John F. Dovidio, Peter Samuel Glick, and Laurie A. Rudman, eds., *On the Nature of Prejudice: Fifty Years after Allport* (Malden, MA: Blackwell, 2005); and Gordon W. Allport, *The Nature of Prejudice* (Reading, MA: Addison-Wesley, 1979); and Rashid, "The Incidental Muslim."

[6] The principles are developed from Diane L. Moore, *Overcoming Religious Illiteracy: A Cultural Studies Approach to the Study of Religion in Secondary Education* (New York: Palgrave Macmillan, 2007).

be understood and could jeopardize his standing as a serious scientist. He thus chooses to present himself as an immigrant, playing into Orientalist tropes of the superstitious Other as a means of protection. The audience is brought on this journey, and then that narrative is undercut. Vaziri presents a vision of the compatibility between religion and science from the perspective of a US military veteran who is fond of Los Angeles sports teams. He is transformed from the Other to the Self, and does so without jettisoning the characteristics that would define him as an Other.

Nearly eight years later, in 2017, *The Legends of Tomorrow* introduced the character of Zari Tomaz. Her introduction takes place in a potential future earth, where being Muslim is criminalized. She has already lost her family, but continues to identify as Muslim. The narrative points out the absurdity of the previous years of suspicion of Muslims, taking them to a potential logical conclusion, particularly after the election of Donald Trump. However, Tomaz's story is not grounded in trauma. After the initial narrative of suspicion of Muslims is disrupted, she becomes a character whose religion is clearly important to her. Yet the story is never *about* her being Muslim. There are the tells of being Muslim for those who know what to look for. As opposed to *Bones*, which was about the explicit expression of Islam, *Legends* takes an approach of showing a Muslim expressing their self as they would in a world that accepts them. Tomaz is able to be more fully Muslim, because it is integrated into every aspect of her actions. She demonstrates how she is not defined in a limiting way by her religion, and that her religion impacts how she exists in the world.

Although beyond the scope of this chapter, it is worth noting that both actors, Pej Vahdat and Tala Ashe, who played Vaziri and Tomaz, respectively, come from Muslim backgrounds and have both said they gave feedback on scripts on how to represent what it means to be Muslim. Both actors, and the characters they play, are of Iranian descent and presumably Shia. The real-life context of the actors, coming from a Muslim religious minority, suggests more of a sensitivity to the diversity of Muslims. That awareness helps to add depth to the characters, who are not confined to majoritarian understandings of Islam.

In the movie *Pitch Black*, Imam is an archetype of an honorable, self-sacrificing leader. Because of his relationship to the lead character, Riddick, Imam can also be read as a "magic negro," who exists to further the development of a white character.[7] While he does help Riddick's development, he also has agency and interests of his own, and he does not exist in the shadow of Riddick. As such, while Imam is grounded in the trope, he is not fully within it, and his character

[7] For a broad and critical understanding of the trope of the "magic negro," see Dokubo Melford Goodhead, "The Resisting Spectator and *The Green Mile*," *Howard Journal of Communications* 33, no. 1 (2022): 45–57.

is doing important racial and religious narrative destabilization. The connection between race and religion cannot be ignored in the context of the United States. Arguably, the Black turn away from Christianity in the United States is tied to ideas of transcending racial and religious boundaries and linkages.[8] Imam's own religious identity, while expressed through Islam, also expresses connections to Christianity, placing him in a real-world discourse. In addition to representing a discourse of Black humanity, Imam also represents the multi-religious extended Black families in the United States, which may include Muslims and Christians. Finally, although the largest racial and ethnic group of Muslims in the United States are Black, most on-screen representations are not, so Imam presents an important corrective to the narrative of Muslims being Arab/Iranian/Central Asian/South Asian.

Finally, Alai's presence in *Ender's Game* is the shortest of all the explicit connections to Islam mentioned so far. It is the void surrounding Alai's religious commitment that gives his presence meaning. His religion is so important to him that he has to declare it at a pivotal moment in the film, when the lead character Ender is going through a transformation. Ender responds to Alai's greeting of "as-salam alaykum" with compassion, and does not express surprise at the phrase. Viewers can read this moment as Alai's religion being important to him, and inconsequential to the team that Ender is constructing. Alai's commitment to his religion is seen as normal, and not in conflict with the science, military, or team-building mission his cohort is on. It is the utter unremarkability of Alai's religion that disturbs the narrative of religion being the only identity a person can have and express. In the cultural matrix of the film, religion is taken seriously and is not limiting to the characters or the narrative.

Conclusion

Each of these examples demonstrates how religious literacy is used to deepen character stories, making the characters more relatable to viewing audiences and effecting a more durable narrative shift. While the examples focus on Muslims, the principles can be applied to other minoritized religious communities in the United States. While the long-running show *The Simpsons* (1989–present) uses satire to both explicitly reinforce and subvert narratives around religion, television shows like *Bel-Air* (2022–2025) and *The Equalizer* (2021–2025) are grounded in showing people living their lives in unremarkable contexts. The daily travails of antisemitism are combined with people supporting their Jewish

[8] Judith Weisenfeld, *New World a-Coming: Black Religion and Racial Identity during the Great Migration* (New York: New York University Press, 2016).

neighbors, and anti-immigrant vandalism is shown with people shopping in bodegas. Characters performing liturgical prayers are also shown running their businesses, partying, and falling in love.

It is these representations that reframe how viewers think of religion, so they are not socialized to think of religion solely through the lens of Christianity. Just as significant is the ability to craft a different narrative for the United States that is more inclusive of marginalized religions.

14

Stories, Stereotypes, and Sitting Shiva

Improving Jewish Representation in TV and Film

Esther D. Kustanowitz

Every now and then, in casual conversation, someone will say something about Jews controlling Hollywood or the media. Usually, the context and intention are more good-natured or joking than hatred-fueled invective, but the charge—a trope that has resurfaced in force as antisemitism globally has increased—can be such a conversational thud that many Jews who work in media have developed joking responses.

"If there were a Jewish media conspiracy, I'd be better paid."

"If Jewish people control the entertainment industry, why did the Academy Museum omit the contributions of Jewish people in its exhibitions?"[1]

"If Jews ruled Hollywood, we'd have more Jewish actors cast in Jewish roles."[2]

Good-humored as these responses may be, the airing of this trope can bristle, as the Jewish people who hear it consider the possibilities within our modern context and experience. In its 2024 audit of antisemitic incidents, the Anti-Defamation League tabulated 9,354 antisemitic incidents across the United States—a 5 percent increase from 2023's 8,873 incidents, a 344 percent increase over the past five years, and a 893 percent increase over a decade ago.[3] So even if, as is likely, the trope-invoking person in your social or professional orbit didn't mean anything hateful by it, we know that the world is not becoming a more tolerant place. We have to consider that a person who introduces the idea of Jewish media control into conversation may, in some measure, believe it.

[1] Sharon Leib Rosen, "Academy Museum of Motion Pictures Course Corrects on Jewish Founders," *The Forward*, January 28, 2022, https://forward.com/news/481078/academy-museum-hollywood-jewish-founders (accessed December 19, 2025). The museum opened "Hollywoodland," an exhibition about Hollywood's founders, in May 2024.

[2] In 2023, much virtual ink was devoted to debating the fairness of non-Jewish actors Helen Mirren and Bradley Cooper playing Israeli Prime Minister Golda Meir in *Golda* and Leonard Bernstein in *Maestro*, respectively. In 2024, both films were Oscar-nominated for their use of makeup to transform the lead actors into the historical figures.

[3] Anti-Defamation League, "Audit of Antisemitic Incidents: Ten-Year Review, 2015–2024," 2024, https://www.adl.org/resources/report/audit-antisemitic-incidents-2024 (accessed December 19, 2025).

Esther D. Kustanowitz, *Stories, Stereotypes, and Sitting Shiva* In: *Modeling Religious Pluralism*.
Edited by: Simran Jeet Singh, Oxford University Press. © Oxford University Press 2026.
DOI: 10.1093/oso/9780197745809.003.0014

It is true that many Hollywood studio heads in the industry's infancy were Jewish by birth, but many among them have earned their influence through hard work, driven by the quest for stability and belonging instilled by their immigrant parents, or informed by their own personal experience fleeing Eastern European persecution. This trauma-fueled origin story influenced some to become assimilationists: They changed their Eastern European Jewish names to feel less Jewish and more American—Poland-born Shmuel Gelbfisz became Samuel Goldwyn, for example—and distanced themselves from Jewish-inflected projects to avoid being linked to an identity that they believed might impede their success. Decades later, the fact that today's cultural producers still experience this legacy of hesitation around Jewish stories is one reason that those stories are not as well-represented on the big and small screens as one might assume them to be. Despite decades of representation in Hollywood leadership spaces, most Jewish stories remain superficial or reinforce the image of Jews as victims.[4]

Having more Jewish-specific stories doesn't necessarily end antisemitic rhetoric, but it does allow for a wider range of Jewish ideas, characters, challenges, and stories to grace our screens. Given the wide geographical reach of primarily US-produced TV and film, some efforts will travel to communities that may be new to Jewish stories. This tasks the creative team with an additional layer of responsibility regarding creative decisions: The choices they make because of time, budget, artistic vision, or lack of knowledge can result in inaccurate or caricatured ideas of what a "Jewish" community or life looks like. When these on-screen portrayals are too broad or reductive, they can cause unintended harm instead of fair representation.

One of the challenges is that defining Jewish identity is not simple. In 2020's Pew Internet Research study on global religious representation, researchers wrote that determining the size of the world's Jewish population is "complicated," because "the number of Jews around the world depends largely on one's definition of Jewishness":

> In our 2013 and 2020 surveys of Jewish Americans, we counted respondents as Jewish if they said either that Judaism is their religion or that they consider themselves Jewish aside from religion (for reasons such as ethnicity, culture or family background); have at least one Jewish parent or were raised Jewish; and don't belong to any other religion. Using that broader definition, there were an estimated 7.5 million Jews of all ages in the U.S. in 2020, about 1.8 million more

[4] Scholar, longtime lecturer for Yad Vashem's International School for Holocaust Studies, and author Rich Brownstein has identified more than four hundred movies about the Holocaust since 1945, which he profiles in his book, *Holocaust Cinema Complete: A History and Analysis of 400 Films.*

than this report's estimate of the number of Americans who identify religiously as Jewish (5.7 million).[5]

The Pew survey also reported that Jewish people "account for less than 0.01% of the population in most countries and territories globally"; and in some countries or territories, Jewish populations are so small that they cannot reliably be measured or the national census may not include "Jewish" as an option.

Jewish identity is not monolithic in any stratum of appearance or experience, yet our on-screen representation remains prone to characters who embody a visual shorthand to indicate their Jewishness: usually dressed and styled as white, male, religious/Orthodox Jews from an Eastern European (Ashkenazi) background. But "Jewish" is more than that.

Data from the Pew Research Center's "Jewish Americans in 2020" study indicate that 17 percent of US Jews live in households where at least one adult or child is Hispanic, Black, Asian, another (non-White) race or ethnicity, or multiracial.[6] While many American Jews present as white both in appearance and in conversations about privilege, many—both in the United States and globally—are not, or do not identify as, white.[7] The same Pew report indicates that two thirds of US Jews identify as Ashkenazi (i.e., their customs come from Central and Eastern Europe). But from there it's a bit more complicated, with 3 percent identifying as Sephardic (i.e., following the Jewish customs of Spain) and 1 percent as Mizrahi (i.e., following the Jewish customs of the Middle East and North Africa). The report adds that "17% say these labels either do not apply to them or that they are just Jewish, while 8% say they follow some other set of Jewish customs, indicate that they are unsure (5%) or otherwise did not answer the question (2%)."[8]

Jewish identity can be intersectional, multiethnic, multicultural, and multi-ideological. So the call for better representation should be about both quality and quantity: Characters should be inclusive of varying experiences and backgrounds, they should be nuanced and three-dimensional, and there should be more of them, so that the burden of representation is not on the shoulders of a single portrayal.

[5] Pew Research Center, "How the Global Religious Landscape Changed from 2010–2020," June 2025, https://www.pewresearch.org/wp-content/uploads/sites/20/2025/06/PR_2025.06.09_global-religious-change_report.pdf.

[6] Pew Research Center, "Jewish Americans in 2020," May 11, 2021, https://www.pewresearch.org/religion/2021/05/11/jewish-americans-in-2020/ (accessed December 19, 2025).

[7] In Israel, the *Jewish Telegraphic Agency/The Times of Israel* reports, there are "more than 200,000 people of African descent," including about 170,000 Ethiopian Jews.

[8] "Israelis of Color Push back against Race-Based, Anti-Israel Narratives Spread Abroad," *Times of Israel*, December 23, 2023, https://www.timesofisrael.com/israelis-of-color-push-back-against-race-based-anti-israel-narratives-spread-abroad/ (accessed December 19, 2025).

Representation: How People See "Jewish" on Screen

When Jewish characters appear on screen, their Jewish life and culture may be a mere flash of an object in the corner—a Hanukkah candelabrum or a star of David encircling a character's neck. Perhaps their purpose is to inject the main narrative with a piece of Jewish wisdom, or to operate as the goofy sidekick. But more substantial portrayals will also impart meaning, especially when characters surprise us with their commitment to Jewish faith and ritual.

When Walter showed up in *The Big Lebowski*, refusing to bowl on Saturday because "I don't roll on Shabbos [another word for Shabbat, the Jewish day of rest]," he explains that he is "shomer Shabbos," observant of the Jewish Sabbath, and therefore abstains from a number of activities, including bowling. It's a moment of strong Jewish identification, and even if it's played for laughs at various points, the observance he describes is deep and important to him.

Jewish characters can be a source of wisdom, meaning, and guidance, as in *The Frisco Kid*, in which Gene Wilder, as a young Polish rabbi en route to a pulpit in San Francisco, teaches his travel companion, a cowboy played by Harrison Ford, about the Torah and about Jewish customs, including a little bit of Yiddish, and awareness of Shabbat restrictions about travel. The comic effect is certainly present, and the moment illustrates the character's earnest love for imparting Jewish meaning to others.

On television, Jewish identity appears in sitcoms and dramas, mostly as shortform comic relief that catalyzes character choices into farce or a web of misunderstandings. *The Nanny* introduced many Americans to the concept of the JAP (Jewish American princess) as "the flashy girl from Flushing" who became an inextricable part of the household, bringing with her a strong, stereotypical Brooklyn accent and tidbits of Jewish identity that clash with the WASPy (White Anglo-Saxon Protestant) household. On one episode of *Frasier*, the eponymous psychologist pretended to be Jewish to impress his girlfriend's mother, roping in his brother and father as Jewish-phrase-spouting accomplices as they hid their Christmas ham in the oven and spiked the wine with sugar to create "Jewish wine." On *Friends*, a "holiday armadillo" helped Ross explain Hanukkah to his half-Jewish son in an attempt to battle the appeal of Christmas with the Jewish winter holiday, while sister Monica merited a line in Phoebe's holiday song because her name helpfully rhymes with "Hanukkah." In each of these examples, we see the presence of a Jewish person as extra-normative, and serving as a fulcrum for conflict. What we don't see in many of these portrayals is a context for these frantic actions.

In the Aaron Sorkin television universe, *The West Wing* regularly imported rabbinic wisdom and Jewish story through the character of Toby Ziegler (Richard Schiff), and Jeremy Goodwin (Josh Malina) led a Passover seder on

"Sports Night." It seems an unwritten rule that long-running supernaturally themed procedural series—such as *Grimm*, *Sleepy Hollow*, *The X Files*, and, of course, *Supernatural*—must include dybbuks, the evil spirits of Yiddish folktales, or a golem, Jewish legend's clay giant built to protect its owner from harm, among the culturally specific monsters of the week.[9]

Even those who cry out for more Jewish stories can't agree on what "Jewish" looks or feels like, thematically or visually. The same creative work can provoke pride for some, but shame for others.

The Marvelous Mrs. Maisel, for example, an Amazon Prime Video original about a secular Jewish woman from the Upper West Side who becomes a comic, drew a range of reactions. "'Marvelous Mrs. Maisel' gets Jewish converts totally wrong," Alexandra Pucciarelli wrote in the *Jewish Telegraphic Agency*.[10] Over at *The Wrap*, Mary Murphy and Michelle Willens wrote that with "Anti-Semitism on the Rise, the Jewishness of 'The Marvelous Mrs. Maisel' Is a Marvel."[11] At *HeyAlma*, Lisa Huberman asked, "When Will 'The Marvelous Mrs. Maisel' Deal with Midge's Privilege?"[12] And *The Washington Post*'s Amanda Lee weighed in with a piece about "How 'The Marvelous Mrs. Maisel' Fights Jewish Stereotypes."[13]

Similarly, the Netflix limited series *Unorthodox*, about a young ultra-Orthodox woman's escape from her insular Brooklyn community to independence in Germany, was hailed, alternately, as groundbreaking and degrading. *The Jewish Journal*'s Leah Aharoni said it "degrades Hasidic Jews into caricatures," adding that "at no point did the creators discuss an attempt to understand or explain what could possibly motivate tens of thousands of individuals to close off in insular communities and reject the trappings of modernity."[14] But *Los Angeles Times* writer Meredith Blake said it "went to remarkable lengths to get Hasidic Jewish customs right,"[15] and *Vulture*'s Jen Chaney called it "a beautiful, immersive portrait of a woman's rebirth."[16]

[9] Esther D. Kustanowitz, "How TV Has Embraced Dybbuks, Golems and Other Jewish Lore," *J: The Jewish News of Northern California*, May 21, 2021, https://jweekly.com/2021/05/21/how-tv-has-embraced-dybbuks-golems-and-other-jewish-lore (accessed December 19, 2025).

[10] Alexandra Pucciarelli, "The Marvelous Mrs. Maisel' Gets Jewish Converts Totally Wrong," *Jewish Telegraphic Agency*, January 2, 2019.

[11] Mary Murphy and Michelle Willens, "Anti-Semitism on the Rise, the Jewishness of 'The Marvelous Mrs. Maisel' Is a Marvel," *The Wrap*, January 6, 2019.

[12] Lisa Huberman, "When Will the 'Marvelous Mrs. Maisel' Deal with Midge's Privilege?" *HeyAlma.com*, December 16, 2019.

[13] Amanda Lee, "How 'The Marvelous Mrs. Maisel' Fights Stereotypes," *Washington Post*, December 6, 2019.

[14] Leah Aharoni, "Netflix's 'Unorthodox' Degrades Hasidic Jews into Caricatures," *Jewish Journal*, April 7, 2020.

[15] Meredith Blake, "Netflix's 'Unorthodox' Went to Remarkable Lengths to Get Hasidic Jewish Customs Right," *Los Angeles Times*, April 7, 2020.

[16] Jen Chaney, "Unorthodox Is a Beautiful, Immersive Portrait of a Woman's Rebirth," *Vulture.com*, March 7, 2020.

That all of these comments could be made about the same two shows illustrates how much baggage individual reviewers bring to their cultural consumption of shows centering the Jewish experience. More recent conversations about 2024's *Nobody Wants This* and the presence of so-named "hot rabbi" Noah (Adam Brody) further illustrate the chasm. The Netflix series is classic rom-com: She's a non-Jewish agnostic sex podcaster, and he's a Reform rabbi who will only marry a Jewish woman: hijinks, miscommunication, ideology clashes, and attraction ensue. Some audiences were triumphant at the visibility for modern Jewish people; others experienced a fear that seems to rhyme with that of the early studio heads, that having these stories in the culture would highlight their discomfort with their own Jewishness, or lead to criticism, stereotyping, and misunderstanding.

Traditions May Vary: Sitting Shiva

One of the key challenges in depicting specific religious representation of any flavor is assuming homogeneity in look, attitude, observance, and character—when, even within a single community, there can be many shades of interpretation and observance. Jewish practice can be solemn and solitary, or celebratory and communal. Some treat Jewish tradition as sacrosanct, while others play in interpretive possibility or reject ritual entirely. Even within a particular ultra-Orthodox Jewish community, customs, dress, and social norms may vary.

With so many variants to Jewish experience, selecting a look and feel for Jewish ritual on screen is less about being precisely in accordance with Jewish law and more about matching or fleshing out the on-screen world.

For instance, shiva, a traditional seven-day period of Jewish mourning observed after a close relative dies, is a great environment for characters with different belief systems to find themselves in the same space for a significant period of time, with tensions, emotions, conflicts, and family secrets just under the surface, waiting to be exposed or explored—a juicy premise for either comedy or drama, or, often, both.

But while shiva means "seven" in Hebrew, non-Orthodox Jewish communities might truncate the period of mourning to a day or two, or none at all. Mourners may hold prayer services with a quorum of community members—with or without women's participation—allowing them to recite the Kaddish, which reaffirms faith while in grief. Mourners may sit on low chairs, visually identifying them as those who grieve, and cover the mirrors, so they don't have to worry about their appearance. Some abstain from listening to music for the entire year after the loss; for others, music is part of the funeral and/or the shiva experience. In Orthodox communities, visitors do not engage the mourner in conversation;

the mourner must initiate. But what shivas share is a purpose: to gather with love (and food) around a mourner.

In the film *This Is Where I Leave You*, based on the book by Jonathan Tropper, the context is comedy. This family of intense siblings under one roof for seven full days of shiva time mourning their late father leads to frustration, explosions, and revelations of family secrets. No one in the family is really religious, so the duration is unusual. But the plot and their parents demand it, so they stay, allowing the cycle of revelation and emotional amplification to reach its peak.

In the Disney Channel kids' series *Andi Mack*, Andi's friend Cyrus—who marked his bar mitzvah in a previous episode—loses his grandmother, and his classmates pay a shiva call. When the kids arrive, Cyrus explains the rituals and the meaning behind them, a deliberate move by series creator and producer Terri Minsky, who told the Los Angeles *Jewish Journal* that she wanted to show that mourning is "cathartic and universal."

> I hope viewers are able to see that even though someone may be different from you or from another culture than you, we all grieve the loss of our loved ones. . . . Even though many in our audience may have never been to a shiva, they can identify with the experience our characters are going through.[17]

It might seem counterintuitive that the cultural specificity of one experience actually might translate as universal. But shiva persists as an oft-visited on-screen setting because even if the particular rituals of Jewish mourning are not universal, the grief and loss that power them are inevitable experiences for people of all faiths or none at all, for the mere fact of our humanity.

Jewish Identity and Authentic Casting

Most contemporary Hollywood productions take authentic casting very seriously when it comes to racial identity: stories featuring Black, Asian American and Pacific Islander (AAPI), Latino, and characters of other ethnicities should be played by actors with similar racial identities. LGBTQ+ characters are usually played by actors with those same identities, but not always; characters with disabilities, increasingly, are played by actors with disabilities. But how do Jewish roles fit into the "authentic casting" picture? Are Jews a racial identity? A community? A family? And in considering on-screen Jewish identity, how can we

[17] Gerri Miller, "Disney Channel's Andi Mack Episode Includes Shiva, Mourning Rituals," *Jewish Journal*, February 5, 2019.

avoid the inadvertent echo of conversations from the previous century around eugenics?

While genetic testing might identify Jewish heritage, identity is not just about DNA. Jews-by-choice (i.e., converts), adopted Jews, and non-Jews raising partly or all-Jewish families might not have "Jewish DNA," but are considered by many to be Jewish because of their commitment to living Jewish lives.

If "Jewish" is a culture and a system of belief and experience, one could argue that anyone *should* be able to play a Jewish character. While a biopic of Leonard Bernstein, for example, might reasonably call for an actor who looks like the conductor they are portraying, insisting on casting "Jewish-looking" actors is problematic, as is augmenting an actor's nose for a "more Jewish" look. These responses echo a racist American past, instead of shaping the present and future of what a Jewish person—or anyone else—looks like to the world.

In her 2021 *Variety* piece addressing the lack of authentic Jewish portrayals, Malina Saval writes that as it is Hollywood's social responsibility to reflect the experiences of ethnic minorities in America, including Asian, Black, Muslim, or Indigenous people, "that same social imperative holds true for the Jewish community":

> Because being Jewish is not about a wig or an accent or talking really loud. It's not about bagels. Being Jewish is about a shared history, a soul, a spirit—in Hebrew we call it a *neshama.* Amidst the terrifying rise of antisemitism, Jews in America do not feel safe. And in truth, we never have. The ways in which we are portrayed on screen yields significant real-life consequences—some positive, but far too many dangerous. The last thing the Jewish community needs right now is hyperbolic misrepresentation of who we actually are. The simple, boring truth: Jews are human.[18]

As Jewish identity becomes more diverse, creating human portrayals of Jewish people requires writers and content creators to do their research and then envision, write, and cast these characters accordingly. For example, casting Daveed Diggs, an actor who is Black and Jewish, as a rabbi counseling congregants in an environmentally catastrophic Florida in AppleTV+'s *Extrapolations* makes two powerful and inclusive statements: that (1) not all Jewish roles and Jewish actors are white, and (2) casting a Jewish actor in a Jewish role can yield a deeply authentic performance.

[18] Malina Saval, "Too Jewish for Hollywood: As Antisemitism Soars, Hollywood Should Address Its Enduring Hypocrisy in Hyperbolic Caricatures of Jews," *Variety*, June 18, 2021.

Accuracy, Authenticity, and Depth

The trappings of Jewish identity are fairly well represented in today's TV and film. We regularly see the groom step on a glass at his wedding as people say, "Mazal tov!"; deli platters heaped high at a bris (ritual circumcision); or a character saying "shalom" (which, like "aloha," means "hello," "goodbye," and "peace"). There's hava nagila, the hora, a Hanukkah candle lighting, a challah. But seldom do we see a system of meaning or belief from our on-screen Jews; their visible Jewish environments are often more about adornment and less about accuracy or substance.

People who have acquired significant Jewish knowledge watch on-screen Jewish identity bracing for mistakes and misrepresentations: Jewish ritual or community serves as an enemy, an extremist force preventing people from individuation. A character declares that a particular prayer is important to her and then pronounces half of the Hebrew words incorrectly. Hebrew letters on Jewish tombstones or Hebrew signs are printed backward. Jewish characters are often drawn broadly—as secular Jews being neurotic, joking about bagels, not having Christmas, and saying "oy vey"; or as ultra-Orthodox Jews maintaining insularity, trying to shut out the temptations of the secular world.

Authentic portrayals of religious and cultural experiences should include characters' daily lives, motivations, and background. How do they connect to faith, family, and friends? Do they live solely as stereotypes, villains, or comedic foils, or do they live a real, nuanced on-screen life?

A production must commit to addressing these questions from the start, retaining consultants who can advise on building out a story's particular Jewish world and with project creators committing to implementing their suggestions. Having Jewish writers, advisors, and consultants—not just rabbis, but knowledgeable Jewish people who are living modern Judaism or specialize in the particular community or time period being depicted—at all stages of production could troubleshoot any Jewish observance or identity moments, check the Hebrew lettering, and adjust dialogue for greater authenticity. (A national speakers' bureau, with an index of consultants' areas of expertise, would be a boon to this work.)

In the comedy *Bad Shabbos*, the representation starts in the film's title.[19] "Shabbos" is a Yiddishized pronunciation of "Shabbat" (the Jewish Sabbath) that is used more in Orthodox communities, and while the family in the film is not strictly Orthodox, the characters operate through a lens of modern Orthodoxy: hosting a traditional Shabbat dinner, the son's girlfriend who is not

[19] As of mid-2025, *Bad Shabbos* was making the Jewish film festival rounds, with limited screening runs in selected cities.

Jewish but is converting and taking her learning seriously, the daughter who hides having driven to her parents' on Shabbat, the younger son who had his sights set on becoming strong enough to join the Israeli Army. As the farce-laden plot rolls out, the family calls on their background, including Talmudic loopholes, to try to handle the extreme position they find themselves in. The conversations, the books on the shelves, and the displayed Judaica items are authentic: At a June 2025 post-screening Q&A I attended in Los Angeles, director and co-writer Daniel Robbins said that all those items were from his parents' house.

> I went to yeshiva for like 12 years, so I was the Jewish consultant and my parents finally think the tuition is worth it, and they're very pleased. In terms of making this movie, we just wanted to make something that was authentic to modern Orthodox Judaism, where we don't usually see it portrayed, where usually Judaism is a joke, or it's us doing crimes. We wanted to show the middle of that for people who take their faith seriously and also engage in a secular world and their faith isn't something to toss away or run away from, but it's something the family finds a way to incorporate into their lives and makes their lives more meaningful, brings them together every week, which is a good thing.

And, as a bonus, Robbins told the audience at the screening, "Christian audiences loved the movie, because it's ultimately pro-faith, faith-based cinema."

On a television series, there is more space to show characters who are on a Jewish journey, evolving and deepening over time. In season 3, episode 9 of the prison drama *Orange Is the New Black*, a rabbi interrogates prisoners to determine if they are Jewish and need kosher food. A comedic montage follows, with a barrage of assumptions about Jews: Inmates claim to observe Rosh Hashanah (while mangling the pronunciation); sing "Hava Nagila"; say, "I call my mother a lot, and I love a bargain"; recite character arcs from *Annie Hall* and *Yentl* as their own personal history; mention a bat mitzvah; and praise Jews for doing a good job controlling the media. The only inmate who passes as Jewish? A nun, thanks to commonalities between her faith and Judaism.

These characters are "playing Jewish," drawing from the little they know about Judaism from pop culture and/or their social environment. The scene brings comedy, and also the question, "What would non-Jewish people—who know little about Judaism—say to convince a rabbi that they were Jewish?" They would snatch at the references they have seen and heard in the culture-at-large, be they benign or malignant.

What's unusual about this portrayal is its next step. Inmate Cindy Hayes decides "to convert for real." She articulates—beautifully and movingly—what she's learned and why she feels connected to Judaism. The scene explains the Jewish conversion process, including the rules around using a *mikveh* (ritual bath) and having three witnesses (a *beit din*). Cindy's story rises above stereotyping and "Jewish for the jokes" into a real connection with faith.

Cindy's journey is not about the kosher food anymore; it's about finding meaning in life and becoming a part of the Jewish people. The character, and the narrative's treatment of "what Jewish looks like," has become a reminder to viewers to challenge their own assumptions about who these characters are and what they find meaningful.

Representation as a Cultural Bridge

In 2021, Ángela Larrea Espinar, a professor in the Department of English Studies at the University of Córdoba in Spain, spoke with the *New York Times* for a story about people outside of the United States who had learned English from watching the TV show *Friends*. That show was particularly helpful, she told the *Times*, because "people who teach foreign languages have gradually shifted over the last two decades from a 'communicative' approach that emphasizes grammar to one that encourages cross-cultural understanding and reflection. 'Culture is a difficult thing to teach, and if you rely on textbooks what you get is stereotypes,' she said."[20]

While it's true that few television series have had the geographical reach and the generational longevity of *Friends*, the content that we consume can also help shape our understanding of the world, especially of the practices, beliefs, and customs that are different from our own. As a Jewish person, I am constantly learning from episodes of *Master of None*, *Ramy*, and *Mo*, and from other Muslim characters who commit to prayer, observe halal, and abstain from alcohol on religious grounds. I also see parallels between their practice and communities—and the younger generation's rejection of their parents' stringencies or their quest to reinterpret religious ritual—and my own. A generational divide about how to keep the faith, or an internal struggle over finding meaning in religious life, is relatable and important to me. Seeing how these characters see their faith makes me appreciate religious pluralism in general, and listening to the lived experiences of others makes boundaries of knowledge and understanding more porous.

When I think about what I'd want people to learn from on-screen portrayals of Jewish people, it's to understand that any singular depiction cannot represent the breadth of Jewish identity and expression, and to hope that it opens a conversation about how that scene resonates with me, my family, or others in my orbit.

[20] Mike Ives, "How 'Friends' Helps People around the World Learn English," *New York Times*, May 29, 2021.

And, on a larger level, I always hope that expanding visibility for one set of particular cultural expressions means a larger representation picture for everyone.

Revisiting Representation in a Pained Present

At every stage in writing this chapter, I struggled with how to identify this moment of searing pain for both the Jewish and Muslim communities worldwide after the events of October 7, 2023. On that day, Hamas invaded Israel; slaughtered twelve hundred people, including women, children, and babies, as well as many teenagers at a music festival; and took hostages. The last of the living hostages were released in October 2025, and the last remains of an Israeli kidnapped on October 7, 2023, were returned to Israel in January 2026. That event launched so much suffering, with families forever undone through violence, and with seeds of conviction and resentment sown for the future.

As we see a Middle East on fire and a world outside that region edging closer to violence and extremism, the conversation around any identity's representation in TV and film may not seem like a priority. Most of us want the violence to end, for our global leaders to be worthy of trust, for innocents to be safe and protected, for accountability to be taken, and for repair to begin. And while nuanced representation will not erase pain or lessen loss, I do believe it can play a part in moving us forward, connecting us, human to human, through our culture.

Whatever our particular identity, affinity, ethnicity, heritage, personality, political inclination, or faith, we look to culture to see our experiences reflected, validated, criticized, and contextualized. If we want to see stories that reflect us responsibly, we have to write, produce, direct, and distribute them. We have to support them with time, talent, money, marketing, and passion, as well as with cross-cultural cohorts of professionals who can help each other with context for religious specificity. And the more accurate, nuanced, and varied our stories are, the better we can invite our rich, diverse cultural experiences, challenges, triumphs, and stories into conversation with each other on screen, and in the world we share.

15
The State of Religious Pluralism in TV and Film

Jody Hassett Sanchez

When the comedic actress Lucille Ball became pregnant in 1952, CBS officials decreed that a pregnant woman could not be seen on network television because it had never been done. *I Love Lucy* was one of the most popular and lucrative weekly programs, so the producers and writing staff made an intriguing decision. They convened a Catholic priest, a rabbi, and a pastor and asked them whether showing a pregnant woman on screen was objectionable. These religious consultants were far less concerned than the network's censors and made it clear they had no religious problems with seeing the star pregnant on screen. The network relented but banned the word "pregnant" on air. Lucy was described on the show as "expecting."[1]

At the time, this approach of hiring religious consultants was considered quite innovative. Today, there is a cottage industry of consultants representing various religions that can be hired to vet a television series or film to ensure that adherents of the featured faith are accurately represented and that the faithful will not be offended or boycott the program. Is this strategy an effective way to pursue religious authenticity on screens big and small today? Does the industry view pluralistic programming as a worthy objective? The US-based filmmakers, scholars, and critics I spoke with suggest there is a growing openness toward spiritually inclusive content. But they caution this is an undertaking that will require a robust effort by those who create, commission, and green-light film and TV projects.

The Current Landscape

The post–World War II period introduced a string of popular sword-and-sandal religious films; Hollywood's lens focused on Biblical epics. More recently that

[1] Daniel S. Levy, "How *I Love Lucy* Changed How America Saw Motherhood," *TIME*, May 8, 2021, https://time.com/6046897/i-love-lucy-little-ricky/ (accessed December 18, 2025).

Jody Hassett Sanchez, *The State of Religious Pluralism in TV and Film* In: *Modeling Religious Pluralism*.
Edited by: Simran Jeet Singh, Oxford University Press. © Oxford University Press 2026.
DOI: 10.1093/oso/9780197745809.003.0015

lens has broadened to include the other two Abrahamic faiths, yet other religions still receive scant attention. David Morgan, professor of religious studies at Duke University, suggests this is because a primary function of mainstream entertainment is to ensure that the audience can comfortably relate to the characters.

> To connect on religious terms is going to be most easily defined if they fit within the parameters of recognized institutional religion. There's just more data and probably your next-door neighbor is Jewish, so you can talk to her, or you went to college with a Muslim kid, and you can touch base with him. Most intellectuals or scriptwriters and entertainers are coming from the middle class. They're going to default to those more recognized structures than they would the small religious movements . . . that are weird in the sense of "they're outside the domain of my experience. I don't really have direct access to them. I don't know those people. I've never worshipped with those people."[2]

Many cultural gatekeepers who do not have a personal connection to religion assume that their audiences also view faith as irrelevant or reserved for the unsophisticated. Tom Lennon, an accomplished documentary filmmaker, has encountered this mindset while working on several films with a religious component. He maintains this bias must be called out before we can expect realistic representations of religion on camera.

> You've got a deep split along class lines (and) spheres of influence. Sometimes the most sophisticated thinkers cannot realize how provincial their thinking is. People should have to explain that dismissal. It's a totally socially sanctioned dismissal, indifference, and even, I'm sorry to say, some sort of laughter and scorn: "Those kinds of beliefs are for the other people, for the poor, the uneducated, the suckers and I'm not a sucker."[3]

This blind spot is particularly problematic because religious believers—historically and globally—are not the outliers, but the majority. Yet this is not consistently reflected in what we see on screen.

Scripts that attempt to be more inclusive of this religious majority can still miss the mark by relying on the formulaic. Cinema critic Jeffery Overstreet, who writes on the interplay of art, faith, and culture, observes, "What I don't see very often is a Christian character for whom their religion is not an agenda aimed at other people. I rarely see a contemplative religious character who isn't out to convert, who isn't out to judge, who isn't out to preach. When I do, I'm

[2] David Morgan, interview by Jody Hassett Sanchez, February 26, 2023.
[3] Tom Lennon, interview by Jody Hassett Sanchez, February 27, 2023.

thunderstruck."[4] Just as concerning is how Islam, the fastest-growing religion in the world, is depicted in US productions. Muslim characters tend to be either villains or extremists. Researchers at the University of Southern California (USC) Annenberg Inclusion Initiative analyzed more than two hundred episodic television series and found that a third of all Muslim men were portrayed as extremists, while Muslim women were often depicted as "fearful and endangered."[5]

Thoughtful Responses

One response to these religious caricatures on screen has been the emergence of Christian production companies that churn out dramas, period pieces, and disaster films. Jon Erwin, who directed *Woodlawn*, *Jesus Revolution*, and several other features, recently started a faith-based movie studio in Hollywood.[6] He is convinced that the future is creating films for specific religious audiences.

> Unless you're making a Marvel movie or *Avatar*, there is no more mainstream. The concept of mainstream is only for these huge movies. For everything else, I feel the way to succeed is to really serve a niche audience. Find some audience that is being under-seen and underserved. It's super helpful if you're a part of that audience.[7]

This notion of writing what you know or, more precisely, what you believe *can* happen on mainstream productions when the creators share the faith of their characters.

Joseph Salzberger, a writer, director, and editor, worked on a film adaptation of Arthur Miller's *The Performance* where crew members brought their faith to the set.

> Part of the main character's background is that he's a second-generation immigrant in 1930s New York. We were really lucky to have had several producers

[4] Jeffrey Overstreet, interview by Jody Hassett Sanchez, February 27, 2023.

[5] Al-Baab Khan, Katherine Pieper, Stacy L. Smith, Ariana Case, and Sam Wheeler, "Erased or Extremists: The Stereotypical View of Muslims in Popular Episodic Series," USC Getty Annenberg Inclusion Initiative, September 2022, https://assets.uscannenberg.org/docs/aii-study-muslim-erased-or-extremists-20220901.pdf (accessed December 15, 2025).

[6] "Jon Erwin Explains Why He's Opening a Faith-Based Movie Studio," *Movieguide.org*, December 22, 2023, https://www.movieguide.org/news-articles/jon-erwin-explains-why-hes-opening-a-faith-based-movie-studio.html (accessed December 15, 2025).

[7] Joshua Ensenias, "*Jesus Revolution* Is a Christian Hit That Takes Lessons from Blumhouse and Paul Thomas Anderson," *Moviemaker*, March 6, 2023, https://www.moviemaker.com/jesus-revolution-christian-hit-blumhouse/ (accessed December 18, 2025).

> with Orthodox Jewish backgrounds on set. They could speak to both how we were handling the script but also how religious rights would have been handled in the home during that time and how the extras [were dressed and behaved].[8]

Audiences and award shows applaud such consistency in period productions, but when it comes to contemporary religious stories, viewers want to see authentic characters who aren't necessarily steadfast in their faith.

Ramy is frequently cited as a series that realistically conveys the conflicts faced by a young man who believes in God but struggles with his faith. Abby Olcese, a frequent commentor on film and faith, describes Ramy, the main character in the series, as having "a really complicated relationship with Islam."

> He's not necessarily practicing and he's not necessarily as strict about it as other people. He's a person around my age who's just trying to be a person. . . . If I see somebody who is Muslim and goes to a mosque once a week but also struggles with wanting to go out with friends and drink or wanting to smoke, that's relatable. I want relatability because that's the thing that I can connect to in my own life.[9]

More showrunners are taking note of *Ramy*'s success, but it's still unusual to see characters for whom religion is not their defining attribute, but just one aspect of their personality.

Amir Hussain, professor of theological studies at Loyola Marymount University, adds to this perspective.

> What's been interesting to me as someone who looks at religion in film, Islam in particular, [is when] you get a character like L.L. Cool J's character on *NCIS: Los Angeles*. His character, Sam Hanna, is actually a Muslim but that's only brought up tangentially. There's also a young woman who wears a hijab. The character's name is Fatima and there's only a little bit of stuff brought in about her religion. . . . She happens to be a Muslim, and she happens to dress differently. One of the last episodes they did was about an Afghan family and an honor killing and that could have been done so wrong in so many different ways, but they handled it really well.[10]

It can be a complex and costly proposition to create programs that organically weave faith and spirituality into the storyline. However, the industry has seen

[8] Joshua Salzberger, interview by Jody Hassett Sanchez, April 4, 2023.
[9] Abby Olcese, interview by Jody Hassett Sanchez, February 24, 2023.
[10] Amir Hussain, interview by Jody Hassett Sanchez, March 7, 2023.

complex stories about sexuality and race succeed and profit, so the barriers are slowly being dismantled.

The Financial Factor

While legacy broadcasters and studios still tend to center Abrahamic faith themes, streaming platforms and cable outlets are increasingly open to projects that present other religions. Professor Morgan reflects on this shift.

> I think that the switch to streaming platforms has only introduced more opportunities for various providers and producers to develop religious programming. It's often not mainstream Christianity anymore but new religious movements, spirituality, neo-paganism, the occult, sort of the questing model, the individual seeker.[11]

These productions are willing to take more risks because they have smaller budgets. Independent films and streaming services usually do not have to recoup the enormous investments that media conglomerates must recover. Olcese, the film critic, agrees.

> If you're making a large-scale studio film and you want it to make a lot of money, you want it to appeal to the broadest audience possible, in the context of international sales. That means you want your movie to do well in places that are not necessarily religious or Christian nations. As a result, you're probably not going to get deep and nuanced takes on forms of faith, whether that's Christianity or Hinduism or Buddhism.[12]

But this cautious approach to religious programming could prove a miscalculation. New research on faith in the entertainment industry from HarrisX confirms that "there's a large swath of the global entertainment consumer that yearns for this kind of content." Their study found that 80 percent of viewers around the world would welcome richer and more diverse religious narratives.[13]

[11] David Morgan, interview by Jody Hassett Sanchez, February 26, 2023.

[12] Abby Olcese interview.

[13] Faith & Media Initiative, *The Global Faith & Entertainment Study*, HarrisX, February 13, 2024, https://www.faithandmedia.com/research/harrisxentertainment (accessed June 28, 2025).

A Wider Lens

Audiences yearning to see religious themes explored thoughtfully on screen can also look beyond traditional narrative films and series. Documentaries, horror, comedy, and animation offer rich alternatives that raise intriguing questions about belief and doubt. Director Scott Derrickson, best known for his supernatural thriller *The Exorcism of Emily Rose*, maintains that the horror genre provides powerful opportunities to raise moral questions.

> I like the fact that it's a genre about confronting evil, confronting what's frightening in the world. It's a genre that takes the mystery in the world very seriously. There are a lot of voices that are broadcasting that the world is explainable. Corporate America limits the world to consumerism. Science can limit it to the material world. Even religion limits it to a lot of theories that can explain everything. I think we need cinema to break that apart and remind us that we're not in control, and we don't understand as much as we think [we] do.[14]

Artful storytelling can push viewers to consider these profound issues about the seen and the unseen without ever explicitly mentioning religion.

The classic comedy *Groundhog Day* has been praised as a powerful spiritual parable by Buddhists, Jews, and Christians.[15] As Bill Murray's character relives the same day repeatedly, he first responds with self-indulgence and nihilism, which prove meaningless. He slowly begins to change and seek out meaning, which lead him to self-awareness and ultimately selflessness. Salzberger, the writer, director, and editor, noted a similar avenue for thoughtful inquiry when he edited the comedy *Welcome to Me* starring Kristen Wiig. "She's dealing with a mental health crisis and being exploited as a reality TV personality in that movie. The movie is not explicitly religious or anything, but to me there's something about the comedy and the tragedy opening up a space for deeper spiritual exploration."[16] This more expansive understanding of religious programming is encouraging. As we evaluate what constitutes religious pluralism in entertainment, mystical and intangible storylines should also be considered.

[14] Steven D. Greydanus, "Interview: Filmmaker Scott Derrickson on Horror, Faith, Chesterton and His New Movie," *National Catholic Register*, July 1, 2014, https://www.ncregister.com/news/interview-filmmaker-scott-derrickson-on-horror-faith-chesterton-and-his-new-movie (accessed December 18, 2025).

[15] Bob Smietana, "After 30 Years, Buddhist-Inspired Message of 'Groundhog Day' Still Holds Spiritual Power," *Religion News*, February 2, 2023, https://religionnews.com/2023/02/02/after-30-years-groundhog-days-buddhist-inspired-message-still-holds-spiritual-power/ (accessed December 18, 2025).

[16] Joshua Salzberger interview, 2023.

Promoting Pluralism

There's no roadmap for encouraging more realistic portrayals of the world's many faiths on screen, but those interviewed for this chapter offer some steps worth consideration. One suggestion is to directly appeal to religious leaders, persuading them to encourage young believers that careers in film and TV can be a worthy vocation. Professor Hussain regularly challenges Muslim audiences about this.

> What I always say is, "Look, you don't want to hear this, but we have enough Muslim doctors, lawyers, engineers. We need more writers, we need more storytellers, we need more journalists. If we want to tell our stories, we have to be the ones to tell those stories. Someone who's not a Muslim isn't going to know these kinds of things that happen in our community."[17]

Hussain also suggests requiring basic religious literacy for today's film students who will be tomorrow's directors and showrunners. He describes how most of his students lack any understanding of world religions. "When I teach religion class, I have to disabuse my students of the notion that all Buddhists are peaceful, that Buddhism is just peace and Zen. I have to talk about what's happening in Myanmar and the Rohingya or that all Muslims are not bad."[18]

Today's television and film productions aren't encumbered by the network censors of *I Love Lucy*'s era, but there's a lingering misperception within the industry that religion is a controversial topic with a finite audience. They believe this despite studies documenting that the majority of respondents define themselves as religious and want to see more people like themselves on screen. These are audiences that will pay to see the kind of programming they seek, as evidenced by the profitability of independent Christian production houses and the success of shows like *Ramy*.

Achieving a broader offering of programs that capture the nuances of multiple religions will require a far more expansive notion of "diversity" in both programming and hiring. When mainstream and independent productions recruit more creatives of every faith, we will see a broader spectrum of characters and there will no longer be a need to hire outside religious "experts." Instead, we can hope for the kind of complex conversations about right and wrong, doubt and deep faith that occur off screen across our country, despite our deep differences.

[17] Amir Hussein interview, 2023.
[18] Ibid.

PART VI
RELIGION IN THE WORKPLACE

I've spent hours and days and months consulting with corporate leaders on making their workplaces more inclusive and welcoming for people of all backgrounds. This work has typically been broad, touching on various experiences and identities, including race, gender, sexual orientation, and more.

Yet, I've noticed something troubling when I suggest they talk about religion and religious identity. Typically, though not always, corporate leaders clam up, saying that they feel comfortable broaching other aspects of diversity, but that religion feels too hot to touch. And typically, though not always, their human resources (HR) departments also discourage me from broaching the topic of religion, deeming it too controversial or divisive or volatile.

I understand the fears of addressing religion in the workplace. Religion is complicated, and many people have strong convictions about it. Discussions about religion can be exceedingly difficult and potentially explosive. But just because a conversation is hard doesn't mean that our best approach is to avoid it. If we have learned anything from our cultural mistakes over the past few decades, it's that we can't make issues go away by pretending they don't exist, and that we're better off when we address them directly.[1]

We spend so much of our daily lives in the workplace, and we spend so much of our time interacting with colleagues in those environments. Given the outsized role that workplaces play in our lives and in our culture, doesn't it follow that these institutions should—at least to some degree—embody the values we are trying to instill and live by in our communities? Moreover, if we don't foster religious pluralism in contexts that are already working toward including and respecting human diversity, then how will we ever develop the skills and abilities to work and live alongside difference in the rest of our lives?

In this section, we bring in leaders who have experience and facility in helping corporate communities talk about religion in the workplace. A shared message

[1] For more on why and how to engage religion in the workplace, see my article in the *Harvard Business Review*: Simran Jeet Singh, "How to Talk about Religion at Work," *Harvard Business Review*, September 16, 2022, https://hbr.org/2022/09/how-to-talk-about-religion-at-work (accessed December 16, 2025).

across their chapters is that everyone is better served when people feel like they can be their authentic selves at work.

Brian Grim, founder and president of the Religious Freedom and Business Foundation, outlines the primary challenges and arguments given by leaders who are skeptical about addressing religion in the workplace. He then offers his ideas on how and why corporate leaders should engage religion meaningfully and effectively.

Jeremy Fricke and Wendy Goldberg draw from their work at the Tri-Faith Initiative, where they cultivated a living laboratory of interreligious engagement. They leverage their learnings to develop a compelling model for religious inclusion, which they describe as the "5B Framework": Belief, Behavior, Belonging, Becoming, and Body.

Similarly, Mark Fowler and Megan Leverage lean into their years of experience helping corporations and businesses enhance religious inclusion in the workplace. The chapter is a case study of their work through the Tanenbaum Center for Interreligious Understanding, including broad lessons and takeaways for others in the space.

Ultimately, the authors of these chapters believe that a pluralistic society makes space for people to live freely, including on the basis of their religious convictions. Being able to do so at work is both crucial and achievable. I am grateful to these leaders who are paving the way forward, and I look forward to the progress we will make in the years to come.

16

Faith-and-Belief Friendly Workplaces

Brian J. Grim

The majority of Fortune 100 companies fail to mention faith or religion as part of workplace belonging efforts.[1] Indeed, faith and core beliefs are taboo topics in many workplaces. But that is changing. In the wake of the pioneering faith-friendly initiatives of companies like American Airlines, American Express, Texas Instruments, Intel, Target, and Tyson Foods, more leading companies are realizing that people's personal faiths and beliefs give meaning and purpose to their work. They are also realizing that including religion as part of their other workplace belonging strengthens overall morale, making it good for the bottom line.

Increasingly, workplace leaders are realizing that their most powerfully impactful "products" are not limited to the products they make or the services they provide. They are seeing that, through their day-to-day operations, they can also export a culture of respect, compassion, and freedom—a different kind of product that both enriches the world and increases brand warmth.

The Religious Freedom & Business Foundation's Faith-Friendly Workplace 'REDI' Index spotlights a wide spectrum of companies where people are encouraged to bring their whole selves to work—including their faith. The corporate shift to acknowledge faith in the workplace is not just confined to the early pioneers; it is also happening in companies like Google, Apple, Salesforce, Accenture, PayPal, and Walmart, where faith-oriented employee resource groups (ERGs) are proliferating.

Workplace chaplains are another visible symbol of this movement, not just in workplaces such as the military, hospitals, athletics, and the US Senate but also in Fortune 100 companies, with Tyson Foods leading the way.

What is at the root of this burgeoning movement?

The short answer is that businesses are recognizing that, for many people, trying to separate their faith from them while at work is as difficult as expecting a person to separate themselves from their race or gender or age. Their faith is as

[1] Brian J. Grim, "Corporates Often Forget Religious Diversity. Here's Why They Should Not," World Economic Forum, January 16, 2020, https://www.weforum.org/agenda/2020/01/religion-diversity-business-inclusion/ (accessed December 18, 2025).

Brian J. Grim, *Faith-and-Belief Friendly Workplaces* In: *Modeling Religious Pluralism*.
Edited by: Simran Jeet Singh, Oxford University Press. © Oxford University Press 2026.
DOI: 10.1093/oso/9780197745809.003.0016

baked into their personhood as these other characteristics, and for some people, even more so. As Julia Oltmanns of Zurich America puts it:

> Over the years, the companies I had worked for had recognized my identity as a woman, but my identity in my faith is more important to me than my gender. Once the organization recognized that importance and supported my expression of my faith at work, I felt encouraged to be an integrated, aligned, values-driven leader in the company, allowing me to reach my full potential.[2]

The Vocation of the Business Leader

A few years ago, I was asked by the Vatican to offer insights on how freedom of religion and belief relates to their seminal document on faith and business, "The Vocation of the Business Leader."[3] When Catholics use the term "vocation," they are usually referring to people who are consecrated into the religious life as priests, nuns, and brothers. Is the Vatican putting businesswomen and businessmen in the same category as nuns and priests? No and yes.

No, the Vatican is not asking them to become celibate as nuns and most priests are called to be. Yes, the Vatican is asking them to see their business work as a calling from God, a vocation in Catholic lingo. The document affirms the sanctity of everyday work and says that creating goods and services that make life better for people honors God and contributes "greatly to the material and even the spiritual well-being of society."

A main point of "The Vocation of the Business Leader" is that people must live a congruent life, one in which everything they do—at work, at home, and at worship—aligns with the expectations of their faith. Of course, not all religions teach the same thing. But, bringing one's full self to work, faith and all, matters not just to Catholics and other Christians but also to people of every faith, from Ahmadiyyas to Zoroastrians.

"The Vocation of the Business Leader" observes that the greatest obstacle to fulfilling this spiritual calling is not corruption, the absence of rule of law, greed, or poor stewardship of resources. Rather, the key barrier to this calling is the all-too-common practice of leading an incongruent, divided life, where faith is checked at the workplace door.

[2] Brian J. Grim, Paul Lambert, and Kent Johnson, eds., "Faith@Work: The Next Big Thing in Corporate America Is Here," Religious Freedom & Business Foundation, 2020, https://religiousfreedomandbusiness.org/faith-at-work-matters (accessed December 18, 2025).

[3] Peter Turkson, K.A., ed., "Vocation of the Business Leader: A Reflection," 5th ed. (Rome: Dicastery for Promoting Integral Human Development, Vatican, 2018), https://www.humandevelopment.va/en/risorse/documenti/vocation-of-the-business-leader-a-reflection-5th-edition.html (accessed December 18, 2025).

Indeed, for people of faith (regardless of religion), such a divided life is inauthentic. It requires that they essentially go "under cover" with their faith, as if their core identity were something shameful. This constraint saps energy, adversely impacts job satisfaction, and degrades performance. For many people of various faiths, perceived restrictions on religious expression at work cause just as much damage as denying the importance of other facets of one's identity that are protected by employment nondiscrimination law in the United States: race, color, national origin, age, disability and genetic information, and sex. Religious inclusion in the workplace is an imperative because people should no sooner be made to hide their religious identities as people with any other protected characteristics should be made to hide unique identities.

Building Bridges across Cultures

At the same time, the business case for faith-and-belief friendly workplaces is overwhelming. As companies globalize, they will need employees who can relate to the daily experience of increasingly diverse customers. For billions of potential customers, including in the world's fastest-growing economies, religious belief and practice are a part of daily life. Having employees who understand the ways that faith and belief are manifest in private and public life will help companies avoid costly missteps and develop products and services better tailored to customer needs, which is an essential part of being competitive.

And it's not *just* about the workplace. What's going on in these arenas strengthens the fabric of civility throughout the world.

It is important to emphasize that faith and business is not just about allowing people to join clubs with others who believe what they believe and making them feel more appreciated (though that is helpful in its own right). It is also about building much-needed bridges across cultures. Taken together, the principles expounded in this volume—directly and indirectly—show how a concerted, strategic focus on workplace religious freedom for all can help strengthen cultures of trust, collaboration, and warmth. These are essential ingredients for team building and business success in the new era that has been indelibly changed by the coronavirus pandemic.

This might seem like a fairy tale in today's culturally divided America. But many in corporate America for whom faith and belief matter have found that collectively protecting and celebrating their freedom to be authentic at work unify rather than divide. Religious freedom for all is the recipe for peace, as research clearly shows.[4] Based on my conversations with industry professionals, the

[4] Brian J. Grim and Roger Finke, *The Price of Freedom Denied: Religious Persecution and Conflict in the 21st Century* (New York: Cambridge University Press, 2011).

single greatest reason companies point to for not having yet joined this movement is that they fear opening the door for religion at work will open a Pandora's box of conflict, especially when religion is coupled with political and culture wars. However, in our experience in working with scores of companies, being free to be your "authentic religious self" decreases conflict while increasing trust, teamwork, and morale. It also makes companies better able to relate to a national marketplace that is becoming more religiously diverse and a global marketplace that is also becoming more religious.

Why Religion in the Workplace Matters

During the pandemic lockdown, we invited people from across corporate America who participated in our First Annual Faith@Work National Conference in 2020 to share their stories of *why* being able to bring their faith to work matters. Here is a summary of the principles that come from their stories, which were published in the online conference proceedings.

First, at the organizational level, all the successful faith and business initiatives in corporate America have the purpose of contributing to the success of the business. As articulated by Ellen Barker, senior vice president at Texas Instruments,[5] their faith ERGs have the same purposes as the company's other belonging initiatives:

1. To promote a collaborative and respectful culture
2. To recruit and cultivate talent
3. To stimulate innovation and engagement
4. To give back to their communities, "believing that stronger companies create stronger communities and stronger communities build stronger companies"

Second, in addition to fulfilling a real-world business need, corporate America's faith and business movement works because it is not about dogma and politics, but about service and celebration. Arguably, this movement is a model for overcoming the polarization that has beset American society.

Third, including faith enhances overall belonging. One example, among many, comes from the leader of the Christian Employee Group at Intel, who not only helped form an interfaith association among the other faith and belief groups—including the agnostic and atheist group—but also spearheaded the annual Martin Luther King, Jr., event as a white Evangelical. Bridges of this sort

[5] Grim, Lambert, and Johnson, "Faith@Work."

are sorely needed. As another example, Faithforce had an event called Multiple Closets, where people of faith who are also members of the LGBTQ+ community shared their experiences of coming out of both closets.

Fourth, the faith-and-business movement takes more than just the form of ERGs. For example, it includes chaplains in hundreds of companies across the country. We are accustomed to seeing chaplains as a regular feature of institutions such as hospitals, prisons, police departments, the military, Congress, and even sports teams. But in business? Yes, indeed.

Airports have chaplains, and so do airlines. American Airlines' chief flight controller is also a priest, workplace chaplain, and the head of their Christian Employee Business Resource Group. Among the Fortune 100, Tyson Foods has the most well-developed chaplaincy program. The objective of the Tyson Foods Chaplain Services program is to live out their culture as a faith-friendly and inclusive company.

Fifth, being religiously inclusive adds ethical resources. People who identify with a faith are not necessarily more ethical or more virtuous than those who do not embrace faith. There are plenty of religious people who do not carry their religion into the workplace. But personal faith itself often involves the aspiration of being guided by a clear ethical compass that focuses on faith, hope, love, and humility. For some people, faith permeates their lives. It changes what they do in business and how they do it. This serves the bottom line because, while people of faith do not have a corner on the market of ethics, they have belief systems that call them to high standards, which is a boon within any business: A healthy, ethical corporate culture must rest on more than written codes and compliance mechanisms. What's needed is a connection with employees' hearts—the core values and beliefs that govern what they do when nobody's looking.

And finally, this will not go away. Religion is one of the few social institutions that accompanies people from cradle to grave. It marks rites of passage in youth, such as baptisms and bar/bat mitzvahs, and it is present in last rites and (in many religions) the hope of resurrection.

In their faith, people are much more complex than typical management training recognizes.

Conclusion

Human souls (however one understands them) are at work every day, impacted by the corporate and social cultures we operate in. We all bring that part of us to work, and these cultures around us have the power to enrich or impoverish our souls. Accenture's tagline is "Creating the most truly human company in the digital age." Ellyn Shook, chief leadership and human resources officer at Accenture, wrote a compelling article on October 28, 2018, titled "Stop Wondering if Faith Is a Workplace Issue. It Is."[6] The date is significant. It is the day after the Tree of Life synagogue mass shooting in Pittsburg that claimed the life of eleven people and wounded six others, including four police officers, during Shabbat morning services. It was the deadliest attack on America's Jewish community in history.

Mass killings like this affect not only friends and family of those killed or hurt, but entire religious communities who feel vulnerable and wonder if their place of worship is next, or if their families are next. Rather than retreat from the horror, Ellyn reached out to colleagues who could help find the words to discuss a way forward together. The faith ERGs at Accenture were there to take the lead and help the company respond in ways that brought both healing and a knowledge that the company stood against religious intolerance and for religious inclusion in the workplace and in society.

How faith and business work in such times is wonderfully captured in a tweet by Salesforce CEO Mark Benioff in response to the 2019 Easter Sunday bombings of churches across Sri Lanka:

> I learned today that a member of our Ohana lost a family member in #SriLanka. Thank you to our Muslim, Buddhist, Jewish, & Hindu Ohana who held a vigil for our whole Christian Ohana. May times of tragedy remind us all that light shines in the darkness (John 1:5) #Faithforce.[7]

By including John 1:5,[8] Mr. Benioff is making explicit reference to Jesus's life being the "light of all people": "The light shines in the darkness, and the darkness did not overcome it."

As companies navigate a constantly changing world, the faiths and beliefs of their employees provide added resources to not only deal with uncertainty and tragedy but also be wells of innovation, values, and resilience.

To be competitive in today's and tomorrow's marketplaces, companies need to set free this force for good by including religion as a full-fledged part of their workplace belonging initiatives.

[6] Ellen Shook, "Stop Wondering if Faith Is a Workplace Issue. It Is," LinkedIn, October 28, 2018, https://www.linkedin.com/pulse/stop-wondering-faith-workplace-issue-ellyn-shook/

[7] Marc Benioff, Twitter, April 30, 2019, https://twitter.com/Benioff/status/1123467506335850496 (accessed December 18, 2025).

[8] Bible, John 1:5, https://biblehub.com/john/1-5.htm (accessed December 18, 2025).

17
Living Interfaith

Applying a Model of Religious Unity in the Workplace

Jeremy Fricke and Wendy Goldberg

As advocates for religious pluralism at the Tri-Faith Initiative, an organization conceived from a visionary dialogue among Omaha's Jewish, Christian, and Muslim leaders following the 9/11 tragedy, we have been pivotal in advancing its unique mission. This groundbreaking project—the world's first intentional co-location of a synagogue, church, mosque, and interfaith center—stands as a beacon of possibility. Our efforts have focused on cultivating an inclusive environment that not only draws spiritual seekers and the religiously curious but also significantly contributes to countering the rise of hate crimes and religious hostility by promoting empathy and understanding. In this chapter, we share insights from our experience, illustrating how the principles of living an interfaith model can serve as a blueprint for enhancing religious unity and inclusion in workplace settings.

Advocating for Marginalized Religious Communities

We have a grand vision of bridging and increasing belonging in neighborhoods throughout the United States and worldwide. Imagine a movement within the workplace that includes religion such that we prioritize new ways of thinking about the people we are with at work, our schools, our hospitals, and everywhere else. Like race, religious identity can shape our worldview, guide our choices, affect how we share ourselves with the world, and influence how others perceive us in our workplaces and communities.

Our vision is to replicate the symbolism of the Tri-Faith Commons in neighborhoods and workplaces across the United States by inviting others to celebrate religious diversity, honor individual and community autonomy, dismantle the orthodoxy/heresy binary, and prioritize belonging.

Tri-Faith has the potential to model how diverse religious communities and the non-religious engage each other in beneficial ways, maintain their distinct identities, and thrive while defending each other's right to thrive. We make space

Jeremy Fricke and Wendy Goldberg, *Living Interfaith* In: *Modeling Religious Pluralism*.
Edited by: Simran Jeet Singh, Oxford University Press.
DOI: 10.1093/oso/9780197745809.003.0017

for those who are affiliated, unaffiliated, and everything in between, affirming that all people relate to religion differently. People need to make decisions for themselves but in a community context. The ability of individuals and communities to make their own decisions is a core ethic for the living interfaith that we advocate for.

Talking about religious diversity can be messy, personal, and even uncomfortable—yet avoiding the topic can deepen the challenge. Religion is often a cause for joy and strife in an individual's life. For many, religion is an essential part of personal and community identity. We cannot create and support diverse and inclusive spaces if we leave something significant out of the conversation. Ian Leslie argues that curiosity is a counterforce to polarization, judgmental attitudes, and defensiveness, whether in interpersonal interactions or at a societal level.[1]

Much of the judgmentalism we see in religiously diverse spaces involves questions about who truly belongs and who gets to represent a religious community. We question internalized attitudes of orthodoxy. As an example, the heinous hate crimes enacted against Black people who attend churches or allies who attend churches supportive of the LGBTQ+ community are attacks not only based on race and sexual orientation but also based on defining who belongs to Christianity and what is considered heretical. Simply denouncing acts of violence committed by those who share our own identities feels like nothing more than empty words that recommit to the binary of orthodoxy and heresy. Although more research needs to be done, we hypothesize that these attitudes are internalized in many Americans, and that *gatekeeping who is a proper representation of a religion is not exclusive to one's own community—it is often applied to communities one is not a part of as well.* Allowing people to shift, change, be fluid, or be different should be a core ethic of interfaith engagement, and is described well in the 5B Framework.

The 5B Framework: Belief, Behavior, Belonging, Becoming, and Body

We know religion means something different to each person, and people relate to religion in their own way. We talk about the beauty and the trauma associated with religion.

We use the 5B Framework to talk about how religion can impact people and how one develops their religious identity. The 3B Framework has been well utilized, and we add the fourth B—Becoming—to account for the continued

[1] Rachel Botsman, "How Can We Have Better Arguments?" *Rethinking with Rachel* (podcast), May 24, 2021, https://link-to-episode.com.

story and shifting relationships with religion(s). We also add the fifth B—Body—to account for the impact that physical experiences and perceptions can have on the way we relate to religion.

1. Belief is our hearts, minds, and morality—the invisible components of religion or non-religion.
2. Behavior is our practices, rituals, holidays, and practical actions.
3. Belonging is our community and connections.
4. Becoming is the changes we make and how our identities intersect and shift.
5. Body is the way we physically interact with the world, and the ways we are perceived by others physically impact the way we engage with religion.

As leaders in the interfaith movement, we lean into all five Bs, but in the experiment of the Tri-Faith Commons, the model has something special to offer in the realms of Belonging and Becoming.[2]

Belonging

One of the challenges of engaging with communities of different religious backgrounds is the invisible boundaries created between communities. The interfaith movement has focused deeply on being welcoming.

Welcoming others is a fantastic first step, but it is really just a first step.

We need to move past welcoming into a place where people genuinely belong.

When we welcome others, we focus on the relationship the "other" has with "our" community. Welcoming is kindness to guests and politeness to visitors. For a relationship between people of different communities, this is always a precursor when the outsider visits the insider community. In other words, welcoming is the process of how we can help others feel more comfortable with us. Being welcoming is extremely important, but *it cannot be our only goal.* Welcoming as an end goal can inadvertently enforce a strict boundary between a community member and guest, destroying the space where one can feel both like a guest and a community member.

Focusing on how we can help others feel comfortable often puts the responsibility of comfort on the guest. Yes, the hope is that the visitor enjoys their time, but being welcoming is woefully empty for many well-intentioned communities.

[2] Jeremy Fricke, "The 5B Framework of Religion & Spirituality," *Tri-Faith Initiative* (blog), April 30, 2023, https://www.trifaith.org/the-5b-framework-of-religion-amp-spirituality/ (accessed December 19, 2025).

It often consists of words of welcome and maybe some food and drink. There's nothing wrong with kind words and coffee—but to make a meaningful change in how we engage with people, we must do more.

What if we became more introspective about the way we engage with others? Rather than putting the responsibility for feeling comfortable with difference on the guest, what if we focused on a responsibility to prepare ourselves for difference? What if we focused more on learning how to be a better guest? Or how to feel more comfortable with guests?

Communities and individuals—especially those that are socially privileged in some way—must reflect on what is needed to be a better visitor. What if our religious institutions taught us how to be brave and humble in spaces where we are underrepresented?

Many people who engage with religious diversity hope for a future where people feel comfortable in one another's spaces while still retaining their identities. But very few visit one another's spaces. It doesn't seem to matter how often the visited space mentions how welcoming they are. The visitor still seems fearful.

It isn't usually a fear of terrorism or hate or bigotry. It is a fear of offending and being the "odd one out." We are so afraid of being wrong that we would rather avoid the other than risk building a relationship on someone else's terms. Those from marginalized religious communities are more likely to spend significant time already being the odd one out. This is not to say that those of us from smaller communities do not have a responsibility to engage with larger religious communities. The point is that those from white, Christian, and/or secular communities have a particular responsibility to be brave enough to be in spaces in which *they* are the minority.

Becoming

We forget we are not static beings; we can and do change. Conversion, deconstruction, leaving religious communities, shifting identities, or even the shifts of belief, behavior, or community association. Religious becoming is about having the freedom to have a narrative based on how one relates to religion. Sharing our narratives breaks our stereotypes and forces us to question the homogeneity of religious experiences.

Religion Is Not a Monolith

We should recognize that even within a given community, there are differences of opinion regarding how people should act or speak. Interfaith engagement must re-evaluate the strategy of "representatives" of various religious traditions who provide the "accurate" interpretation of a religion. Religious tropes are often inaccurate and lead to binary thinking, which can be easily manipulated in times of crisis.

We must teach bravery, humility, and the responsibility to be engaged with other religious backgrounds. In our communities and organizations, we must start to teach this responsibility and engage with those of different religious backgrounds.

Bridgebuilding is a fluid and natural cultural exchange within religiously diverse spaces. Healthy and productive conflict is appreciated across religious lines of difference in nearly every scripture. Difficult conversations to seek understanding are a sign that someone cares. It's a powerful signal of trust.

Religious Diversity at Work

Workplace initiatives that include religious diversity foster creativity, fresh perspectives, and understanding to protect, promote, and welcome the participation of all people. Beneficiaries include people of all professional backgrounds, including organization leaders, community members, educators, physical and mental health practitioners, artists, religious communities, and scholars.

Religion is a personal and community identity, but human resources (HR) practitioners rarely include it in workplace policies. "Seven in ten Americans (70%) identify as Christian, including more than four in ten who identify as white Christian and more than one-quarter who identify as Christian of color. Nearly one in four Americans (23%) are religiously unaffiliated, and 5% identify with non-Christian religions."[3] "Religiously unaffiliated" includes atheists, agnostics, or those with no particular religion. Pew Research notes that the "absence of a religious affiliation does not necessarily indicate an absence of religious beliefs or practices." On the contrary, most "religiously unaffiliated" report they believe in God, and most describe themselves as religious, spiritual, or both.[4] Workplace efforts rarely acknowledge the role of religion in public discourse and societal organization and structure. People are uncomfortable talking about religion where they work. This is to American society's detriment.

[3] Robert P. Jones, Natalie Jackson, Diana Orcés, and Ian Huff, *The 2020 Census of American Religion* (Washington, DC: Public Religion Research Center, 2021), 7, https://www.prri.org/wp-content/uploads/2021/07/PRRI-2021-Religion-Report.pdf (accessed December 19, 2025).

[4] Cary Funk and Greg Smith, *"Nones" on the Rise: One-in-Five Adults Have No Religious Affiliation* (Washington, DC: Pew Research Center, 2012), https://www.pewresearch.org/wp-content/uploads/sites/7/2012/10/NonesOnTheRise-full.pdf (accessed December 19, 2025).

Existing Models for Incorporating Religious Diversity in the Workplace

Existing models for incorporating religious diversity span a spectrum, from a call to embedding religious principles into management and values-based instruction to recognizing how society privileges, marginalizes, and discriminates based on religion in hopes of encouraging an improvement in behavior, engagement, and policies to promote pluralism. The taboo of religious belonging in the workplace will transform into organizations embracing religious diversity as good for people and profits.

Real or perceived, religious discrimination is an all-too-common experience of people of diverse religious backgrounds in the workplace. Schneider et al. offer that perceived religious discrimination in the workplace is relatively common:

> Nearly one-third of all workers surveyed reported having experienced religious discrimination at work to some degree: Muslims, Jews, and evangelical Christians were especially likely to report religious discrimination in the workplace. More than half of Jewish and Muslim workers and more than a third of evangelical Christians report religious discrimination. Follow-up interviews with Muslim, Jewish, nonreligious, and Christian respondents revealed how minority and majority religious traditions describe similar categories of religious discrimination, including verbal microaggressions and stereotyping, social exclusion, and othering, and negative experiences tied to observing religious holidays or displaying religious symbols.[5]

With a clear, effective strategy around workplace community building based on religious diversity, it is likely this discrimination would have had reduced the negative impact on the communities.

Employee resource groups, or ERGs, are a popular method to broach diversity in the workplace. Interfaith ERGs exist to acknowledge and learn about employees' religious identities, so employees understand other faith worldviews. Interfaith ERGs have the potential to boost employee morale, attract and retain employees, and serve as a business resource. Razaki et al. suggest interfaith dialogue in ERGs is critical to success at multinational corporations and must be incorporated to support strategic objectives in the global marketplace.[6] Interfaith ERGs are composed of employees who connect based on shared characteristics,

[5] Rachel C. Schneider, Deidra Carroll Coleman, Elaine Howard Ecklund, and Denise Daniels, "How Religious Discrimination Is Perceived in the Workplace: Expanding the View," *Socius* 8 (2022): https://doi.org/10.1177/23780231211070920.

[6] Khalid Razaki, Anne Drougas, and Mohamed Askar, "Religion and Interfaith Dialogue: The Forgotten Pedagogical DEI Initiative in Business Education and Strategic Planning," *Journal of Higher Education Theory and Practice* 22, no. 10 (2022): 38–52.

affinity, values, and life experiences and can focus on cultural understanding and community outreach. Workplaces that value religious diversity and have interfaith ERGs often offer kosher or halal food, provide floating holidays, provide training on religious literacy, or hire an interfaith chaplain who offers spiritual or social support.

QUESTIONS FOR HR PRACTITIONERS TO CONSIDER

- Is religion part of your employee engagement survey or business needs assessments?
- How can your business strategy include cultural competency training?
- How can your employees be experts in navigating tensions, contradictions, and conflicts?
- Have you considered what ethical practices invite folks to express their religious identity?

Strategic objectives frequently ignore different belief systems and the opportunity to promote freedom of thought and belief, including the belief systems of those with no religion. A typical response to increased religious diversity in the workplace is restricting or acknowledging any religion—in other words, ignoring religion, regardless of how important, influential, or central it is to someone's life. We do not believe ignoring religious differences leads to equity or equality.

According to the Public Religion Research Institute (PRRI) in 2019, nearly a quarter of Americans (22 percent) seldom or never interact with someone who does not share their religion.[7] It is normative for organizations to consider a belief system or religion as a monolith or to privilege denominations of Christianity. Too often, employees, especially religious minorities, are expected to leave essential aspects of themselves at home, which affects their sense of belonging, minimizes their potential contribution to the community, and denies them a supportive and psychologically safe work environment.

In 2015, Pew Research projected that world marketplaces will become more religious and religiously diverse by 2050. The United States, China, Japan, India, and Germany will shift from economies dominated by majority Christians to Hindus, Muslims, Buddhists, and the unaffiliated.[8] In the United States, younger

[7] Robert P. Jones and Maxine Najle, *American Democracy in Crisis: The Fate of Pluralism in a Divided Nation* (Washington, DC: Public Religion Research Institute, 2019), 13, https://www.prri.org/wp-content/uploads/2019/02/Democracy-in-Crisis-3-Pluralism-1.pdf (accessed December 19, 2025).

[8] Conrad Hackett, Alan Cooperman, and Katherine Ritchey, *The Future of World Religions: Population Growth Projections, 2010-2050* (Washington, DC: Pew Research Center, 2015), https://assets.pewresearch.org/wp-content/uploads/sites/11/2015/03/PF_15.04.02_ProjectionsFullReport.pdf (accessed December 19, 2025).

generations are more religiously diverse and expect employers to welcome religious differences as an opportunity to learn about worldviews and hear each other's narratives.

People expect religious communities to be homogeneous—this isn't the case. For workplace initiatives to be effective, they must illuminate the gaps in understanding between people. Examining identities must be singular and intersectional since we are both unique humans *and* a combination of more than one identity. Religion cannot be understood from a single perspective, and religious identity is often connected to religious institutions while increasingly tangled with political identity. Often people do not have the vocabulary and understanding to talk about religion without robust, honest, frank, and constructive dialogue and deliberation to advance the public interest in pluralism. And when people lack the skills and curiosity to seek understanding, it becomes polarizing and potentially hostile. Polarization and hostility manifest in the workplace as fear, apprehension, and safety concerns by employees.

We can summarize most of this chapter as follows: Life is complicated, people are complicated, and religion is complicated. Our advice is to be open to discomfort and nuance and be curious about how people relate to religion in the workplace. The 5B model leans into complexity. Sometimes it has less to do with what we generally consider "religious" because religion does not sit in a bubble outside our other identities, upbringing, and culture.

The most practical action that organizations can take to be more equitable and inclusive of religious diversity is to prioritize a flexible and empathetic environment. In our experience, that means the following:

1. Recognize the internal diversity of religious communities as a priority for inclusive organizations.
2. Question and reflect on an orthodoxy/heresy mindset.
3. Rather than overly defining religion or questioning how sincere someone may be, focus on how people engage with religion through the 5B Framework—Belief, Behavior, Belonging, Becoming, and Body.
4. Assume something is more complex than it may seem.

This moment requires a movement for religious pluralism that invites bridging and belonging in neighborhoods and workplaces across the United States. We aim to advance public interest in religious pluralism and prepare more citizens with the vocabulary and understanding to talk about religion and signal to our neighbors they are seen and can bring their whole selves to our relationships.

18

Religious Pluralism in the Workplace

A Conscious Decision

Reverend Mark E. Fowler and Megan Leverage

In the wake of the devastation of Hurricane Sandy in 2012, the Depository Trust & Clearing Corporation (DTCC) relocated from lower Manhattan to a new office space in Jersey City, New Jersey. When they moved to their new location, a group of employees approached Nadine Augusta, the former head of DTCC's Global Diversity & Inclusion and Corporate Social Responsibility. In a private meeting, one of the employees disclosed, "In the old location, we used to be able to reserve a conference room to pray during the day. In this new space, however, everything is glass and clear—so there isn't a place where we are comfortable praying privately because everything is so open."[1] In this pivotal moment, Nadine faced a crucial question: *What can we do to ensure that all our employees have a safe, comfortable environment to honor the practices of their beliefs?*

Nadine had learned about Tanenbaum while attending a presentation at The Conference Board, and she decided to reach out to Tanenbaum's Workplace program.[2] Nadine was interested in finding an answer to her question and exploring more fully how the reality of religious diversity could be better integrated into the policies and practices at DTCC. To get a fuller understanding of religious accommodations at DTCC, we first conducted a policy review, including an examination of their new office with a specific focus on the space designated for prayer. Upon review, Tanenbaum suggested removing desks and office materials, and providing a clear indication of the east direction for prayer purposes. Tanenbaum also proposed adding cabinetry within the room for employees to store sacred objects, texts, and prayer rugs. In this way, the quiet room would support a religiously diverse workforce. Tanenbaum presented these suggestions to DTCC's Diversity Council, chaired by former CEO Mike Bodson, who

[1] Tanenbaum, "But, Where Can I Pray?" (New York: Tanenbaum, 2018).

[2] Founded in 1992, Tanenbaum promotes justice and builds respect for religious difference by transforming individuals and institutions to reduce prejudice, hatred, and violence. As a secular and non-sectarian nonprofit, Tanenbaum works to promote religious peacebuilders who help counter extremism and violence in armed conflicts, and tackles religious bullying of students, harassment in workplaces, and disparate health treatment for people based on their beliefs.

Reverend Mark E. Fowler and Megan Leverage, *Religious Pluralism in the Workplace* In: *Modeling Religious Pluralism*. Edited by: Simran Jeet Singh, Oxford University Press. © Oxford University Press 2026.
DOI: 10.1093/oso/9780197745809.003.0018

promptly found a larger room for group prayer. DTCC emphasized the importance of accommodating religious practices for employee well-being and business success in their *2017 Annual Report*, and impacted employees shared their appreciation for the company addressing their needs.

Over the past twenty-five years, Tanenbaum has developed models for cultivating religiously inclusive workplaces, and our work with DTCC illustrates the practical applications of these models: notably the identification of potential bias through Tanenbaum's 10 Bias Danger Signs® and the implementation of our maturity model, the Corporate Religious Diversity Assessment (CRDA).[3]

The CRDA, developed in collaboration with the Religious Freedom & Business Foundation (RFBF), offers a comprehensive framework for a company's self-evaluation to foster religious pluralism in their work environments.

Creating a religiously inclusive workplace is a decision. It starts with an acknowledgment of the culture the company strives to create regarding the religious and spiritual diversity of its workforce, and reviewing, updating, or creating the policies and practices that make that cultural goal a reality.

Identifying and Combating Bias

Tanenbaum's 1999 survey, and the joint Tanenbaum and the Society for Human Resource Management (SHRM) 2001 survey, revealed a significant gap between employee expectations and employer accommodations of religion. In the 1999 survey, 89 percent of employees expressed the importance of companies providing personal days for religious observance, including time off for holidays. The 2001 survey showed that "Christian holidays are the only official holidays in 99% of workplaces. And only 25% of respondents' organizations permit holiday swapping, such as working on Ash Wednesday in exchange for taking time off on Yom Kippur." This comparison shows the misalignment between the requirements of employees and the actual provisions made by employers, illuminating the need for a closer examination of non-accommodation in the workplace.[4]

The data from the 1999 survey created the foundation for Tanenbaum's 10 Bias Danger Signs, which presents a vital framework for organizations to assess

[3] Tanenbaum, "10 Bias Danger Signs," Workplace Resources, https://tanenbaum.org/about-us/what-we-do/workplace/workplace-resources/ (accessed March 1, 2024); and Tanenbaum and Religious Freedom & Business Foundation, "Corporate Religious Diversity Assessment," https://crdatool.com (accessed March 1, 2024).

[4] Yosie Saint-Cyr, "Religious Diversity in the Workplace," HR Info Desk, November 2002, https://www.hrinfodesk.com/preview.asp?article=8835 (accessed May 13, 2024); and Society for Human Resource Management, *Religion and Corporate Culture: Accommodating Religious Diversity in the Workplace* (Alexandria, VA: Society for Human Resource Management, 2008).

and proactively address potential religion-based bias. Designed to bridge the gap between human resources' (HR's) perception of accommodation and the real experiences of religious employees facing non-accommodation, these warning signs alert employers to the most common areas of bias in the workplace across religious traditions. From challenges related to attire and devotion to issues with scheduling and socializing, each sign represents a critical aspect that impacts the experience of belonging for people of various religious beliefs in the workplace. By considering these danger signs, organizations can identify areas for evaluation and take proactive measures to create a more welcoming and inclusive environment. This model serves as a guide to help organizations prepare and respond to the religious needs of employees. It ensures their policies and practices align with the actual experiences of their religiously diverse workforce.

In October and November of 2013, Tanenbaum conducted eleven qualitative interviews with a cross-section of DTCC's leaders and employees about their experiences of religion in the DTCC workplace. Participants were asked questions based on Tanenbaum's 10 Bias Danger Signs, exploring issues of attire, devotion, diet, holidays, icons, employee networks, prayer, ridicule, scheduling, and socializing. These interviews informed our recommendations to DTCC on creating a religious diversity strategy. The interviews helped reveal that DTCC had a strong foundation of inclusion and revealed some areas for development.

Engaging in a comprehensive review allows companies to create a realistic strategy for creating a religiously inclusive culture for their employees. Here are some examples.

Scheduling

Scheduling bias refers to a form of workplace discrimination where work shifts and meeting schedules fail to consider or accommodate holidays and religious/spiritual observances. This bias becomes apparent when the scheduling process overlooks or neglects the importance of religious and non-religious practice, leading to conflicts between work commitments and an individual's ability to observe and celebrate days of personal significance.

In Tanenbaum's interviews with DTCC employees, they expressed that their employer accommodated their needs to take off work for religious observances. Employees indicated that their colleagues and supervisors did not regularly schedule meetings or events during times when they were unavailable, and when this occurred, they provided meeting notes and relevant materials to absent employees. Some employees were looking forward to DTCC's forthcoming paid-time-off policy, expressing favorable opinions about this change that would permit better flexibility. Taken together, DTCC demonstrated exceptional proficiency in scheduling, addressing the primary concern identified in our survey research on American workers.

Diet

Diet bias is evident in the workplace when work-sponsored gatherings provide limited or insufficient options for individuals with dietary requirements, such as kosher, halal, or vegetarian diets. Without asking about dietary needs, this bias potentially excludes those who adhere to specific cultural, religious, or personal dietary restrictions. Diet bias can impact an employee's ability to fully participate in and enjoy communal activities.

In the interviews, some employees had attended DTCC events where they could not find food that fit their religiously mandated dietary restrictions. For example, several employees mentioned that the cafeteria in Jersey City offers kosher and vegetarian dietary options, but not halal options. And kosher options were only offered after employees requested this addition. Nearly all employees said that, to their understanding, it was not policy or standard practice to send out emails asking about dietary needs or restrictions before company or departmental events where food would be provided.

Following the interview feedback, we recommended training sessions for navigating religious diversity in the workplace and building competencies for respectful communication with a specific emphasis on asking all employees about their dietary needs. DTCC accepted and acted on that recommendation and provided a number of trainings for all employees.

Devotion

Devotion bias refers to a form of workplace discrimination that arises when employees face challenges or obstacles in seeking accommodations for practices such as prayer, meditation, or reflection during the workday. One example of devotion bias is when employees seek permission for breaks during the workday for religious purposes and it is not permitted. Another example includes lack of access to a suitable and private space within the workplace for religious practices. Devotion bias can hinder employees' abilities to freely observe their faith at work.

In their New York City office, DTCC already had practices in place where employees could reserve a conference room to observe prayer rituals during the day. DTCC took a positive first step by providing a quiet room for employees in its Jersey City office. However, not all employees knew it existed. For example, some employees thought that the only way to obtain a space to pray was if their manager was willing to reserve a conference room. Some employees mentioned that the new office space in Jersey City made finding private space for prayer more difficult (e.g., glass walls, lower cubicle walls, and smaller offices), and they, too, seemed unaware of the quiet room.

Employees raised additional issues about the quiet room. Some commented that the quiet room was very small and therefore could not accommodate group prayer sessions. Several employees mentioned that they left DTCC premises and went to nearby religious institutions to pray. Of these employees, some indicated that this was their preference, while one indicated that they would have preferred having a space to pray within the DTCC office. Lastly, DTCC employees working in other offices outside of Jersey City expressed their concern about not being able to reserve a consistent space where they could pray, reflect, or meditate.

Upon review, Tanenbaum commended DTCC for establishing a quiet room in their Jersey City offices. To improve their policies and practices around the aspect of devotion, we recommended DTCC clearly communicate about the quiet room via email, intranet postings, and orientation discussions with new employees. To optimize the room's usefulness, we recommended a system for reserving the room and guidelines for its use, including open access, scheduling through HR or a managed intranet system, and restrictions on group activities (due to limited space). We advised DTCC to consider creating similar quiet rooms across all its locations, ensuring adherence to the standardized guidelines. In cases where a quiet room was not feasible, we proposed directing employees to DTCC policies and providing information on local houses of worship.

We then presented all our findings to DTCC's Diversity Council, which as mentioned was chaired by their former CEO, Mike Bodson. When Tanenbaum shared the information about the contemplation room, Bodson turned to the person next to him and said, "Can't we find a bigger room?" And they did—within a week.

Our survey research revealed that DTCC's experience with religion-based bias aligned with broader workplace trends. In 2013, Tanenbaum published the results of its national report, *Survey of American Workers and Religion*, conducted in partnership with Public Religion Research LLC, which focused on non-accommodation in the workplace. The findings revealed that over one third (36 percent) of workers have personally experienced or witnessed religious non-accommodation in their workplace. The most prevalent instances include being required to work on the Sabbath or religious holidays (24 percent) and attending company-sponsored events lacking kosher, halal, or vegetarian options (13 percent). Less than half of all workers report the presence of key policies related to religious diversity, such as flexible work hours for religious observance or prayer (44 percent) and a policy allowing employees to "swap holidays" (21 percent).

Against this backdrop, DTCC's commendable efforts in addressing these common forms of bias stand out, reflecting a commitment to building respect for religious differences.[5]

Building Respect for Religious Difference

In their *2017 Annual Report*, DTCC highlighted the significant accomplishments of their long-standing partnership with Tanenbaum, showcasing collaborative work conducted over several years. One notable aspect was DTCC's ongoing proactive approach to address religion-based bias. For example, Rahul Bhalerao, director of IT business value management, mentioned in the report that being a practicing Hindu, his vegetarian diet had never been an issue at work. He stated, "Being a vegetarian has never been an issue during any team luncheons or other corporate events, as these dietary needs are easily taken care of. Such gestures make you feel included."[6]

Marc Masri, executive director and area lead for IT, who identified as an Orthodox Jew, similarly emphasized DTCC's accommodation of his religious dietary needs in addition to his scheduling requirements. Masri reflected, "Having the flexibility to honor my religious traditions gives me peace of mind and greater confidence to be myself at work. It makes me more effective at my job, and it allows me to bring a diverse perspective to the initiatives I lead. I've created a similar environment for my team, and it's so gratifying to see how this motivates them to contribute even more to our success."[7]

DTCC's *2017 Annual Report* recognized the business case for promoting freedom of religion and belief and religious pluralism in the workplace. As the report summarized, "As the focus on workplace diversity and inclusion evolves, the inclusion of dimensions such as religion have grown in importance. When employees feel free to be themselves and have the ability and flexibility to honor their religious obligations and traditions at work, it translates into business advantage and success."[8]

Beyond the workplace, former CEO Michael Bodson emphasized in the report the importance of external initiatives connected to DTCC's core values: "We also gave back to the local communities where we work through volunteerism and philanthropy, closely aligning our activities with our CSR [corporate social responsibility] pillars."[9]

[5] Tanenbaum and Public Religion Research, *What American Workers Really Think about Religion* (New York: Tanenbaum, 2013).

[6] DTCC, *Turning Headwinds into Tailwinds: 2017 Annual Report* (New York: DTCC, 2017).

[7] Ibid.

[8] Ibid.

[9] Ibid.

Building upon the success of the collaborative efforts with organizations like DTCC, Tanenbaum and the RFBF jointly introduced the CRDA in 2018. As the first internal evaluation tool for efforts on religion and diversity, equity, and inclusion, the CRDA was crafted as a maturity model to empower companies to assess their strategies on religious diversity in the workplace. DTCC's proactive engagement and exemplary practices served as a model, influencing the development of the CRDA's four criteria:

1. Non-Discrimination and Non-Harassment on the Basis of Religion or Belief
2. Religious Accommodation and Inclusion
3. Promoting Sustainable and Innovative Business through Protecting Freedom of Religion or Belief (FoRB)
4. Protecting and Promoting Freedom of Religion or Belief (FoRB) in Our Communities

Since its inception, the CRDA has provided companies with a comprehensive framework, drawing inspiration from DTCC's journey, to evaluate past and present efforts and create a roadmap for the future road ahead. Upholding the values of the freedom of religion or belief and religious pluralism, the CRDA encourages companies to actively embrace the religious dimension of diversity, equity, and inclusion, recognizing its positive impact on both the workplace and beyond.[10]

When Tanenbaum started its work to support companies in their journeys to include religion in their diversity and inclusion strategies, we were often met with resistance. Litigation avoidance was the primary lens through which companies considered their policies and practices as they related to their religiously diverse workforce. *If we're not being sued, everything is probably okay.*

Today, we continue to see the evolution of religion and religious identity recognized as a critical part of corporate strategies to build and respond to religiously diverse workforces and marketplaces. Forty percent of Tanenbaum member companies are exploring and launching faith-based employee resource groups of various configurations from individual groups to interfaith and inter-belief groups. There are multiple convenings where employees of all faiths and none gather to gain skills and perspective on how to create inclusive workplaces. Tanenbaum convenes a symposium for chief diversity officers, chief HR officers, general counsels, and executive sponsors of faith-based employee resource

[10] Tanenbaum and Religious Freedom & Business Foundation, "Corporate Religious Diversity Assessment."

groups to consider future action for the policies, practices, and cultures that will be necessary for the ever-expanding religiously diverse workforce.

It is imperative that we continue to support this evolution within diversity, equity, inclusion, and belonging. This is the same path that all of the other identity areas have walked and are walking today. Now is the time for us to continue to make the decision that workplaces, where employees of all faiths and none know they are respected, are worth the effort.

PART VII
RELIGION AND PHILANTHROPY

There's an account of Guru Nanak's life in which he meets a wealthy merchant who is proud of everything that he's accumulated. He gives Guru Nanak a tour of his home, boasting all throughout. At the end, Guru Nanak gives him a needle and says, "Can you do me a favor? Hold onto this needle for now and give it back to me in the afterlife."

In trying to explain that this is not possible, the merchant understands the Guru's wisdom. *What's the point of hoarding wealth? We can't take any of it with us.* In realizing the error of his ways, the merchant becomes generous, sharing his wealth with those in need.

This is one of the many accounts that inspires Sikhs to give freely and openly. I first heard it as a child, and I've heard it hundreds of times since. Over the years, as I have studied other religious traditions, I have observed that stories like this are plentiful, and that people lean on them for guidance and inspiration.

Generosity continues to be an animating force in religious communities. So much of the giving we see in our world is connected to faith, from humanitarian aid to philanthropic grant making. And yet, there is a tension between religion and philanthropy that often goes unspoken. Philanthropies don't always trust religious institutions or faith-based organizations, and many foundations are reticent to support them financially.

Will they use our funds to proselytize? Does giving to religiously affiliated efforts mean we're privileging one religion over others? Given these risks, are we better off not funding any faith-based organizations?

These questions are understandable, and the logic is, too. But this approach leaves so much impact on the table. Here's what I've learned about philanthropy through many colleagues who are much smarter and far more seasoned than me: While philanthropy is an important engine for social and cultural change, too much of it is hindered by self-imposed limitations on how it deals with religion and religious communities.

In this section, we explore the complex relationship between religion and philanthropy, which is simultaneously complementary yet conflicting, fraught yet enriching. We also consider ways that philanthropy can navigate its core tension with religion with an eye toward advancing religious pluralism for the common good.

Jason Garrett's chapter examines religious pluralism and philanthropy through a lens of power, which he argues is often missing from these conversations. Garrett, senior vice president of faith, bridging, and belonging at Freedom Together Foundation, argues that when we account for power, interventions for progress will consider new methods, including transformation through praxis and an asset-based approach.

Farhan Latif and Catherine Orsborn outline the benefits of engaging religion rather than avoiding it, and how they have approached this connection through their work with the El Hibri Foundation. Latif serves as president for the foundation, and Orsborn is director of program operations. They also present challenges and opportunities that they have faced, with practical examples and recommendations of how to engage religion effectively.

Allison K. Ralph, who consults on pluralism and belonging, makes the case for why the philanthropic sector is critical for building religious pluralism. Her chapter lays out ideas, strategies, and resources for how philanthropy serving organizations can better engage religion and religious communities.

Each of these chapters acknowledges the very real tensions that exist between religion and philanthropy. Each of them also implores us to embrace these tensions and recognize that ignoring religion because it's uncomfortable leaves us all worse off. I find it instructive and reassuring to see that people with so much experience in this field have wisdom and guidance for how we might navigate these waters effectively.

19
A New Path
Pairing Power and Religious Pluralism

Jason Garrett

The Critical Gap

While it may seem unusual for a mosque to wield power via a religiously pluralistic membership organization, this pathway emerged as the most viable option for the Dar al-Farooq Islamic Center, a mosque in Bloomington, Minnesota. Just as morning prayers began on August 5, 2017, a firebomb crashed through the window of the mosque and exploded in a room adjacent to where the imam was located. Fortunately, no one was injured physically, but the emotional and psychological trauma led to fear, a steep decline in weekly attendance, and an inclination among some members to remain quiet about this injustice. As expressed by the perpetrator during a trial two years later, the intent behind the bomb was to scare Muslims out of the country and let them know, "You're not welcome here."[1]

What does religious pluralism look like for members of the Dar al-Farooq Mosque suffering from the trauma of a terrorist attack? Pluralism is different from diversity in that it requires a positive response to diversity.[2] The Aspen Institute goes even further with religious pluralism, noting how it is defined by the existence of diverse religious communities and non-believers who have opportunities to thrive and defend each other's right to thrive.[3] But we must also ask how one thrives or grows toward their individual and communal purpose when their mere existence is obstructed by forces of fear, domination, and exclusion?

[1] Elizabeth McKenna, "Shifting Power by Sharing Power: A Case Study of Relational Organizing in Saint Paul, MN," The P3 Lab at Johns Hopkins University, December 15, 2021, https://d3n8a8pro7vhmx.cloudfront.net/hahrie/pages/1200/attachments/original/1639510118/Deep_Dive_Isaiah.pdf?1639510118r (accessed December 17, 2025).

[2] Global Centre for Pluralism, "Who We Are," https://www.pluralism.ca/who-we-are/ (accessed April 11, 2023).

[3] Aspen Institute, "The Politics of Vulnerability," February 17, 2026, https://www.aspeninstitute.org/wp-content/uploads/2025/05/Politics-of-Vulnerability.pdf.

Jason Garrett, *A New Path* In: *Modeling Religious Pluralism*. Edited by: Simran Jeet Singh, Oxford University Press. © Oxford University Press 2026. DOI: 10.1093/oso/9780197745809.003.0019

Over the past two decades, I have worked to help people build communities of belonging where they have power, experience love, and can thrive, primarily in faith institutions as a licensed Christian minister, in nonprofit organizations as a community organizer, and in three of the country's largest foundations as a program officer for civic engagement and, currently, as a senior vice president for faith, bridging, and belonging. While I have been a part of meaningful changes that have improved the lives of millions across the United States, my positioning in these three communities—faith institutions, nonprofit organizations, and foundations—has helped me to see a critical gap that undermines the work of all three constituencies, undercuts the promise of religious pluralism, and imperils our democracy. On one hand, foundations and secular organizations have often failed to see how the adoption of religious pluralism could significantly advance their diverse strategic interests. On the other hand, some faith communities and philanthropic institutions have been hesitant to pair pluralism with power—the ability to achieve a purpose and move beyond dialogue to action. The critical gap, therefore, is where pluralism and power fail to meet.

I contend that making gains to advance religious pluralism and implementing effective philanthropic strategies would be propelled greatly if the three aforementioned communities could work collaboratively at the intersection of pluralism and power. By doing so, a stronger democracy, the opportunities for people to thrive, and religious pluralism will be more within our reach, as exemplified by the story of the Dar al-Farooq Mosque.

Pairing Power with Religious Pluralism

The challenges faced by the Dar al-Farooq Mosque started well before the terrorist attack and existed long afterward, and those challenges speak to questions of belonging. For years, the mosque was denied the ability to use most of the building they purchased, despite full utilization by the Lutheran Church that occupied it before them. Muslim children faced deep resistance when attending the nearby public park, leading the mosque to build a new playground on its site. These dynamics—manifested within government policies or within overt acts of discrimination—were driven by actors who did not believe Muslims belonged. Belonging is about membership and power, and the members of the mosque were clear they neither belonged to Bloomington, Minnesota, nor had the power to change their status.[4]

john a. powell, director of the Othering and Belonging Institute, talks about how membership is the greatest good of society, because from there flow all other

[4] McKenna, "Shifting Power by Sharing Power," 2021.

decisions.[5] powell elevates the importance of co-creation, or the ability to co-create the organizations, systems, and structures that shape one's future and the ability to influence outcomes.[6] Co-creation is an action that involves agency and is deeply connected to power, which is derived from the Latin *poetere*, meaning "to be able." Phrased differently, Reverend Dr. Martin Luther King, Jr., said, "Power, properly understood, is the ability to achieve purpose."[7]

Too often, there is an aversion to power that severely undermines progress toward religious pluralism. However, power is complex and exists in different forms. Usually, the resistance to power is to one particular form of power, which community organizers call "power over" or "dominant power." Dr. King helps to parse through the reservations and misunderstanding around power when he said, "What is needed is a realization that power without love is reckless and abusive and that love without power is sentimental and anemic."[8] In a way, religious pluralism unpaired with power is sentimental and anemic as well, because pluralism without power can create the conditions for dialogue but not necessarily the capacity to thrive.

Pluralism must be paired with two specific types of power, "power within" and "power with." The former recognizes the importance of cultivating an individual's capacity to grow and achieve a given purpose, and the latter recognizes that power, like love and belonging, is best designed to be a communal endeavor. "Power with" views power as shared instead of absolute, and it embraces democracy and belonging. Dialogue and deliberation are important, but suffering calls for a response that starts with dialogue, yet it does not stop there; suffering demands movement toward action around a common goal.[9] For the sake of this article, I would suggest the common goal or shared vision for philanthropy, faith groups, and nonprofit organizations could be expressed by a commitment to address human suffering and actualize love, thriving, and belonging.

The narrative of Dar al-Farooq Mosque is an example of an organization operating at the intersection of religious pluralism and power, and its story is described in more detail in a case study about ISAIAH, one of the largest faith-based community organizing coalitions in the United States designed to support collective training, acting, and co-creation of an alternative future.[10] By the end

[5] john a. powell and Stephen Menendian, "The Problem of Othering: Towards Inclusiveness and Belonging," *Othering and Belonging*, 2016, http://www.otheringandbelonging.org/the-problem-of-othering/ (accessed December 18, 2025).

[6] Ibid.

[7] Clayborne Carson, *The Autobiography of Martin Luther King, Jr.* (New York: Grand Central Publishing, 2001).

[8] Ibid.

[9] Jung M. Sung, "Capitalism as Religion and Religious Pluralism: An Approach from Liberation Theology," *JSTOR* 34 (2014): 155–165, https://www.jstor.org/stable/24801361.

[10] McKenna, "Shifting Power by Sharing Power," 2021.

of the story, a transformation occurs with the Muslim members of ISAIAH: They experience agency in a critical meeting with the mayor, they become members within an organization practicing religious pluralism and providing mutual support for thriving, and they see why power is an essential ingredient to address injustices and to create the conditions for thriving.

Barriers to Religious Pluralism

There are a number of barriers that obfuscate the path to working at the intersection of pluralism and power, and I have seen the myriad ways in which foundations, faith institutions and non-profit organizations have been challenged by these obstacles.

The historic and contemporary role of faith institutions with oppression, domination, economic exploitation, or even genocide may give one pause around engaging faith groups, and understandably so. Yet, I have found in philanthropy that a rubric of skepticism and apprehension is unequally applied to faith groups. While hosting a focus group within a foundation about the role of faith and social change, a participant adamantly raised the issue of "red lines" and asserted we should not work with a group of Catholic churches on one issue because they worked against the foundation on a different priority. Another person highlighted how our foundation worked with governments around the world in spite of various disagreements, and so he asked, "How is working with the Catholic Church any different?" The question was followed by silence, but the wrestling with the tension was notable.

The culture and systems within philanthropy and secular organizations, by and large, are not designed to support religious pluralism. In over a decade of working in philanthropy, I have seen countless trainings that create the conditions for pluralism by helping to learn about dynamics with different identities related to race, gender, sexuality, and immigration status. Nevertheless, I have never seen a similar training on religion within philanthropy. Foundation application processes have made great strides to consider the inclusion of racial diversity, people with disabilities, and gender in leadership, among others, but most do not include an opportunity (not the obligation) to include information about faith. Hiring processes are mindful of multiple aspects of diversity, including geographic and educational diversity, but rarely religious diversity.

Furthermore, philanthropic organizations and secular nonprofits have serious challenges with appreciating the value of spiritual power. Too often, the path to addressing suffering focuses on technical instruments such as the rule of law, universal right to vote, or freedom of expression.[11] Those things may remove

[11] Wilhem Guggenberger and Bala Kumar Hrudayaraj, *Democracy, Religion, and Pluralism Theological Responses* (Innsbruck: Innsbruck University Press, 2022), https://library.oapen.org/

barriers to thriving, but they do not provide the fuel to persevere down a path toward an alternative future. People are motivated more by their beliefs, values, and where they find meaning and less so by legislation or technical solutions. Religion is important or somewhat important for 77 percent of Americans, and nine in ten Americans believe in a higher power.[12] This greater power, or Soul Force as one frame for the transcendent offered by Dr. King, was a key driver for Mahatma Gandhi in the drive for independence from the British, for Dr. King in the civil rights movement, and for Nelson Mandela in the anti-Apartheid movement.

As we see from those movements, exercising power requires productive friction to contest the dominant forces that benefit from societal inequities and to create a different social arrangement.[13] Theological education normally lacks the ability or willingness to train students at the intersection of pluralism and power, and broader cultural forces, while well intentioned many times, prefer the avoidance of power versus distinguishing the different types of power.

Political theorist Danielle Allen suggests freedom from domination requires an equal share of control over the institutions that govern our lives, not just technical solutions to protect our democratic rights.[14] Social difference without domination, in her view, identifies the importance of having social patterning that does not consistently result in one group having direct or reserve control over another group.[15] Stated differently, when talking about an ideal form of pluralism, political scientist Michael Parenti states that "the opportunities and resources necessary for the exercise of power are inclusively rather than exclusively distributed and that neither the enjoyment of dominance nor the suffering of deprivation is the constant condition of any one group."[16]

This concept of difference without denomination is critical to religious pluralism because it addresses the unintentional and intentional ways in which domination prevails and, thereby, diminishes any type of pluralism. Frederick

bitstream/id/152b50ef-b79d-46d9-83ed-7dfdd02149a7/10.15203-99106-082-6.pdf (accessed December 18, 2025).

[12] Pew Research Center, *Importance of Religion and Religious Beliefs* (Washington, DC: Pew Research Center, 2015), https://www.pewresearch.org/religion/2015/11/03/chapter-1-importance-of-religion-and-religious-beliefs/ (accessed December 18, 2025).

Pew Research Center, *When Americans Say They Believe in God, What Do They Mean?* (Washington, DC: Pew Research Center. 2018), https://www.pewresearch.org/religion/2018/04/25/when-americans-say-they-believe-in-god-what-do-they-mean/ (accessed December 18, 2025).

[13] Mary L. Friedline, "Pluralism and the Roots of Social Conflict: Rethinking Rails," *MDPI*, December 29, 2018, https://doi.org/10.3390/rel10010020.

[14] Rohini Somanathan and Danielle Allen, eds., *Difference without Domination: Pursuing Justice in Diverse Democracies* (Chicago: University of Chicago Press, 2020).

[15] Ibid.

[16] Michael Parenti, "Power and Pluralism: A View from the Bottom," *Journal of Politics* 32, no. 3 (August 1970): 501–530, https://www.jstor.org/stable/2128829.

Douglass speaks to the strategy needed to dismantle this power in his "West India Emancipation" speech, which merits a fuller context than it is typically given. "If there is no struggle there is no progress. Those who profess to favor freedom and yet deprecate agitation are men who want crops without plowing up the ground; they want rain without thunder and lightning. . . . Power concedes nothing without a demand. It never did and it never will."[17] Coupling "power within" and "power with" is the mechanism that can move us from difference with denomination to difference without denomination. Yet, too often, I find faith groups and philanthropic institutions are uncomfortable with the plowing and agitation that are necessary to arrive at this stage. Promoting bridging and building work is essential, and that work is evident in the story of the Dar al-Farooq Mosque. "Power with" embodies bridging and building, but it does so without leaving behind the plowing that is necessary to reckon with the deep roots of domination.

Religious Pluralism's Path of Progress

A path of progress is marked by positive developments and certain markers that foreshadow progress in a particular area. In many ways, the markers of progression toward religious pluralism and power will be defined by how we address the aforementioned barriers on the path. One step, as noted by the Aspen Institute, is the need for literacy and skills to navigate the religious diversity in our environment. An added value would be to connect this learning with an intersectional analysis and asset-based approach.[18] The intersectional analysis highlights the ways in which individual identities intersect and impact how people are perceived, treated, and belong. Most often, class, gender, race, sex, and sexuality have been the identities of focus, not religion. Yet, the terrorist attacks in recent years at Emanuel A.M.E. Church in Charleston, South Carolina; the Tree of Life Synagogue in Pittsburgh, Pennsylvania; and the Dar al-Farooq Mosque in Bloomington, Minnesota, illustrate how a faith identity can stimulate acts of oppression as well. At the same time, the communities represented by these institutions continue to encounter oppressive forces due to other aspects of their identity, such as race, immigration status, and culture. Efforts to fight for religious pluralism, political equality, or racial justice, for instance, must be mutually reinforced rather than pursued separately. By doing so, diverse groups can seize opportunities to unite and act against dominant forces who set out to

[17] Frederick Douglass, *Two speeches, by Frederick Douglass: one on West India emancipation, delivered at Canandaigua, Aug. 4th, and the other on the Dred Scott decision, delivered in New York, on the occasion of the anniversary of the American Abolition Society, May, 1857* (Rochester: C.P. Dewey, 1857).

[18] Aspen Institute, "The Politics of Vulnerability," 2026.

foment division and undermine pluralism by utilizing similar methods of exclusion against them all.

The intersectional analysis ought to be balanced with an asset-based approach. Intersectional analyses inform us about the nature of the problems, but they rarely provide the needed motivation to move toward a shared vision. An asset-based approach recognizes that we have all the capacity, expertise, and resources that an alternative future requires.[19] Philanthropic and nonprofit institutions often work with faith groups to combat discrimination against those communities; however, they often do so in a rent-a-collar fashion that temporarily engages those faith groups, primarily for their utility with advancing a particular issue. Spiritual power, however, is often not the impetus for funding or partnership, and it certainly is not perceived as a valid strategic approach. For those faith, secular, and philanthropic institutions that do pursue an asset-based approach, sometimes it is their only method for approaching change. I would caution against this imbalance, because an asset-based approach untethered to an intersectional analysis may not address the roots of domination and, thus, would compromise any durable change around pluralism and political equality.

Praxis at the intersection of pluralism and power is another essential ingredient. Educator and philosopher Paulo Freire's orientation around praxis can be instructive in this effort, as he asserts dialogue consists of both reflection and action and keenly notes that if one half of this duo is sacrificed, the other half suffers.[20] After the presidential election of Donald Trump in 2016, I noticed a trend in philanthropy and the organizations we serve. I witnessed how one body of emerging organizations focused on dialogue and bridging conversations to address deep divides, and another set of organizations focused on activism to address injustices. In line with Freire's observation, I saw the two sides suffer due to a lack of balance in their praxis: There was either too much conversation unsubstantiated in transformative action or too much action unrefined by taking time for reflection. This dynamic of separation, especially in a religiously pluralistic context, is the status quo; closing this gap will advance religious pluralism significantly.

Lastly, praxis flourishes when planted in containers in which people can cultivate durable communities and practice democracy. The members of Dar Al-Farooq Mosque were able to engage in this praxis model within the context of ISAIAH, which functioned as a place where they could belong, relate to others, and be a part of something greater. Belonging is best "created when we join with other people in producing something that makes a place better."[21] The detriment

[19] Peter Block, *Community: The Structure of Belonging* (San Francisco: Berrett-Koehler, 2009).
[20] Paulo Freire, *Pedagogy of the Oppressed* (New York: Continuum, 2000).
[21] Block, *Community*.

of many bridging efforts is that people come as individuals to be trained or as a group to dialogue, but those efforts lack a context of belonging where the participants can engage in the collective praxis work to address suffering and help their community thrive. Faith institutions, organizing coalitions such as ISAIAH, and other membership-oriented nonprofit organizations are some of the richest grounds to build the social fabric in our nation, exercise power, and experience pluralism, in part because the depth of relationships forged over long periods of time allows for more trust, growth, and connection.

A New Story

I visited Dar al-Farooq Mosque in the winter of 2023, six years after the bombing. A lot had changed since the feeling of powerlessness overwhelmed the imam after the terrorist attack. Religious pluralism helped to lay the foundation for a community of belonging within ISAIAH, but it was pluralism paired with power that opened the door to a new path, one in which the mosque built "power within" through leadership and democracy training, and "power with" in collaboration with thousands of members of ISAIAH. Together, they influenced and co-created the organizations, systems, and policies affecting their communities in Minnesota. Opportunities to thrive were more abundant for their members, in part because ISAIAH harnessed the assets of a diverse community and engaged in productive tension to counter the forces that sought to silence, oppress, or simply ignore them. As I listened to their story from the imam, I felt an energy, a power, an unwavering confidence that made me realize that, perhaps, the perpetrator had failed. It was a new story, one of belonging, power, and thriving.

20

A Case for Faith-Integrated Philanthropy

Farhan Latif and Catherine Orsborn

A few years ago, on a trip to Saudi Arabia, I was looking for dates to gift my friends and family.[1] A friend took me to a lush, expansive date farm outside of Madinah. Traditions maintain that the date farm was born out of a well, dating back to the time of the Prophet Muhammad (may peace and blessings be upon him), and was a beautiful example of Muslim philanthropy. For fourteen hundred years, this well and date farm were entrusted from generation to generation to be of benefit to communities over time. A small gift of land, a well, and date palms survived and thrived to produce the dates I purchased, while the proceeds were further distributed to feed the poor. This example illustrates how I think about philanthropy: investments that bear fruit for generations.

Faith plays an important role in my own motivation and in the way we approach philanthropy at the El-Hibri Foundation (EHF), where I serve as president. In this chapter I argue that by engaging faith-inspired institutions in an intentional and integrated way, philanthropies will see greater impact when it comes to advancing inclusion and creating social change. By drawing upon the experiences and learnings of a philanthropy inspired by Muslim values, I demonstrate some of the outcomes and best practices to guide this engagement and to advance the mutually beneficial relationship between faith inspired institutions and philanthropy for the long haul.

Engaging Religion: What's the Benefit?

While this volume as a whole speaks to the question in much greater depth, it is worth making a few points at the start of this chapter regarding the value proposition of engaging religion through philanthropy. One perspective is that the intricacies and challenges of engaging and supporting faith communities overcomplicate philanthropic giving, and therefore it is simpler to not engage at

[1] This chapter was written from the first-person perspective of Farhan Latif and was co-written with Dr. Catherine Orsborn. Additional research and support were provided by Brie Loskota and Patrick Cates.

Farhan Latif and Catherine Orsborn, *A Case for Faith-Integrated Philanthropy* In: *Modeling Religious Pluralism*. Edited by: Simran Jeet Singh, Oxford University Press. © Oxford University Press 2026.
DOI: 10.1093/oso/9780197745809.003.0020

all, to avoid the potential pitfalls. As Allison K. Ralph articulates in "But What if They Preach?" there are numerous reasons funders choose to avoid religion, including concerns regarding constitutionality, proselytizing, and the potential of social stances that differ from that of the funder.[2] These concerns should not be dismissed. At the same time, what we would lose in the social change sector by not engaging religion makes the labor of navigating these concerns worthwhile.

As Scott Appleby has argued, religion itself is "ambivalent."[3] In short, it can be utilized to cause harm or to advance good. My argument here is not that faith-inspired institutions are inherently good, but that philanthropy would benefit from intentional engagement of faith-inspired communities and institutions. Pew studies show that an overwhelming majority of the global population affiliates with a religious identity. Though religious affiliation may be declining in Europe and the United States, globally it remains strong.[4] Given this reality, the question for philanthropy is not *whether* to engage religion, but *how*.

A 2021 report from the Bridgespan Group posits that faith-inspired nonprofits account for approximately one third of all nonprofits, and faith-inspired organizations comprise about 40 percent of overall social safety net spending.[5] Faith-inspired organizations have long been key players in both addressing issues of social change while also meeting the direct needs of communities within their reach. For minority communities in the United States, faith-inspired institutions play an especially important role, given essential factors such as trust and access.

During the height of the COVID-19 pandemic, for example, faith institutions were critical to meeting food and economic needs while also serving as testing and vaccine distribution centers across the country.[6] One could share many more examples of how faith-inspired organizations have made positive contributions to the social sector. A recent report from the World Economic Forum highlights

[2] Allison K. Ralph, "But What if They Preach? A Guide for Funding Faith-Inspired Grantees with Boundaries and Integrity," Aspen Institute Inclusive America Project, September 2021, https://www.aspeninstitute.org/wp-content/uploads/2025/05/What-if-they-Preach-Report.FINAL2_.pdf (accessed December 18, 2025).

[3] Scott Appleby, *The Ambivalence of the Sacred: Religion, Violence and Reconciliation* (New York: Rowman & Littlefield, 2000).

[4] Pew Research Project, "Key Findings from the Global Religious Futures Project," December 21, 2022, https://www.pewresearch.org/religion/2022/12/21/key-findings-from-the-global-religious-futures-project/ (accessed December 18, 2025).

[5] Jeri Eckhart Queenan, Peter Grunert, and Devin Murphy, "Elevating the Role of Faith-Inspired Impact in the Social Sector," Bridgespan Group, 2021, 9, https://www.bridgespan.org/insights/role-of-faith-inspired-impact-in-the-social-sector (accessed December 17, 2025).

[6] Uzma Syed, Olivia Kapera, Aparajita Chandrasekhar, et al., "The Role of Faith-Based Organizations in Improving Vaccination Confidence & Addressing Vaccination Disparities to Help Improve Vaccine Uptake: A Systemic Review," *Vaccines* 11, no. 2 (2023): 449, https://doi.org/10.3390/vaccines11020449.

a number of these contributions, which would have been missed if faith-inspired institutions had been sidelined.[7]

Through the Lens of a Philanthropy Inspired by Muslim Values: A Unique Perspective

EHF is a case study in the benefits and lessons from the intentional engagement of faith-inspired institutions and philanthropy. EHF is a funder and also receives co-investment funding from larger philanthropies, so we approach the topic as both a funder and a grantee to offer a unique perspective on the ways in which faith and philanthropy can interact to better serve society.

EHF was founded by Ibrahim El-Hibri, a Muslim man of Lebanese descent, and his wife Elisabeth, a Catholic woman of German descent. They made their way from Germany to the United States in 1979 and found success in the private sector, running purpose-driven companies that improved and saved lives via medical and technological advancements. The El-Hibri family established an endowment for the foundation in 2001 and hoped to help create a space for Muslim belonging in the United States. At the same time, they committed to contributing to the good of society as a whole through engagement across lines of difference. EHF's story was inspired by their experience of providing safe haven to Jewish families during the Holocaust, and later living through war in Lebanon. The work that the foundation does today has been shaped by a rootedness in a socially active understanding of faith.

For me, the question of how faith and philanthropy interact is deeply personal. The way I think about philanthropy is grounded in love for humanity and the impact of one's work in perpetuity. In Islam, there are three things that are said to bring benefit to the deceased. One is that your children pray for you. Another is the education you provided to others. And a third is the impact you leave behind through philanthropy. Giving in perpetuity is a long-standing tradition within the Islamic faith, and the roots of philanthropic giving have deep connections to other faith traditions and teachings.

I grew up living in Muslim-majority cities of Karachi, Dubai, and Doha, as well as in cities where I was a religious minority. When I ultimately decided to attend college in the United States, I found myself one day watching a group of Muslim students being removed from the university library for trying to offer their sunset prayer in a tiny corner in the back of the library. This prompted

[7] World Economic Forum Global Agenda, "The Role of Faith in Systemic Global Challenges," June 2016, https://www3.weforum.org/docs/WEF_GAC16_Role_of_Faith_in_Systemic_Global_Challenges.pdf (accessed December 17, 2025).

me to start a club on campus, as advised by the administration, and I became the president of the Muslim Student Association. My first day as president was September 11, 2001.

As I watched in horror and grief, mourning the three thousand innocent lives lost, I did not realize the backlash that was set in motion. The next day, a philosophy professor pushed a Muslim student down the steps and flushed a copy of the Quran in the toilet. My aunt, who was walking to work that morning, was called the N-word, and told to go back where she came from, because she was wearing a headscarf. At school, people threw beer bottles on my car. And on a national level, we could see an uptick in hate crimes, mosques being burnt, and innocent brown people being attacked, like the Sikh man who was shot because he was wearing a turban. Life became exceptionally hard for Black Muslim communities who at times became a double or triple minority, subjected to racism and Islamophobia.

It was also during this time that I was physically attacked outside my apartment, beaten down and almost run over by a vehicle. I am fortunate to have survived an attack by religious extremists. Having received death threats and intimidation tactics, and finally being physically assaulted, I have experienced firsthand how religion can be misused to inflict pain and suffering. But my lived experience tells a different story of how faith can play an incredibly positive role in people's lives and in society. This was a difficult time for me, and simultaneously, it was a time when I experienced tremendous allyship from other faith communities—Jewish, Christian, and people of no faith—who became fearless allies and helped stand up for and partner with our communities.

I share my own story in these paragraphs because I believe it is important to articulate where I am coming from, how I think about philanthropy, and what motivates me. These experiences drove me to undertake social change work, which is deeply grounded in my own faith teachings and practices, and eventually led me to lead a philanthropy that also infuses faith values to funding social transformation.

The US Philanthropic Landscape: Challenges and Opportunities

EHF has strategically dedicated a portion of our funding toward faith-inspired nonprofits, with a focus on Muslim-led organizations and ally organizations that are doing work directly impacting American Muslim communities. By looking at the current state of philanthropic affairs from our unique vantage point as a philanthropy inspired by Muslim values, we can shed light on the paradoxes that emerge in the current landscape, and the opportunities for a more thoughtful and productive relationship between philanthropy and faith communities.

The experience of Muslim-inspired institutions is unique within the broader landscape of religious institutions. This has, in part, to do with the ways in which Muslim identity has been politicized and racialized in the United States. While corporate philanthropy tends to eschew religion, looking at religion as risky business, institutional philanthropy has been more willing to consider faith-inspired organizations in their giving portfolios, although there has been a trend in foundations shedding their faith portfolios altogether. When they do fund faith-inspired organizations, institutional philanthropy often situates religion within particular silos, with some philanthropies approaching religion through the lens of religious freedom, and others treating Muslim communities in particular as a racial, rather than religious, category.

One subset of foundations has emphasized the issue of religious freedom and its connection to individual freedom of expression. This area of giving, outside of the most extreme wings of far-right activism, generally includes Muslim religious freedom under this umbrella, seeking to enable Muslims to have free exercise of their own sincerely held religious beliefs.

At times, however, these funders—while comfortable with the broad category of religion—have difficulty with the particulars of Islam and, in some cases, with Muslims. There are notable examples where Islam is treated not as a religion but as a political ideology, and Muslims as members of diverse racial backgrounds, as detailed by Asma Uddin in "When Islam Is Not a Religion."[8] It is also important to note that funding for Islamophobia has also occurred through anti-Muslim groups who have backed attacks on Muslim communities.[9] This has created a wariness from Muslim nonprofits in seeking funding from socially conservative philanthropies, and there are also concerns among Muslims about co-optation for conservative aims.

Another subset of foundations, generally operating within a socially progressive framework, has been historically more amenable to including Muslims in their conversations and as grantees. However, they often treat Muslims as a racialized category, rather than a religious one. The racialization of Muslims is a real issue with data to support this construction.[10] However, it is incomplete and sometimes confusing, especially for Muslim Americans. While these funders do

[8] Asma T. Uddin, *When Islam Is Not a Religion: Inside America's Fight for Religious Freedom* (New York: Pegasus Books, 2019).

[9] For context and specific examples of anti-Muslim groups funding Islamophobia, see Matthew Duss, Yasmine Taeb, and Ken Gude, *Fear Inc., 2.0*, Center for American Progress, February 2015, https://www.americanprogress.org/article/fear-inc-2-0/ (accessed December 17, 2025).

[10] See, for example, Sahar Aziz, *The Racial Muslim: When Racism Quashes Religious Freedom* (Oakland: University of California Press, 2021).

understand the racialization of Muslim communities, they do not fully grasp the uniqueness of the religious particularities of Muslims.

Both approaches are limiting, creating identity silos for American Muslims and operating with major blind spots when it comes to a holistic view of American Muslim identities. When Muslim identity is seen only through either a faith lens or a racial lens, philanthropies are missing out on a more holistic approach to social transformation. For Muslims in the United States, religion is a cross-cutting identity that cannot be neatly fit into a box of faith or of race.[11]

All philanthropy is undergoing upheaval at present, causing reflection that perhaps the silos and verticals into which giving has been streamlined in the past are not the best fit for the present moment and into the future. It is simpler, in the complex and ever-changing world that we live in, to put projects and people into particular work streams and verticals. However, for many communities, issues are cross-cutting and cannot be fit into a particular silo. For example, there isn't just "Muslim" work and there isn't just environmental work. What is missing from the current philanthropic approach is a way to integrate the issues of real people and real communities that crosscut philanthropic portfolios and strategies. The current conversation among foundations involves becoming more grantee-centric, owning past mistakes, leaning into experimentation, and trying to create a future that is broader and creates more space for cross-cutting identities. This is where the experience of EHF can be illustrative.

A path forward on faith and philanthropy must see a religious community's identity as integrated and as a cross-cutting category of being and belonging. It is not only about faith, though faith is an aspect. And it is not only about race or a sociological category of being, though that is an aspect as well. By seeing faith communities through a lens of multifaceted identity, the philanthropic sector can engage faith-inspired organizations and communities in a more holistic and impactful way.

What Is a Different Way? A Faith-Engaged Lens on Philanthropy

In the remainder of this chapter, I will offer the experience of EHF as a faith-engaged lens on philanthropy, integrating the cross-cutting experience of American Muslim communities in particular into a funding strategy. I am

[11] It is worth noting here that the American Muslim community is highly diverse when it comes to race and ethnicity, with no single racial or ethnic group as a majority. See Pew Research Center, "U.S. Muslims Concerned about Their Place in Society, but Continue to Believe in the American Dream," July 26, 2017, https://www.pewresearch.org/religion/2017/07/26/demographic-portrait-of-muslim-americans/ (accessed December 17, 2025).

arguing for a shift from looking at religion as a theoretical category of identity, which is easily siloed, to religion as a lived identity,[12] which provides a more integrated and holistic lens on how philanthropy can interact with religion.

I want to clarify two frames I will be referencing here. The first frame is a sociological one—faith is a lived experience, not solely theoretical, and the experience of faith communities is embedded in the everyday lives and sociopolitical realities of individuals and groups. The second is the values frame when we are talking about faith-inspired work. No one approaches social change work from a value-neutral position, though at times, secular paradigms are treated as neutral by default. Whether an individual or a nonprofit organization is approaching their work from a faith lens or a secular one, each is infusing values and deeply held beliefs into the work that they are doing. From this perspective, faith communities should not be treated as "other" within the nonprofit landscape, but rather as bringing one among many sets of values into the work.

These two frames—of values and of lived religion—are woven together in how we think about and approach the role of faith in philanthropy.

Today, our work at EHF is focused on investing in cross-sector leaders and institutions that are advancing inclusion and working for the common good, with a special focus on faith communities. Muslims are 1–2 percent of the country; thus, the community's survival is predicated on the guarantees of the US Constitution, under which the free exercise of religion is protected. There are resonance and coherence with Muslim values and American foundational documents.

Our investments focus on both Muslim and ally organizations that seek to advance the well-being and inclusion of American Muslims in the larger social fabric of the United States. We also provide our grantees and partners with capacity-building training and coaching, some of which is focused on technical skills and some of which is focused on a holistic sense of leadership development.

In both our grantmaking and programmatic work, EHF works with a diversity of partners across the United States. For example, the Inner-City Muslim Action Network (IMAN) has built a holistic approach to community development focused on health, wellness, and healing, rooted in Islamic values while offering services and organizing communities well beyond those that identify as Muslim. Emgage cultivates Muslim civic engagement nationwide and advocates on policies that impact American Muslim communities and their neighbors. And the Shoulder to Shoulder Campaign mobilizes faith allies to work alongside Muslim communities in addressing Islamophobia. These are just a few of our diverse grantees, dealing with issues from political engagement to health

[12] For further reading on the concept of lived religion, see David Hall, *Lived Religion in America: Toward a History of Practice* (Princeton, NJ: Princeton University Press, 1998).

and wellness to social cohesion work. Each of these organizations exemplifies the way trust and access to faith communities (realities of lived religion) and a values-oriented framework have combined to create critical impact across multiple sectors. A large portion of our grantees are faith-inspired and are working across a variety of sectors and issue areas.

During the height of the pandemic, EHF added an entire funding stream on responding to the multiple challenges communities were experiencing with COVID-19. This provided my team and me the opportunity to visit our grantees working on the fallout from COVID-19. During this time, I remember visiting the ADAMS Center, the largest mosque in the Washington, DC, area, and instead of the usual sight of people praying, I saw healthcare providers serving people of all faiths and backgrounds as a community-based vaccine distribution site. I knew that this was happening not only at mosques but also at synagogues, churches, gurdwaras, and temples in big cities and across rural areas.

What was clear was that, throughout the COVID-19 pandemic, faith-inspired communities all over the country used their social capital to build trust around the vaccine and help to dispel myths. They also addressed food and economic insecurity, supporting those in need regardless of faith or background. They turned houses of worship into food pantries and COVID testing and vaccination sites. While it is hard to tell a story of all faith communities, it is important to stress that for so many congregations this was the story of their faith community. Once again, it is important to note the Bridgespan statistics, showing that faith communities provide 40 percent of social safety net spending in the United States. This was apparent in the COVID-19 pandemic.

EHF approaches giving through a values frame that is informed by faith. This is not a new idea. In truth, much philanthropy was initially given out of an expression of individuals' own values, tied to their religious beliefs, and done out of a desire to see good carried out in the world. Philanthropy has been intimately tied with individuals' faith commitments from the beginning.

One component of EHF's faith-engaged philanthropy is optimism and hope regarding the possibilities of change. Religious communities believe in the possibility of transformation grounded in a deep understanding of the barriers that maintain the status quo in the world as it currently exists. This faith-rooted lens guides us as we look to call attention to the wrongs of the world and to maintain hope as we work to correct them. There is no room for despair, and there is a general acceptance of the idea that we will not see perfection within our lifetimes. In fact, we cannot be certain we know what perfection looks like. The struggle is to improve the world and to prevent harm while knowing that imperfection is also the nature of life.

Another component of EHF's faith-engaged philanthropy is to grapple with difference in a way that is meaningful rather than something to be erased or flattened. Diversity of identity and belonging, including that of both thought and action, is divinely ordained from an Islamic perspective. Current trends in polarization seek to solidify stark lines between political camps with highly policed boundaries that are reinforced by ongoing purification of rhetoric. This may be a useful political tool for those squarely within a camp, but it creates deeper divides, limiting the ability to build bridges or foster cooperation. A faith-engaged approach to philanthropy sees difference as an opportunity for exploration and to deepen our own understanding. For pluralism to flourish, it requires investing in spaces where difference can productively be engaged. As Brie Loskota has said, "[P]luralism is what happens when diversity builds relationships."[13]

All of this is grounded in an ethic of humility. Ultimately the call of faith-engaged philanthropy is to remember that human beings are limited. We are not responsible for seeing through every outcome, but rather, planting and watering the seeds within our ability while we are here on earth.

By drawing upon faith values ourselves, and by working with faith-inspired nonprofit organizations that are working across issues and sectors, we have seen incredible results. Faith-engaged philanthropy has breakthroughs to offer, as I have seen through our work at EHF over the years. When we intentionally and thoughtfully engage faith communities, we will see continued progress related to race, polarization, and fragmentation, as well as on other pressing issues of collective concern, such as health, climate change, immigration and forced migration, food insecurity, and beyond. We need all hands on deck. If we leave faith communities off the table due to uncertainty or fear, we will lose out on the good these communities can offer.

Recommendations

As the field of philanthropy moves forward in conversations around engaging and funding faith-inspired institutions, I have three primary recommendations based upon the experience of EHF.

First, rather than dissolving faith portfolios, philanthropies should integrate faith as a cross-cutting factor across portfolios of work. Siloing faith to its own portfolio shortchanges what faith has to offer, and by intentionally integrating it across issue areas in a way that is similar to how other core values such as representation, fairness, and broad participation, are often treated as cross-cutting considerations, philanthropies can benefit from the unique approaches and

[13] Ruhee Jaffer, "Los Angeles Holds 4th Annual Day of Religious Pluralism," *The Ismaili*, May 28, 2019, https://the.ismaili/usa/los-angeles-holds-4th-annual-day-religious-pluralism (accessed December 17, 2025).

community embeddedness of faith-inspired organizations as key stakeholders when it comes to social change.

Second, engage faith actors in setting the table on various issue areas of funding, rather than adding them as an afterthought onto a pre-formed framework. Deeply engaging faith communities in creating the frameworks in the first place will allow for frameworks that include faith perspectives and lived experiences in a more integrated, cross-cutting way. Faith communities should be part of designing philanthropic and social change—not privileged beyond other voices, but given equal weight in bringing their perspectives and experiences into the conversation and design, as part of philanthropy's broader commitment to ensuring that a wide range of perspectives and lived experiences meaningfully shape its work. For example, if philanthropy convenes on climate change and brings together various stakeholders, do not omit the faith actors in those early-stage conversations, given the trust, access, and unique perspectives and experiences these actors bring to the table on a multitude of issues.

Finally, one thing I have learned throughout my work in this space is that we figure out how to navigate complexity when we feel it is important to do so. I am certainly not advocating for funding any and all faith-inspired work, as it is necessary to apply rigorous assessments in making funding decisions no matter the nature of the organization under consideration. But my recommendation to fellow funders and social change practitioners is to lean into the complexity that often comes along with engaging faith-inspired organizations. The payoffs are worth the investment.

21

Let's Talk about It

Philanthropy-Serving Organizations' Role in Promoting Pluralism

Allison K. Ralph

Philanthropy is squeamish about religion. Most of the largest private and public grantmakers, even those that are or were historically faith-inspired, avoid religion or publicly minimize its influence. Philanthropy-serving organizations (PSOs) tend to avoid religion as well. These convenors reflect the avoidance from member grantmakers, keeping religion off conference agendas. This effectively solidifies a widespread tendency to treat religion as a taboo—a social norm that amounts to a prohibition.

Avoiding religion is deeply problematic. Philanthropic institutions cannot hope to meet their strategic goals if they cannot attend to the myriad ways that religion infuses human society.

This volume is dedicated to showing and promoting what positive religious pluralism could look like and how to achieve it. The work of racial justice, religious freedom, dismantling faith-based hate, and other aspects of religious pluralism relies primarily on the nonprofit sector as well. Religious pluralism therefore lies also on the shoulders of the philanthropic sector that supports it.

Religions and religious communities play a role in shaping current social ills and discontents on global, national, and local levels. Just to name a few: Climate change, polarization, racism, and anti-democratic sentiment all are influenced by religion in some way. White Christian Nationalism ties up the last two of these together, attacking fundamental processes of democracy like voting access in order to reinforce racist hierarchies.[1] The extraordinary success of the Religious Right has sparked oppositional social movements like Moral Mondays. As an effect, polarization levels rise.[2] Climate change politics are deeply linked to

[1] Andrew L. Whitehead and Samuel L. Perry, *Taking America Back for God: Christian Nationalism in the United States* (New York: Oxford University Press, 2020).

[2] Ruth Braunstein, "A Theory of Political Backlash: Assessing the Religious Right's Effects on the Religious Field," *Sociology of Religion*, November 15, 2021, srab050, https://doi.org/10.1093/socrel/srab050.

Allison K. Ralph, *Let's Talk about It* In: *Modeling Religious Pluralism*. Edited by: Simran Jeet Singh, Oxford University Press. © Oxford University Press 2026. DOI: 10.1093/oso/9780197745809.003.0021

similar religio-political alignments.[3] Interreligious conflict deepens geopolitical disputes in India, Israel, and Myanmar.

Religious communities also work powerfully together to find solutions to those ills. Organizations like the Center for Christianity and Public Life help committed Christians bring traditions of discipleship, that is, trying to behave as Christ would have done, into the public sphere by modeling humility and service.[4] Other nonprofits, like Interfaith Power & Light, work to unite many diverse faith communities together to address the climate crisis.[5] Some multifaith organizations explicitly build relationships to reduce polarization.[6] Moreover, religious ways of believing, behaving, or belonging are deeply meaningful to most people that grantmakers want to help. Up to 40 percent of the nonprofit sector is faith inspired—going far beyond houses of worship to include both grantmakers and grantees doing secular work.[7]

Given this landscape, how can grantmakers expect to make any headway on issues that are deeply shaped by religion without acknowledging religion? Institutional grantmakers' avoidance of religion seems almost incomprehensible.

Almost incomprehensible, but not quite. Religion is a fraught subject, a minefield of personal and collective hurts. It can be difficult enough to navigate that subject on an interpersonal level, and there are historical reasons why professional philanthropy feels the need to avoid religion.

But, philanthropic culture has made similar shifts to address important issues before and can do so again. Our national and philanthropic conversation about race has shifted from an emphasis on "colorblindness" in the 1990s to an emphasis on understanding and addressing how race shapes our society and affects us personally.[8] Race and racially inflected social realities are not going

[3] "Bible Demands Action on Climate Change, Evangelicals Say in New Report," *Washington Post*, August 30, 2022, https://www.washingtonpost.com/religion/2022/08/30/evangelicals-climate-change-bible/ (accessed December 19, 2025).

[4] The Center for Christianity & Public Life, "The Center for Christianity & Public Life," https://www.ccpubliclife.org (accessed October 13, 2023).

[5] Interfaith Power & Light, "About," September 9, 2021, https://interfaithpowerandlight.org/about/ (accessed December 19, 2025).

[6] See, for example, Interfaith America, "Interfaith America," https://www.interfaithamerica.org (accessed October 13, 2023); and Sisterhood of Salaam Shalom, "Sisterhood of Salaam Shalom," https://sosspeace.org (accessed June 29, 2025).

[7] Jeri Eckhart Queenan, Peter Grunert, and Devin Murphy, "Elevating the Role of Faith-Inspired Impact in the Social Sector," Bridgespan Group, January 2021, https://www.bridgespan.org/insights/library/philanthropy/role-of-faith-inspired-impact-in-the-social-sector (accessed December 19, 2025); and Brad R. Fulton, "Religious Organizations: Crosscutting the Nonprofit Sector," in *The Nonprofit Sector: A Research Handbook*, 3rd ed., edited by Walter W. Powell and Patricia Bromley (Stanford, CA: Stanford University Press, 2020), 579–597.

[8] Cheryl Dorsey, Jeff Bradach, and Peter Kim, "The Problem with 'Color-Blind' Philanthropy," *Harvard Business Review*, June 5, 2020, https://hbr.org/2020/06/the-problem-with-color-blind-philanthropy (accessed December 19, 2025); and Malkia Devich Cyril, Lyle Matthew Kan, Ben Francisco Maulbeck, and Lori Villarosa, "Mismatched: Philanthropy's Response to the Call for Racial Justice," Philanthropic Initiative for Racial Equity, 2020, https://racialequity.org/mismatched/ (accessed December 19, 2025).

to disappear if we ignore them. Religion and religiously inflected social realities won't disappear either.

There are real consequences if the field of philanthropy cannot adjust to address religion in its work. PSOs have a particular, powerful role to play. Let me give a real example.

In 2022, I came across a PSO for a medium-sized, religiously diverse metropolitan area that is regularly affected by antisemitism. I was chatting amiably with a staff member about how religion intersects with institutional philanthropy, gauging interest in further conversation. They told me their PSO did not generally include religion in their thinking about strategy, membership, or programming, noting simply, "It just didn't come up."

As we chatted about why it should, the staff member recalled that one local Jewish family foundation only participates in their member programming through a consultant. They shared that the funder bars the consultant from mentioning their foundation. I asked why. The answer was that the funder is *afraid of being seen as a Jew with money and being attacked.*[9] That admission took my breath away.

Without any intent at all, the avoidance of religion by a PSO effectively excluded a Jewish funder in the very moment when hate crimes against Jews are on the rise across the country; and in that community, when Jewish voices and presence are most needed; and when Jews most need connection and partnership. The staff at the PSO had not thought about it before. Their oversight was not intentional, but it did have an effect. I suspect similar exclusions of religious people and faith-inspired organizations occur across the field.

These kinds of damaging exclusions are inevitable when we avoid religion. But there is also a flip side to the coin, positives that can come if funders and the PSOs who serve them can learn to attend to where religion already exists within and influences their portfolios.

PSOs, as convenors of funders and powerful curators of conversations, have an opportunity to break the taboo on religion, allow space for learning and curiosity, and help grantmakers find the tools and resources they need to navigate a religiously infused world. This is not an exhortation for philanthropy to promote religion, religious ideas, religious people, or religious institutions. This is not an exhortation for philanthropy to change its strategic goals. This is an exhortation for philanthropy to move thoughtfully in a religiously infused world.

After a definitional exercise, I will explore more deeply:

- Why philanthropy is squeamish about religion
- Why religion is already in philanthropic portfolios
- Where religion already exists in the philanthropic sector

9 Allison K. Ralph, personal communication with regional PSO, September 5, 2021.

- The opportunity for PSOs
- Resources to begin the work
- Finally: a caution

What Are "Philanthropy" and "Religion"?

Both philanthropy and religion can mean different things to different people.

In this chapter I am discussing institutional philanthropy rather than individual charity, that is, public or private nonprofit organizations that give grants.[10] There are many types of grantmakers, ranging from corporate and private foundations to public charities that both receive and give grants. Some grantmakers have hundreds of staff, while others rely only on volunteer time. I will use the terms funder, grantmaker, and foundation interchangeably.

For the sticky subject of "religion," I am building on the definition developed by Benjamin Marcus: Religion is "not only what religious communities and individuals believe but also how they act (behaviors) and create community (belonging)."[11] Because this chapter addresses how philanthropy avoids all discussion of religion's social effects, I am also referring to how religion influences wider society via its influence on individuals (e.g., positions on policy issues, levels of toleration of difference, or participation in various social movements). Third, with the terms "faith-based" or "faith-inspired," I am referring to organizations whose religious values shape their organizational identity.[12] I will generally use the term "faith-inspired" as it includes organizations with strong or mild effects of religious identity on organizational culture.[13]

Religion Is Already in Philanthropic Portfolios

Religion is already in philanthropic portfolios via the three realities mentioned above: people themselves, religious influence on society, and faith-inspired nonprofits. This is true regardless of whether grantmakers have given religion explicit attention.

[10] Allison K. Ralph, Brad R. Fulton, and Samuel Allen, "Faith-Based Public Foundations: Identifying the Field and Assessing Its Impact," *The Foundation Review* 14, no. 1 (March 1, 2022): https://doi.org/10.9707/1944-5660.1600. I am not discussing Donor Advised Funds (DAFs) in this chapter.

[11] "Six Guidelines for Teaching about Religion," *Education Week*, April 4, 2016, https://www.edweek.org/education/opinion-six-guidelines-for-teaching-about-religion/2016/04 (accessed June 29, 2025).

[12] Robert Ressler, Brad R. Fulton, and Pamela Paxton, "Activity and Identity: Uncovering Multiple Institutional Logics in the Nonprofit Sector" (paper presented at the Association for Research on Nonprofit Organizations and Voluntary Action annual meeting, virtual, 2020).

[13] Eckhart Queenan, Grunert, and Murphy, "Elevating the Role of Faith-Inspired Impact in the Social Sector."

First, target beneficiaries of philanthropic strategies may be highly religious. People in communities of color, Indigenous peoples, rural communities, and some communities of immigrants and refugees are more likely to be religious than other populations.[14] To support those communities, grantmakers must understand their experiences as inflected by religion and its intersections with race, ethnicity, and socioeconomic and immigration status.

Second, the past and present influence of religious values, movements, communities, and organizations on every aspect of American society is immense. Even as membership in religious communities is declining overall, some now-minority religious communities are growing rapidly; for example, both Muslim and Catholic affiliation is on the rise.[15] Some religious communities exert an influence stronger than their numbers alone through their civic engagement activities.[16] Some of this influence strengthens our social bonds—some weakens our social bonds.

Third, faith-inspired grantees already exist. They are doing the work and doing it well. The nonprofit sector itself is about 35–40 percent religious or faith-inspired organizations. This includes more than 350,000 houses of worship,[17] and about 228,000 faith-inspired organizations doing something other than

[14] Ninety-one percent of Black and 84 percent of Latino Americans told Pew Research in 2014 that religion is important in their lives, significantly more than the 75 percent of White respondents. Pew Research Center's Religion & Public Life Project, "Religious Landscape Study," https://www.pewresearch.org/religion/religious-landscape-study/ (accessed May 22, 2023). Although both urban and rural areas are three quarters or more religious, urban areas are more religiously diverse, but slightly less religious overall, than rural areas. See Arin Pinkus, "Religious Stereotypes vs. Reality in Urban, Suburban, and Rural America," American Communities Project, April 15, 2022, https://www.americancommunities.org/religious-stereotypes-vs-reality-in-urban-suburban-and-rural-america/ (accessed December 19, 2025). The Institute for Social Policy and Understanding (ISPU) reports that American Muslims say their faith is very important to them in higher numbers than any group but Evangelicals. ISPU, "American Muslim Poll 2022: A Politics and Pandemic Status Report," https://www.ispu.org/american-muslim-poll-2022-1/ (accessed May 22, 2023).

[15] Americans are undoubtedly leaving religion; see "The Fastest Growing US Religious Affiliation? 'None,' Poll Says," *The Hill*, https://thehill.com/homenews/state-watch/585764-the-fastest-growing-us-religious-affiliation-none-poll-says/ (accessed May 23, 2023). At the same time, numbers of Catholics and Muslims are on the rise in the United States. See A.J. Willingham, "By 2040, Islam Could Be the Second-Largest Religion in the US | CNN Politics," CNN, January 10, 2018, https://www.cnn.com/2018/01/10/politics/muslim-population-growth-second-religious-group-trnd/index.html (accessed December 19, 2025); and Catholic News Agency, "U.S. Catholic Population Shows Growth, Especially in the South," https://www.catholicnewsagency.com/news/252998/us-catholic-population-shows-growth-trends-southward (accessed May 23, 2023).

[16] Public Religion Research Institute (PRRI) Staff, "A Christian Nation? Understanding the Threat of Christian Nationalism to American Democracy and Culture," *PRRI* (blog), February 28, 2023, https://www.prri.org/research/a-christian-nation-understanding-the-threat-of-christian-nationalism-to-american-democracy-and-culture/ (accessed December 19, 2025); Philip Bump, "Analysis | A New Lens into the Overlap of Religion and Right-Wing Politics," *Washington Post*, February 8, 2023, https://www.washingtonpost.com/politics/2023/02/08/religion-christian-right-wing-politics/ (accessed December 19, 2025); and Ruth Braunstein, *Prophets and Patriots: Faith in Democracy across the Political Divide* (Berkeley: University of California Press, 2017).

[17] Clifford A. Grammich, Erica Dollhopf, Mary Gautier, et al., "U.S. Religion Census—Religious Congregations and Membership Study, 2020 (County File)," OSF, 2023, https://doi.org/10.17605/OSF.IO/ET2A5.

worship.[18] The latter grouping includes your local YMCA, rooted in Christian history and values but open to all comers; Dancing Earth Creations, a contemporary dance studio celebrating Indigenous-inspired modern dance; and the award-winning Inner-City Muslim Action Network (IMAN) that provides social services and advocates for more resources in the communities they serve.[19] Faith-inspired organizations have been shown to be just as professional as, and often better resourced than, their secular counterparts. There are faith-inspired organizations in every major category of the National Taxonomy of Exempt Entities, from a small percentage in arts and environment to a large portion of health and human services.[20] The 2021 report from Bridgespan, "Elevating the Role of Faith-Inspired Impact in the Social Sector," speaks to the prevalence of faith-inspired organizations in this sector, highlighting that faith-inspired organizations make up about 40 percent of safety net service providers in many cities.[21]

Indeed, in cases where target beneficiaries are highly religious, those communities may best be served by faith-inspired organizations that are more trusted and more culturally competent than secular organizations that are external to those communities.[22] When philanthropic organizations attempt to work across these lines without doing some cultural competency learning of their own, lines of communication can break down and grant processes can be disrupted. The end result is that the people whom philanthropy is trying to serve are hurt and organizational goals are unmet.[23]

Where Religion Already Exists in the Philanthropic Sector

Faith-inspired grantmakers exist across the philanthropic sector as well. Twenty percent of all active American grantmakers are faith inspired.[24] Among private

[18] Ressler, Fulton, and Paxton, "Activity and Identity."

[19] YMCA, "YMCA," https://www.ymca.org (accessed June 29, 2025); Dancing Earth Creations, "Dancing Earth Creations," https://www.dancingearth.org (accessed June 29, 2025); and John D. and Catherine T. MacArthur Foundation, "Rami Nashashibi," October 11, 2017, https://www.macfound.org/fellows/class-of-2017/rami-nashashibi (accessed December 19, 2025)

[20] Ressler, Fulton, and Paxton, "Activity and Identity."

[21] Eckhart Queenan, Grunert, and Murphy, "Elevating the Role of Faith-Inspired Impact in the Social Sector."

[22] Ibid.; and Brie Loskota, "Bridging Religious Divides: Understanding the Influence of Faith and Religion on Social Strength and Civic Engagement" (paper presented at the Council on Foundations annual meeting, Miami, FL, May 1, 2019).

[23] Allison K. Ralph, "But What if They Preach? A Guide for Funding Faith-Inspired Grantees with Boundaries and Integrity," August (Washington, DC: Aspen Institute, 2021).

[24] Brad R. Fulton and Allison K. Ralph, "Faith-Based Private Foundations: Identifying the Field and Assessing Its Impact" (paper presented at the Association for Research on Nonprofit and Voluntary Action annual meeting, Raleigh, NC, 2022).

foundations, that number rises to 28 percent. In a field where "religion" is a taboo subject, the number of faith-inspired grantmakers and organizations is surprisingly large. For PSOs, especially those focusing on people, localities, or issues that are highly influenced by religion, we might expect 20 percent or more of members to have a faith identity themselves. However, new research performed by students at Indiana University under the direction of Brad Fulton shows that PSOs that are not specifically religious have between 2 and 10 percent faith-inspired grantmakers among their members.[25] One wonders how many faith-inspired grantmakers have felt unwelcome in such spaces, like the Jewish funder who hid their identity for fear of overt antisemitism.

In addition to grantmaking organizations that hold a faith identity, staff and boards of grantmakers are just as likely to have a religious identity. Internal cultures of strict secularism quash people's ability to bring their whole selves to work openly. That has a number of effects. As Reverend Jennifer Bailey says, "[F]aith is already in the room," and people's religious orientation, and/or their distrust of other people's religious orientation, affects grantmaking and partnership decisions.

Strict secular cultures can also diminish the effectiveness of grantmaking programs that are intended to benefit minority communities. Here's an example. Some secular philanthropies have portfolios that are intended to support minoritized religious communities and have hired staff from those communities to run them. This is a great idea on its face. However, more than one such program officer told me they feel oppressed in their own workplace because the faith part of their identity is disallowed: Religious garb and acts are frowned on during the workday, and discussion of tenets of the faith relevant to the grantmaking work for the community get shut down. In other words, these philanthropic organizations are promoting the same oppression inwardly they intend to ameliorate outwardly.

Why Is Philanthropy Squeamish about Religion?

I see three main reasons why philanthropic organizations and philanthropic culture generally avoid religion.

1. The culture of institutional philanthropy in America developed alongside sweeping movements for organizational professionalization,

[25] "Faith in Philanthropy," Funder Groups, Indiana University O'Neill School of Public and Environmental Affairs, https://fip.oneill.indiana.edu/funder-groups/index.html (accessed March 4, 2026).

secularization, and modernization. These intertwined movements shunned anything overtly religious as backward and unprofessional. These are false dichotomies, but the assumption that to be religious is to be unprofessional is still common in the nonprofit sector.

2. Staff and board members have legitimate concerns about whether to engage faith-inspired organizations. They may also lack skills to talk about religion in diverse settings.
3. Religion and its effects on society are complex. Religious communities and leaders have played central roles in creating and healing our deepest personal and collective wounds. Religious communities are internally diverse. Moving thoughtfully takes work, and when staff are already burdened with heavy workloads, adding another dimension to the work seems impossible.

The first point here explains why a sense of disdain might animate secular organizations against religion. It does not excuse it. Avoiding religion altogether actively contributes to many of the problems funders are trying to solve. If philanthropic organizations are going to make headway on the issues they care about, they are almost certainly going to have to attend to religion in some way.

The second two points are real issues. It is very appropriate for staff and board members to think carefully about whether and how to engage with religious communities or faith-inspired organizations. I and others have written elsewhere about the legitimacy of these concerns.[26]

To be clear, I am not suggesting that funders should promote religion or religious ideas or communities. I am not arguing that every funder should focus on religion in their strategic plan. I do not suggest that funders should necessarily work with faith-inspired organizations despite values conflicts arising from religious difference. What I am arguing is that grantmakers should be able to assess how religion already intersects with their work, and what attention or partnerships are necessary to be effective. PSOs can help them develop the tools and skills to do this well.

The Opportunity for Philanthropy-Serving Organizations

PSOs exist to support their members in developing skills for grantmaking, content knowledge, and peer-to-peer relationships. PSOs also curate and moderate philanthropic culture in how they convene and what they talk about. Whatever

[26] Ralph, "But What if They Preach?"; Eckhart Queenan, Grunert, and Murphy, "Elevating the Role of Faith-Inspired Impact in the Social Sector"; and Ralph, Fulton, and Allen, "Faith-Based Public Foundations."

the grantmaking specialty (e.g., health, democracy, environment, a specific locality, diversity and belonging, racial equity, aging, immigration, disability, poverty, homelessness, or food insecurity), religious people, organizations, and movements have a part to play. Grantmakers need access to tools to help them attend to religion where it already exists in their portfolios. More than anything, grantmakers need the space to be able to learn—to ask open questions, learn how and when to partner with faith-inspired grantees, and see their target beneficiaries as people whose religion is important to them. PSOs have incredible power to create the space for this learning.

I recognize that I am asking a lot of PSOs. PSOs that avoid religion are reflecting their member grantmakers, members who pay in dues and who might *stop* paying if they feel content is unhelpful. PSOs themselves are often diverse communities, in which bringing up a notoriously personal, emotional, politics-laden subject may seem like a bad idea. Many staff and board members at PSOs may not feel equipped to open topics such as "religion and women's rights" or "religion, politics, and climate justice."

Resources

Luckily, there are some resources already that can help PSOs to better serve their members. The philanthropic field itself is diverse, and not all of these resources may be appropriate for specific PSOs. They are at least a place to start.

- The Aspen Institute Religion & Society program has created a set of starter resources on a variety of topics to support PSOs in developing helpful conference content.
- Philanthropy for Active Civic Engagement (PACE) is a PSO in its own right that spent four years running a learning community in this area (the Faith In/And Democracy Fund). It is now offering consulting to other PSOs and has a new how-to guide.[27]
- Twenty-eight percent of private foundations (the type of organization that makes up most PSO member rolls) are faith inspired. They may be able to help PSOs navigate open conversations at the intersection of philanthropic strategy and religion in society. Working groups or communities of practice may be good ways to open doors to a few of the most interested funders, and

[27] Philanthropy for Active Civic Engagement (PACE), "Faith In/And Democracy," https://www.pacefunders.org/faith/ (accessed June 29, 2025); and PACE, "A Funding Guide for Faith and Democracy," https://form.jotform.com/PACEproject/faithguide (accessed June 29, 2025).

test topics and discussion formats in small-group settings, before bringing them to the full community.

- Philanthropy and the Black Church project, cosponsored by the Center for the Church and the Black Experience at Garrett Seminary and the Lake Institute on Faith & Giving at Indiana University, aims to build a strong connection between the field of philanthropy and Black religious institutions, which are the center of social and civic power in Black America. For organizations interested in racial equity and justice, real partnership with Black religious institutions is a must.
- The Council on Foundations' Values-Aligned Philanthropy project is an excellent model for engaging members on a difficult topic and providing a set of tools and resources to help them find solutions. This project helps member funders learn the skills to discern for themselves how to set barriers around funding grantees that may be considered hate groups. This topic is deeply entwined with religion on both the subject of hate directed at or coming from faith groups and the subject of working with faith-inspired nonprofits.[28]
- One PSO, the Philanthropy Roundtable, has published a range of articles and tools addressing areas of connection between religion and its members' interests: on the social capital of faith communities, how philanthropy can reinforce existing religious nonprofit efforts, providing mental health resources to religious leaders who are de facto counselors, and other topics.[29]
- For basic resources on building partnerships with religious communities, see the Center for Religion and Civic Culture (CRCC) at the University of Southern California's "Tools" section of its website. The CRCC is renowned for its very practical tip sheets and tools.
- One caution for all PSOs and grantmakers: Philanthropic institutions that do not have a religious identity cannot and should never presume to dictate theology or doctrine to religious individuals or communities or to faith-inspired organizations. Acts like these will sour any relationship.

Conclusion

Religion affects everything around us, including our collective abilities to live with each other in a diverse, democratic society. To move strategically,

[28] Council on Foundations, "Values Aligned Philanthropy," https://cof.org/program-initiative/values-aligned-philanthropy (accessed December 19, 2025).

[29] A search of "faith" on their website reveals twenty pages of results as of today. Philanthropy Roundtable, search results for "Faith," https://www.philanthropyroundtable.org/search/faith (accessed June 29, 2025).

grantmakers need the skills and willingness to attend to where religion already intersects with their portfolios. PSOs have an incredible opportunity to cultivate these skills within their own diverse communities.

To do so would be to promote effective and equitable ways of contending in diverse and democratic societies. It would be to promote religious pluralism.

References

Aharoni, Leah. "Netflix's 'Unorthodox' Degrades Hasidic Jews into Caricatures." *The Jewish Journal*, April 7, 2020. https://jewishjournal.com/commentary/opinion/314712/netflixs-unorthodox-degrades-hasidic-jews-into-caricatures/.

Allport, Gordon W. *The Nature of Prejudice*. Reading, MA: Addison-Wesley, 1979.

Almasy, Steve, and Konstantin Toropin. "Oklahoma Man Found Guilty of Hate Crime in His Neighbor's Death." CNN, February 2, 2018. https://www.cnn.com/2018/02/07/us/oklahoma-stanley-vernon-majors-trial/index.htm.

Alsultany, Evelyn. *Arabs and Muslims in the Media: Race and Representation after 9/11*. New York: New York University Press, 2012.

Alsultany, Evelyn. "Arabs, Muslims, and Arab Americans: Constructing an Evil Other." In *The Routledge Companion to Media and Race*, edited by Christopher Campbell, 241–249. New York: Routledge, 2016.

Alsultany, Evelyn. "Challenging Stereotypes." In *How to Watch Television*, edited by Ethan Thompson and Jason Mittell, 91–98. New York: New York University Press, 2020.

Alsultany, Evelyn. "Representations of Arabs and Muslims in Post-9/11 Television Dramas." In *The Colorblind Screen*, edited by Sarah Nilsen and Sarah E. Turner, 140–166. New York: New York University Press, 2020.

American Academy of Religion. *AAR Guidelines for Teaching about Religion in K-12 Public Schools in the United States*, April. Atlanta, GA: American Academy of Religion, 2010.

American Academy of Religion. *AAR Religious Literacy Guidelines: What U.S. College Graduates Need to Understand about Religion*, September. Atlanta, GA: American Academy of Religion, 2019. https://aarweb.org/resource/aar-religious-literacy-guidelines-2/.

American Civil Liberties Union. "Sikh Religious Musicians Settle with US Airways after Wrongful Removal from Flight." 2009. https://www.aclu.org/press-releases/sikh-religious-musicians-settle-us-airways-after-wrongful-removal-flight.

American Civil Liberties Union. "Nationwide Anti-Mosque Activity." N.d. https://www.aclu.org/other/nationwide-anti-mosque-activity.

Anderson, Jeffrey E. *Conjure in African American Society*. Baton Rouge: Louisiana State University Press, 2005.

Andrus, Marc. *Brothers in the Beloved Community: The Friendship of Thich Nacht Hanh and Martin Luther King, Jr.* Berkeley, CA: Parallax Press, 2021.

Anti-Defamation League. "Joint Statement of Solidarity by Jewish Communal Organizations." April 1, 2020.

Anti-Defamation League. "Audit of Antisemitic Incidents: Ten-Year Review, 2015–2024." 2024. https://www.adl.org/resources/report/audit-antisemitic-incidents-2024.

Anti-Defamation League. "Who We Are." N.d. https://www.adl.org/who-we-are.

Appleby, R. Scott. "Essay." In *The Ambivalence of the Sacred: Religion, Violence, and Reconciliation*, 8. Lanham, MD: Rowman & Littlefield, 2000.

Araujo, Ana Lucia. *Humans in Shackles: An Atlantic History of Slavery*. Chicago: University of Chicago Press, 2024.

Arendt, Hannah. *The Human Condition*. Chicago: University of Chicago Press, 1958.

Asad, Talal. *Formations of the Secular: Christianity, Islam, Modernity*. Stanford, CA: Stanford University Press, 2003.

Asian American Christian Collaborative. "Statement on Anti-Asian Racism in the Time of Covid-19." March 2020. https://www.asianamericanchristiancollaborative.com/read-statement.

Asian American Christian Collaborative. "National Rally: Stand for AAPI Lives and Dignity 3/28/21." https://www.asianamericanchristiancollaborative.com/rally.

Aspen Institute. "The Politics of Vulnerability." February 17, 2026. https://www.aspeninstitute.org/wp-content/uploads/2025/05/Politics-of-Vulnerability.pdf.

Augustine, Sarah. *The Land Is Not Empty: Following Jesus in Dismantling the Doctrine of Discovery*. Nashville, TN: APG Sales and Distribution, 2021.

Aziz, Sahar. *The Racial Muslim: When Racism Quashes Religious Freedom*. Berkeley: University of California Press, 2021.

Bacon, Perry Jr. "Democrats Are Wrong About Republicans. Republicans Are Wrong About Democrats." *FiveThirtyEight*, June 26, 2018. https://fivethirtyeight.com/features/democrats-are-wrong-about-republicans-republicans-are-wrong-about-democrats/.

Bajaj, Monisha, Ameena Ghaffar-Kucher, and Karishma Desai. "Brown Bodies and Xenophobic Bullying in US Schools: Critical Analysis and Strategies for Action." *Harvard Educational Review* 86, no. 4 (Winter 2016): 481–505.

Baker, Kelly J. *Gospel According to the Klan: The KKK's Appeal to Protestant America, 1915-1930*. Lawrence: Kansas University Press, 2017.

Bare, Daniel R. *Black Fundamentalists: Conservative Christianity and Racial Identity in the Segregation Era*. New York: New York University Press, 2021.

Benioff, Marc. Twitter, May 1, 2019. https://twitter.com/Benioff/status/1123467506335850496.

Bell, Carole V. "Talking Racial Politics Online." In *Parasocial Politics: Audiences, Pop Culture, and Politics*, edited by Jason Zenor, 133–152. Lanham, MD: Lexington Books, 2014.

Bender, Courtney, and Pamela Klassen, eds. *After Pluralism: Reimagining Religious Engagement*. New York: Columbia University Press, 2010.

Bennett, Hermit L. *African Kings and Black Slaves: Sovereignty and Dispossession in the Early Modern Atlantic*. Philadelphia: University of Pennsylvania Press, 2019.

Berger, Peter L. *The Desecularization of the World: Resurgent Religion and World Politics*. Washington, DC: Ethics and Public Policy Center, 2008.

Bernard, Diane. "The Creator of Mount Rushmore's Forgotten Ties to White Supremacy." *Washington Post*, July 2, 2020. https://www.washingtonpost.com/history/2020/07/03/mount-rushmore-gutzon-borglum-klan-stone-mountain/.

Bible. Daniel 2:1–47. New International Version.

Bible. John 1:5. https://biblehub.com/john/1-5.htm.

Bible. Romans 13:1–10. New International Version.

"Bible Demands Action on Climate Change, Evangelicals Say in New Report." *Washington Post*, August 30, 2022. https://www.washingtonpost.com/religion/2022/08/30/evangelicals-climate-change-bible.

Blake, Meredith. "Netflix's 'Unorthodox' Went to Remarkable Lengths to Get Hasidic Jewish Customs Right." *Los Angeles Times*, April 7, 2020.

Blakemore, Erin. "How Mahatma Gandhi Changed the Face of Political Protest." *National Geographic Culture*, May 4, 2021. https://www.nationalgeographic.com/culture/article/mahatma-gandhi-changed-political-protest.

Block, Peter. *Community: The Structure of Belonging*. San Francisco: Berrett-Koehler, 2009.

Blyden, Edward Wilmot. *Christianity, Islam and the Negro Race*. Edinburgh: Edinburth University Press, 1967.

Boaz, Daniel N. *Banning Black Gods: Law and Religions of the Africa Diaspora*. University Park: Pennsylvania University Press, 2021.

Borja, Melissa, and Kayla Zhang. "'Please Love Our Asian American Neighbors': Christian Responses to Anti-Asian Racism during the COVID-19 Pandemic." *Theology Today* 79, no. 4 (2023): 370–389.

Botsman, Rachel. "How Can We Have Better Arguments?" *Rethinking with Rachel* (podcast), May 24, 2021. https://link-to-episode.com.

Braunstein, Ruth. *Prophets and Patriots: Faith in Democracy across the Political Divide*. Berkeley: University of California Press, 2017.

Braunstein, Ruth. "A Theory of Political Backlash: Assessing the Religious Right's Effects on the Religious Field." *Sociology of Religion*, November 15, 2021, srab050. https://doi.org/10.1093/socrel/srab050.

Brooks, Arthur. "Political Polarization." *New York Times*, March 2, 2019. https://www.nytimes.com/2019/03/02/opinion/sunday/political-polarization.html.

Brown, Brené. *Braving the Wilderness: The Quest for True Belonging and the Courage to Stand Alone*. New York: Random House, 2019.

Brown, Vince. *The Reaper's Garden: Death and Power in the World of Atlantic Slavery*. Cambridge, MA: Harvard University Press, 2008.

Brueggemann, Walter. *The Prophetic Imagination*, 2nd ed. Minneapolis, MN: Fortress Press, 2021.

Bump, Philip. "Analysis | A New Lens into the Overlap of Religion and Right-Wing Politics." *Washington Post*, February 8, 2023. https://www.washingtonpost.com/politics/2023/02/08/religion-christian-right-wing-politics/.

Burkett, Randall K. *Garveyism as a Religious Movement: The Institutionalization of a Black Civil Religion*. Metuchen, NY: Scarecrow Press, 1978.

Burwell v. *Hobby Lobby Stores*, 573 U.S. 682 (2014). https://supreme.justia.com/cases/federal/us/573/682/.

Butler, Anthea. *Women in the Church of God in Christ: Making a Sanctified Word*. Chapel Hill: University of North Carolina Press, 2007.

Butler, Jon. *Awash in a Sea of Faith: Christianizing the American People*. Cambridge, MA: Harvard University Press, 1990.

Cahill, Thomas. "The Peaceful Crusader." *New York Times*, December 25, 2006. https://www.nytimes.com/2006/12/25/opinion/25Cahill.html.

CAIR. "CAIR at a Glance." N.d. https://www.cair.com/about_cair/cair-at-a-glance.

Campa, Andrew. "Fire, Vandalism Rock Buddhist Temple in Little Tokyo." *Los Angeles Times*, February 26, 2021, sec. California. https://www.latimes.com/california/story/2021-02-26/higashi-honganji-fire.

Campbell, Christopher. "Representation: Stuart Hall and the 'Politics of Signification.'" In *The Routledge Companion to Media and Race*, edited by Christopher Campbell, 11–18. New York: Routledge, 2016.

Carson, Clayborne. *The Autobiography of Martin Luther King, Jr.* New York: Grand Central Publishing, 2001.

Casanova, José. "Rethinking Public Religions." In *Rethinking Religion and World Affairs*, edited by Monica Duffy Toft, Alfred Stepan, and Timothy Samuel Shah, 25–35. New York: Oxford University Press, 2012.

Center for Christianity & Public Life. "The Center for Christianity & Public Life." N.d. https://www.ccpubliclife.org.

Chaney, Jen, "Unorthodox Is a Beautiful, Immersive Portrait of a Woman's Rebirth." *Vulture.com*, March 7, 2020.

Charron, Cate. "Sikh Prayer Service Emphasizes Community, Inclusion One Year after the FedEx Shooting." *Indianapolis Star*, April 10, 2022. https://www.indystar.com/story/news/local/indianapolis/2022/04/10/sikh-prayer-service-community-fedex-shooting-anniversary/9492218002/.

Chireau, Yvonne Patricia. *Black Magic: Religion and the African American Conjuring Tradition*. Berkeley: University of California Press, 2006.

Clegg, Claude A. *The Life and Times of Elijah Muhammad*. Chapel Hill: University of North Carolina Press, 2014.

Clinton, Bill. "State of the Union address." Archives.gov. https://clintonwhitehouse4.archives.gov/WH/New/other/sotu.html.

Coleman, Will. *Tribal Talk: Black Theology, Hermeneutics, and African/American Ways of "Telling the Story."* University Park: Pennsylvania State University Press, 2000.

Considine, Craig. "Finding Tolerance in Akbar, the Philosopher-King." *Huffpost*, April 10, 2013. https://www.huffpost.com/entry/finding-tolerance-in-akba_b_3031746.

Corley, Cheryl. "Bayard Rustin: The Man Who Organized the March on Washington." *NPR All Things Considered* (broadcast), August 15, 2013.

Council on Biblical Manhood and Womanhood. *The Nashville Statement*. N.d. https://cbmw.org/nashville-statement/#preamble.

Council on Foundations. "Values Aligned Philanthropy." N.d. https://cof.org/program-initiative/values-aligned-philanthropy.

Crosby, Alana. "Reconstructing Religious Liberty in a Time of Religious and Secular Extremes." *Adventist Review*, November 14, 2023. https://adventistreview.org/news/reconstructing-religious-liberty-in-a-time-of-religious-and-secular-extremes/.

Crummell, Alexander. *Africa and America: Addresses and Discourses*. Springfield, MA: Willey & Co., 1891.

Curtice, Kaitlin B. *Living Resistance: An Indigenous Vision for Seeking Wholeness Every Day*. Grand Rapids, MI: Brazos Press, 2023.

Daniels, Alex. "Grant Maker Bolsters Human Connection as a Way to Take on Polarization." *The Chronicle of Philanthropy*, May 4, 2021. https://www.philanthropy.com/article/grant-maker-bolsters-human-connection-as-a-way-to-take-on-polarization.

Darling-Hammond, Sean, Eli K. Michaels, Amani M. Allen, David H. Chae, Marilyn D. Thomas, Thu T. Nguyen, Mahasin M. Mujahid, and Rucker C. Johnson. "After 'the China Virus' Went Viral: Racially Charged Coronavirus Coverage and Trends in Bias against Asian Americans." *Health Education & Behavior*, September 10, 2020, 109019812095794. https://doi.org/10.1177/1090198120957949.

Dellinger, Jeff. "303 Creative Case a "Cynical Ploy" for Discrimination, CFI Tells SCOTUS." *Cfi*, August 19, 2022. https://centerforinquiry.org/press_releases/303-creative-case-a-cynical-ploy-for-discrimination-cfi-tells-scotus/.

Dent, Sabrina, and Corey Walker, eds. *African Americans and Religious Freedom: New Perspectives for Congregations and Communities*. Washington, DC: Freedom Forum, 2021.

De Silva, Padmasiri. "Tolerance and Empathy." In *Religious Tolerance, Education and the Curriculum*, edited by Elizabeth Burns Coleman and Kevin White (Rotterdam: SensePublishers, 2011), 99–110. https://doi.org/10.1007/978-94-6091-412-6_8.

Devich Cyril, Malika, et al. "Mismatched: Philanthropy's Response to the Call for Racial Justice." Philanthropic Initiative for Racial Equity, 2020. https://racialequity.org/mismatched/.

Deyle, Steven. *Carry Me Back: The Domestic Slave Trade in American Life*. New York: Oxford University Press, 2005.

Dickerson, Dennis C. "Gandhi's." *Journal of African American History* 104, no. 1 (2019): 59–83.

Dignity for Everyone. "Punta Del Este Declaration on Human Dignity for Everyone Everywhere: Seventy Years after the Universal Declaration of Human Rights." December 2018. https://www.dignityforeveryone.org/about/.

Dorsey, Cheryl, Jeff Bradach, and Peter Kim. "The Problem with 'Color-Blind' Philanthropy." *Harvard Business Review*, June 5, 2020. https://hbr.org/2020/06/the-problem-with-color-blind-philanthropy.

Douglass, Frederick. *Two speeches, by Frederick Douglass; one on West India emancipation, delivered at Canandaigua, Aug. 4th, and the other on the Dred Scott decision, delivered in New York, on the occasion of the anniversary of the American Abolition Society, May, 1857*. Rochester, N.Y: C.P. Dewey, American Office, 1857.

Dovidio, John F., Peter Samuel Glick, and Laurie A. Rudman, eds. *On the Nature of Prejudice: Fifty Years after Allport*. Malden, MA: Blackwell, 2005.

DTCC. *Turning Headwinds into Tailwinds: 2017 Annual Report*. New York: DTCC, 2017.

Du Bois, W.E.B. (William Edward Burghardt), ed. *The Negro Church. Report of a Social Study Made under the Direction of Atlanta University; Together with the Proceedings of the Eighth Conference for the Study of the Negro Problems, held at Atlanta University, May 26th, 1903*. 1903. https://docsouth.unc.edu/church/negrochurch/dubois.html.

Du Bois, W.E.B. *Black Reconstruction*. Millwood, NY: Kraus-Thomson Organization, 1976.

Du Bois, W.E.B. "Of Dawn of Freedom." In *The Souls of Black Folk*, chap. 2. Project Gutenberg, January 1986. https://www.gutenberg.org/files/408/408-h/.

Duss, Matthew, Yasmine Taeb, and Ken Gude. *Fear Inc., 2.0*. Center for American Progress, February 2015. https://www.americanprogress.org/article/fear-inc-2-0/.

Dvorak, Katharine L. *An African-American Exodus: The Segregation of the Southern Churches*. Brooklyn, NY: Carlson, 1991.

Eck, Diana. *A New Religious America: How a "Christian Country" Has Now Become the World's Most Religiously Diverse Nation*. New York: HarperSanFrancisco, 2001.

Eckhart Queenan, Jeri, Peter Grunert, and Devin Murphy. "Elevating the Role of Faith-Inspired Impact in the Social Sector," 9. Bridgespan Group, 2021. https://www.bridgespan.org/insights/role-of-faith-inspired-impact-in-the-social-sector.

Eckhart Queenan, Jeri, Peter Grunert, Devine Murphy, and Brie Loskota. "Bridging Religious Divides: Understanding the Influence of Faith and Religion on Social Strength and Civic Engagement." Paper presented at the Council on Foundations annual meeting, Miami, Florida, May 1, 2019.

Encinias, Joshua. "*Jesus Revolution* Is a Christian Hit That Takes Lessons from Blumhouse and Paul Thomas Anderson." *Moviemaker*, March 6, 2023. https://www.moviemaker.com/jesus-revolution-christian-hit-blumhouse/.

Ensaaf and Benetech Human Rights Data Analysis Group. *Violent Deaths and Enforced Disappearances during the Counterinsurgency in Punjab, India: A Preliminary Quantitative Analysis*. 2009. https://hrdag.org/indiafaqs/.

Escobar, Melvin. "Loving-Kindness: May All Beings Be Happy." *Lion's Roar*, September 20, 2022. https://www.lionsroar.com/loving-kindness-may-all-beings-be-happy/.

Evanzz, Karl. *The Messenger: The Rise and Fall of Elijah Muhammad*. New York: Pantheon Books, 1999.Faith & Media Initiative. *The Global Faith & Entertainment Study*. HarrisX, February 13, 2024. https://www.faithandmedia.com/research/harrisxentertainment.

Faith in Philanthropy. *Funder Groups*. https://fip.oneill.indiana.edu/funder-groups/index.html.

"The Fastest Growing US Religious Affiliation? 'None,' Poll Says." *The Hill*, December 14, 2021. https://thehill.com/homenews/state-watch/585764-the-fastest-growing-us-religious-affiliation-none-poll-says/.

Franklin, John Hope. *George Washington Williams: A Biography*. Fayetteville: University of Arkansas Press, 1985/2012.

Freire, Paulo. *Pedagogy of the Oppressed: 50th Anniversary Edition*, 4th ed. New York: Bloomsbury Academic, 2018.

Fricke, Jeremy. "The 5B Framework of Religion & Spirituality." *Tri-Faith Initiative* (blog), April 30, 2023. https://www.trifaith.org/the-5b-framework-of-religion-amp-spirituality/.

Friedline, Mary L. "Pluralism and the Roots of Social Conflict: Rethinking Rails." *MDPI*, December 29, 2018. https://doi.org/10.3390/rel10010020.

Fulton, Brad R. "Religious Organizations: Crosscutting the Nonprofit Sector." In *The Nonprofit Sector: A Research Handbook*, 3rd ed., edited by Walter W. Powell and Patricia Bromley, 579–597. Stanford, CA: Stanford University Press, 2020.

Funk, Cary, and Greg Smith. *"Nones" on the Rise: One-in-Five Adults Have No Religious Affiliation*. Washington, DC: Pew Research Center, 2012. https://www.pewresearch.org/wp-content/uploads/sites/7/2012/10/NonesOnTheRise-full.pdf.

Galtung, Johan. "Cultural Violence." *Journal of Peace Research* 27, no. 3 (August 1990): 291–305.

Garay, Jesus. "These Posters Protesting Trump Were Created by the Man Responsible for Obama's 'Hope' Artwork." *Guff*, 2016. https://guff.com/these-posters-protesting-trump-were-created-by-the-man-responsible-for-obamas-hope-artwork.

Gardner, Eric. *Black Print Unbound: The Christian Recorder, African American Literature, and Periodical Culture*. New York: Oxford University Press, 2015.

Gerbner, Katharine. *Christian Slavery: Conversion and Race in the Protestant Atlantic World*. Philadelphia: University of Pennsylvania Press, 2018.

Gerstein, Josh. "Court Mulls FBI Mosque Surveillance." *Politico Magazine*, December 8, 2015. https://www.politico.com/blogs/under-the-radar/2015/12/court-mulls-fbi-mosque-surveillance-216529.

Gin Lum, Kathryn. *Heathen: Religion and Race in American History*. Cambridge, MA: Harvard University Press, 2022.

Glendon, Mary Ann. *A World Made New*. New York: Random House, 2000.

Global Centre for Pluralism. "Who We Are." https://www.pluralism.ca/who-we-are/.

Gomez, Michael A. *Exchanging Our Country Marks: The Transformation of African Identities in the Colonial and Antebellum South*. Chapel Hill: University of North Carolina Press, 1998.

Goodhead, Dokubo Melford. "The Resisting Spectator and *The Green Mile*." *Howard Journal of Communications* 33, no. 1 (2022): 45–57.

Goodrich, Luke. *Free to Believe: The Battle over Religious Liberty in America*, sneak peek excerpt. Colorado Springs, CO: WaterBrook, 2019. https://waterbrookmultnomah.com/wp-content/uploads/pdf/Sneak-Peek-Free-to-Believe-1.pdf.

Goodstein, Laurie. "Around Country, Mosque Projects Meet Opposition." *New York Times*, August 8, 2010, A1. https://www.nytimes.com/2010/08/08/us/08mosque.html.

Goodwin, Megan. "The Field Is Not One/The Body Is Smart: Rethinking Theory in the Study of Religion." In *Key Categories in the Study of Religion—Contexts and Critiques*, edited by Rebekah King. Sheffield, UK: Equinox, 2022. https://www.equinoxpub.com/home/view-chapter/?id=39436.

Gottschalk, Paul. *The Earliest Diplomatic Documents on America: The Papal Bulls of 1493 and the Treaty of Tordesillas Reproduced and Translated*. Berlin: Paul Gottschalk, 1927.

Gottschalk, Peter, and Gabriel Greenberg. *Islamophobia and Anti-Muslim Sentiment: Picturing the Enemy*. Lanham, MD: Rowman & Littlefield, 2018.

Grammich, Clifford A., Erica Dollhopf, Mary Gautier, et al. "U.S. Religion Census—Religious Congregations and Membership Study, 2020 (County File)." 2023. https://doi.org/10.17605/OSF.IO/ET2A5.

Greater Good Science Center. *Bridging Differences Playbook*. Berkeley: University of California, 2021. https://greatergood.berkeley.edu/images/uploads/Bridging_Differences_Playbook-Final.pdf.

Greenberg, Kenneth S., ed. *Nat Turner: A Slave Rebellion in History and Memory*. Oxford: Oxford University Press, 2003.

Greene, J.P., A. Cheng, and I. Kingsbury. "Education and Anti-Semitism." Education Reform Faculty and Graduate Students Publications, 2021. https://scholarworks.uark.edu/edrepub/121.

Grewal, Zareena. "1965 and the Global Afterlife of Malcolm X." *American Studies* 54, no. 2 (2015): 9–20.

Greydanus, Steven D. "Interview: Filmmaker Scott Derrickson on Horror, Faith, Chesterton and His New Movie." *National Catholic Register*, July 1, 2014. https://www.ncregister.com/news/interview-filmmaker-scott-derrickson-on-horror-faith-chesterton-and-his-new-movie.

Grim, Brian J. "Corporates Often Forget Religious Diversity. Here's Why They Should Not." World Economic Forum, January 16, 2020. https://www.weforum.org/agenda/2020/01/religion-diversity-business-inclusion/.

Grim, Brian J., and Roger Finke. *The Price of Freedom Denied: Religious Persecution and Conflict in the 21st Century*. New York: Cambridge University Press, 2011.

Grim, Brian J., Paul Lambert, and Kent Johnson, eds. "Faith@Work: The Next Big Thing in Corporate America Is Here." Religious Freedom & Business Foundation, 2020. https://religiousfreedomandbusiness.org/faith-at-work-matters.

Guggenberger, Wilhem, and Bala Kumar Hrudayaraj. *Democracy, Religion, and Pluralism: Theological Responses.* Innsbruck: Innsbruck University Press, 2022. https://library.oapen.org/bitstream/id/152b50ef-b79d-46d9-83ed-7dfdd02149a7/10.15203-99106-082-6.pdf.

Hackett, Conrad, Phillip Connor, Marcin Stonawski, and Vegard Skirbekk. *The Future of World Religions: Population Growth Projections, 2010-2050.* Washington, DC: Pew Research Center, 2015. https://assets.pewresearch.org/wp-content/uploads/sites/11/2015/03/PF_15.04.02_ProjectionsFullReport.pdf.

Haig, Terry. "Buddhists Sites and Temples Are Vandalized in Montreal." Radio Canada International, March 5, 2020. https://www.rcinet.ca/en/2020/03/05/buddhists-sites-and-temples-are-vandalized-in-montreal/.

Hall, David. *Lived Religion in America: Toward a History of Practice.* Princeton, NJ: Princeton University Press, 1998.

Hall, Katie. "Police Investigating Vandalism at Buddhist Temple in North Austin." *Austin American-Statesman*, April 29, 2020. https://www.statesman.com/news/20200429/police-investigating-vandalism-at-buddhist-temple-in-north-austin.

Hall, Stuart. "Ethnicity: Identity and Difference." *Radical America* 23, no. 4 (1991): 9–20.

Haraway, Donna. "Situated Knowledges: The Science Question in Feminism and the Privilege of Partial Perspective." In *Simians, Cyborgs, and Women: The Reinvention of Nature*, 183–202. New York: Routledge, 1991.

Harding, Vincent. *There Is a River: The Black Struggle for Freedom in America.* New York: Harcourt Brace Jovanovich, 1981.

Harding, Vincent. "Vincent Harding: Creating America." Children's Defense Fund National Conference. YouTube video, October 19, 2012, 2:51. https://www.youtube.com/watch?v=T6W42KLpNgQ.

Hatch, Nathan O. *The Democratization of American Christianity.* New Haven, CT: Yale University Press, 1989.

Haynes, Stephen R. *Noah's Curse: The Biblical Justification of American Slavery.* New York: Oxford University Press, 2007.

Hazzard-Donald, Katrina. *Mojo Workin': The Old African American Hoodoo System.* Urbana: University of Illinois Press, 2013.

Hehir, J. Bryan. "Why Religion? Why Now?" In *Rethinking Religion and World Affairs*, edited by Monica Duffy Toft, Alfred Stepan, and Timothy Samuel Shah, 15–24. New York: Oxford University Press, 2012.

"Heschel, Abraham Joshua." The Martin Luther King, Jr. Research and Education Institute. https://kinginstitute.stanford.edu/heschel-abraham-joshua.

Hewstone, Miles, Mark Rubin, and Hazel Willis. "Intergroup Bias." *Annual Review of Psychology* 53, no. 1 (2002): 575–604.

Hindu American Foundation. "Hindu American Foundation Launches 'Fight Hate. Educate.' Campaign." December 19, 2019. https://www.hinduamerican.org/press/hindu-american-foundation-fight-hate-educate-campaign.

Hines, Jason. "Liberty Twice Removed." *Spectrum Magazine*, February 25, 2021. https://spectrummagazine.org/views/2021/liberty-twice-removed.

Hinnershitz, Stephanie. *Race, Religion, and Civil Rights: Asian Students on the West Coast, 1900-1968.* New Brunswick, NJ: Rutgers University Press, 2015.

Holden, Vanessa M. *Surviving Southampton: African American Women and Resistance in Nat Turner's Community.* Urbana: University of Illinois Press, 2021.

Holt, Mack P. *The French Wars of Religion, 1562-1629.* Cambridge: Cambridge University Press, 1995.

Hong, Jane. "The Asian American Movement and the Church." *Journal of Asian American Studies* 25, no. 1 (February 2022): 63–94. https://doi.org/10.1353/jaas.2022.0002.

hooks, bell. *Reel to Real: Race, Class and Sex at the Movies*. New York: Routledge, 2009.

hooks, bell. *Black Looks: Race and Representation*. New York: Routledge, 2015.

Horton, Donald, and R. Richard Wohl. "Mass Communication and Para-Social Interaction: Observations on Intimacy at a Distance." *Psychiatry* 19, no. 3 (1956): 215–229.

Horton, S.B. "To the Honorable Members of the Senate and House of Representatives of the General Assembly, Baton Rouge, La." *Official Journal of the Proceedings of the Senate of the State of Louisiana at the First Regular Session of the Third General Assembly under the Adoption of the Constitution of 1898; Begun and Held in the City of Baton Rouge, May 11, 1908*, 101–104. Baton Rouge, LA: Daily State Publishing Company, State Printers. https://www.google.com/books/edition/Official_Journal_of_the_Proceedings_of_t/h1hBAQAAMAAJ (digitized by the University of Chicago).

Huberman, Lisa. "When Will the 'Marvelous Mrs. Maisel' Deal with Midge's Privilege?" *HeyAlma.com*, December 16, 2019.

Hughes, Langston. "Let America Be America Again." *Poets.org*, 1935. https://poets.org/poem/let-america-be-america-again.

Human Rights Watch (Asia). "Dead Silence: The Legacy of Human Rights Abuses in Punjab." 1994. https://www.hrw.org/report/1994/05/01/dead-silence-legacy-abuses-punjab.

Hurston, Zora Neale. *Tell My Horse*. Philadelphia: J.B. Lippincott, 1938.

Hussain, Umer, and George B. Cunningham. "Why Muslim Women Choose to Wear Headscarves while Participating in Sports." *The Conversation*, February 23, 2022. https://theconversation.com/why-muslim-women-choose-to-wear-headscarves-while-participating-in-sports-176441.

Hussein, Amir. Interview by Jody Hassett Sanchez, March 7, 2023.

Ibrahim, Dina. "Maybe Brown People Aren't So Scary if They're Funny: Audience Readings of Arabs and Muslims." In *The Colorblind Screen*, edited by Sarah Nilsen and Sarah E. Turner, 167–188. New York: New York University Press, 2014.

Independence Hall Association. "Historic Documents." https://www.ushistory.org/DOCUMENTS/index.html.

Ingraham, Christopher. "The Non-Religious Are Now the Country's Largest Religious Voting Bloc." *Washington Post*, July 14, 2016. https://www.washingtonpost.com/news/wonk/wp/2016/07/14/the-non-religious-are-now-the-countrys-largest-religious-voting-bloc/.

Interfaith America. "Interfaith America." https://www.interfaithamerica.org.

Interfaith Power & Light. "About." September 9, 2021. https://interfaithpowerandlight.org/about/.

Islamophobia Is Racism. "Resource for Teaching and Learning about Anti-Muslim Racism in the United States." https://islamophobiaisracism.wordpress.com.

ISPU. "American Muslim Poll 2022: A Politics and Pandemic Status Report." https://www.ispu.org/american-muslim-poll-2022-1/.

"Israelis of Color Push back against Race-Based, Anti-Israel Narratives Spread Abroad." *Times of Israel*, December 23, 2023. https://www.timesofisrael.com/israelis-of-color-push-back-against-race-based-anti-israel-narratives-spread-abroad/.

Ives, Mike. "How 'Friends' Helps People around the World Learn English." *New York Times*, May 29, 2021.

Jacobsen, Douglas, and Rhonda Hustedt Jacobsen. *No Longer Invisible: Religion in University Education*. New York: Oxford University Press, 2012.

Jakobsen, Janet R., and Ann Pellegrini, eds. *Secularisms*. Durham, NC: Duke University Press, 2008.

Jelks, Randal Maurice. *Faith and Struggle in the Lives of Four African Americans*. London: Bloomsbury Academic, 2019.

Jhutti-Johal, Jagbir, and Hardeep Singh. *Racialization, Islamophobia and Mistaken Identity: The Sikh Experience*. London: Taylor & Francis, 2019.

"John Kerry Would Study Religion." C-SPAN, August 7, 2013. https://www.c-span.org/video/?c4461670/user-clip-john-kerry-study-religion.

Johnson, Walter. *Soul by Soul: Life inside the Antebellum Slave Market.* Cambridge, MA: Harvard University Press, 1999.

Johnston, Robert. "Southern Baptist Convention Resolutions on Abortion 1971-2009." N.d. https://www.johnstonsarchive.net/baptist/sbcabres.html.

"Jon Erwin Explains Why He's Opening a Faith-Based Movie Studio." *Movieguide.org*, December 22, 2023. https://www.movieguide.org/news-articles/jon-erwin-explains-why-hes-opening-a-faith-based-movie-studio.html.

Jones, Alonzo. *The National Sunday Law, Argument of Alonzo T. Jones before the United States Senate Committee on Education and Labor at Washington, D.C.* December 13, 1888. Oakland, CA: American Sentinel, 1889. http://www.bible-sabbath.com/Sabbath-Sunday/NationalSundayLaw-Jones.pdf.

Jones, Robert P. *White Too Long: The Legacy of White Supremacy in American Christianity.* New York: Simon & Schuster, 2020.

Jones, Robert P., and Maxine Najle. *American Democracy in Crisis: The Fate of Pluralism in a Divided Nation.* Washington, DC: Public Religion Research Institute, 2019. https://www.prri.org/wp-content/uploads/2019/02/Democracy-in-Crisis-3-Pluralism-1.pdf.

Jones, Robert P., Natalie Jackson, Diana Orcés, and Ian Huff. *The 2020 Census of American Religion.* Washington, DC: Public Religion Research Center, 2021. https://www.prri.org/wp-content/uploads/2021/07/PRRI-2021-Religion-Report.pdf.

Joshi, Khyati. *White Christian Privilege: The Illusion of Religious Equality in America.* New York: New York University Press, 2020.

Kapur, Sudarshan. *Raising Up a Prophet: The African American Encounter with Gandhi.* Boston: Beacon Press, 1992.

Karpowitz, C., J. Quinn Monson, and K. Patterson. "Who's In and Who's Out: The Politics of Religious Norms." *Politics and Religion* 9, no. 3 (2016): 508–536. https://doi.org/10.1017/S1755048316000456.

Kasimow, Harold. *Interfaith Activism: Abraham Joshua Heschel and Religious Diversity.* Eugene, OR: Wipf & Stock, 2015.

Kendi, Ibram X. *How to Be an Antiracist.* New York: Penguin Random House, 2019.

Kennedy v. *Bremerton School District*, 597 U.S. 507 (2022). https://www.supremecourt.gov/opinions/21pdf/21-418_i425.pdf.

Khan, Al-Baab, Katherine Pieper, Stacy L. Smith, Ariana Case, and Sam Wheeler. "Erased or Extremists: The Stereotypical View of Muslims in Popular Episodic Series." USC Getty Annenberg Inclusion Initiative, September 2022. https://assets.uscannenberg.org/docs/aii-study-muslim-erased-or-extremists-20220901.pdf.

Khan, Zeba. "When Racism Goes Viral: The Coronavirus and Modern Muslim Orientalism." *MuslimMatters.org* (blog), February 1, 2020. https://muslimmatters.org/2020/02/01/coronavirus-racism-china/.

King, Coretta Scott. Interview by Blackside Inc. November 21, 1988. Washington University Libraries, Film and Media Archive, Henry Hampton Collection.

King, Martin Luther, Jr. *Where Do We Go from Here: Chaos or Community?* Boston: Beacon Press, 2010.

Klein, Hebert. *The Atlantic Slave Trade*, 2nd ed. Cambridge: Cambridge University Press, 1999/2010.

Koppelman, Andrew M. "Gay Rights vs. Religious Liberty? The Unnecessary Conflict: Introduction." In *Gay Rights vs. Religious Liberty? The Unnecessary Conflict.* 2020.

Kumar, Deepa. *Islamophobia and the Politics of Empire.* New York: Haymarket Books, 2012.

Kustanowitz, Esther D. "How TV Has Embraced Dybbuks, Golems and Other Jewish Lore." *J: The Jewish News of Northern California*, May 21, 2021.

Kwong, Lucas. "Lamenting Sanctified Sinophobia, Demanding Transformation." *ISAAC* (blog), December 24, 2020. https://isaacweb.org/lamenting-sanctified-sinophobia-demanding-transformation/.

Kwong, Lucas. "'God Bless Mr. Truman': Christian Nationalism's Impact on Anti-Asian Hate." *ISAAC* (blog), January 7, 2021. https://isaacweb-org.fhs00040.managedword.com/2021/01/07/god-bless-mr-truman-christian-nationalisms-impact-on-anti-asian-hate/.

Kwong, Lucas. "An Open Letter on Anti-Asian Racism & Christian Nationalism." Against Christian Xenophobia. N.d. https://www.againstchristianxenophobia.com/against-christian-xenophobia.

Lai, Michael. "Asian American Church Zoom-Bombed with Racial Slurs and Pornographic Images during Good Friday Service." *AsianFeed*, April 3, 2021. https://www.asianfeed.com/article/michaellai//2021/04/asian-american-church-zoom-bombed-good-friday.

Laycock, Douglas. "Religious Liberty and the Culture Wars." *University of Illinois Law Review* 3 (June 2014): 839–880. https://illinoislawreview.org/wp-content/ilr-content/articles/2014/3/Laycock.pdf.

Lee, Amanda. "How 'The Marvelous Mrs. Maisel' Fights Stereotypes." *Washington Post*, December 6, 2019.

Lennon, Tom. Interview by Jody Hassett Sanchez, February 27, 2023.

Leslie, Dwayne. "Why Uganda Should Consider the Greatest Commandment." *Huffington Post*, March 18, 2014. https://www.huffpost.com/entry/why-uganda-should-conside_b_4984262.

Levy, Daniel S. "How *I Love Lucy* Changed How America Saw Motherhood." *Time*, May 8, 2021.

London, Samuel G., Jr. *Seventh-day Adventists and the Civil Rights Movement*. Jackson: University of Mississippi Press, 2010.

Loskota, Brie. "Understanding Religious Literacy Content Creators and Providers in Education, Journalism and New Media: A Report for the Arthur Vining Davis Foundations." The Arthur Vining Davis Foundations, Aspen Institute Inclusive America Project, and USC Center for Religion and Civic Culture, 2021. https://www.aspeninstitute.org/wp-content/uploads/2021/08/Understanding-Religious-Literacy-FINAL.pdf/.

Luscombe, Bellina. "MacKenzie Scott Gave away $6 Billion Last Year. It's Not as Easy as It Sounds." *Time*, May 25, 2021. https://time.com/6050873/mackenzie-scott-profile/.

Maarif, Ahmad Syaffii. *Islam Humanity and the Indonesian Identity*. Leiden: Leiden University Press, 2018.

MacRobert, Iain. *The Black Roots and White Racism of Early Pentecostalism in the USA*. New York: St. Martin's Press, 1988.

Manhattan Declaration. *The Manhattan Declaration: A Call of Christian Conscience*. N.d. https://www.manhattandeclaration.org.

Masuzawa, Tomoko. *The Invention of World Religions: Or, How European Universalism Was Preserved in the Language of Pluralism*. Chicago: University of Chicago Press, 2005.

Matory, James Lorand. *Black Atlantic Religion: Tradition, Transnationalism, and Matriarchy in the Afro-Brazilian Candomblé*. Princeton, NJ: Princeton University Press, 2005.

McKenna, Elizabeth. "Shifting Power by Sharing Power: A Case Study of Relational Organizing in Saint Paul, MN." P3 Lab at Johns Hopkins University, December 15, 2021. https://d3n8a8pro7vhmx.cloudfront.net/hahrie/pages/1200/attachments/original/1639510118/Deep_Dive_Isaiah.pdf?1639510118r.

McKenzie, Keisha. "A Tale of Two Briefs: How Current Adventist Legal Strategy Fails the Good Samaritan Test." *Adventist Today* 25, no. 2 (2017): 9–11.

Melling, Louise. "The New Faith-Based Discrimination." *Boston Review*, December 14, 2022. https://www.bostonreview.net/articles/the-new-faith-based-discrimination/.

Michel, Debbie. "Religious Liberty Leaders Emphasize Connecting with the Marginalized." *Adventist Review*, October 24, 2019. https://adventistreview.org/news/religious-liberty-leaders-emphasize-connecting-with-the-marginalized/.

Miller, Emily McFarlan. "Asian American Christians Denounce Anti-Asian Racism amid Coronavirus." *Religion News Service*, April 2, 2020. https://religionnews.com/2020/04/02/asian-american-christians-release-statement-against-anti-asian-racism-amid-coronavirus/.

Miller, Gerri. "Disney Channel's Andi Mack Episode Includes Shiva, Mourning Rituals." *Jewish Journal*, February 5, 2019.

Mir, Shabana, and Loukia K. Sarroub. "Islamophobia in U.S. Education." In *The Routledge International Handbook of Islamophobia*, edited by Irene Zempi and Imran Awan, 298–309. Abingdon, UK: Routledge, 2019.

"Montreal Police Suspect Hate-Crimes after Vandals Hit Buddhist Temples, Chinatown." *CBC News*, March 4, 2020. https://www.cbc.ca/news/canada/montreal/vandalism-temples-1.5485151.

Moore, Diane L. *Overcoming Religious Illiteracy: A Cultural Studies Approach to the Study of Religion in Secondary Education.* New York: Palgrave Macmillan, 2008.

Moore, Diane L., chair. "Guidelines for Teaching about Religion in K-12 Public Schools in the United States." AAR Religion in the Schools Task Force, 2010. https://hwpi.harvard.edu/files/hds2/files/aark12curriculumguidelines3.pdf.

Moore, R.I. *The War on Heresy.* Cambridge, MA: Belknap Press of Harvard University Press, 2012.

Morgan, David. Interview by Jody Hassett Sanchez, February 26, 2023.

Morgenstein Fuerst, Ilyse R. *Indian Muslim Minorities and the 1857 Rebellion: Religion, Rebels, and Jihad.* London: I.B. Tauris, 2017.

Morgenstein Fuerst, Ilyse R. "Survivals: The Stakes of Religious Literacy." *Method & Theory in the Study of Religion* 34, no. 5 (2022): 435–445. https://doi.org/10.1163/15700682-bja10078.

"Most Americans Say Nation Is Deeply Divided over Values, Poll Says." *PBS NewsHour*, October 16, 2020. https://www.pbs.org/newshour/nation/most-americans-say-nation-is-deeply-divided-over-values-poll-says.

Mudimbe, V.Y. *The Invention of Africa: Gnosis, Philosophy, and the Order of Knowledge.* Bloomington: Indiana University Press, 1988.

Muir, Ben. "Oxbow Pastor's Comments, Behavior Raise Concerns." *Watertown Daily News*, June 27, 2020. https://www.nny360.com/communitynews/faithperspectives/oxbow-pastor-s-comments-behavior-raise-concerns/article_767b2476-d820-5a89-8b69-06644565c0d2.html.

Murphy, Mary, and Michelle Willens. "Anti-Semitism on the Rise, the Jewishness of 'The Marvelous Mrs. Maisel' Is a Marvel." *The Wrap*, January 6, 2019.

Nadine, Naber. "'Look, Mohammed the Terrorist Is Coming!' Cultural Racism, Nation-based Racism, and Intersectionality of Oppressions after 9/11." In *Race and Arab Americans Before and After 9/11: From Visible Citizens to Visible Subjects*, edited by Amaney Jamal and Nadine Naber, 276–304. Syracuse: Syracuse University Press, 2008.

Nacos, Brigitte Lebens, and Oscar Torres-Reyna. *Fueling Our Fears: Stereotyping, Media Coverage, and Public Opinion of Muslim Americans.* Lanham, MD: Rowman & Littlefield, 2007.

Nash, Gary B. *Forging Freedom: The Formation of Philadelphia's Black Community, 1720-1840*, paperback ed. Cambridge, MA: Harvard University Press, 1991.

National Library of Medicine. "1978: American Indian Freedom of Religion Legalized." Native Voices: Native Peoples' Concepts of Health and Illness, US National Institutes of Health. https://www.nlm.nih.gov/nativevoices/timeline/545.html.

Nelson, William Stuart. "The Interfaith Origins of the Civil Rights Movement." In *Churches, Blackness, and Contested Multiculturalism*, edited by R.D. Smith, W. Ackah, and A.G. Reddie, 57–72. New York: Palgrave Macmillan, 2014. https://doi.org/10.1057/9781137386380_5.

Newhouse, Alana. "Everything Is Broken: And How to Fix It." *Tablet Magazine*, January 2021. https://www.tabletmag.com/sections/news/articles/everything-is-broken.

Newhouse, Alana. "Brokenism." *Tablet Magazine*, November 2022. https://www.tabletmag.com/sections/news/articles/brokenism-alana-newhouse.

Niebuhr, H. Richard. *The Social Sources of Denominationalism*. New York: World Publishing, 1972.

"O Come All Ye Faithful." *The Economist*, November 3, 2007. https://www.economist.com/special-report/2007/11/03/o-come-all-ye-faithful.

Olcese, Abby. Interview by Jody Hassett Sanchez, February 24, 2023.

Onishi, Bradley. *Preparing for War: The Extremist History of White Christian Nationalism—And What Comes Next*. Minneapolis, MN: Broadleaf Books, 2023.

Overstreet, Jeffrey. Interview by Jody Hassett Sanchez, February 27, 2023.

Parenti, Michael. "Power and Pluralism: A View from the Bottom." *Journal of Politics* 32, no. 3 (August 1970): 501–530. https://www.jstor.org/stable/2128829.

Patel, Eboo. "The New Identity Politics of Religion." *Interfaith Observer*, February 1, 2017. https://www.theinterfaithobserver.org/journal-articles/2016/6/6/the-new-identity-politics-of-religion.html.

Patterson, Orlando. *Slavery and Social Death*. Cambridge, MA: Harvard University Press, 1982, Chapter 2.

Pew Research Center. "Asian Americans: A Mosaic of Faiths." August. Washington, DC: Pew Research Center, 2012.

Pew Research Center. *Importance of Religion and Religious Beliefs*. Washington, DC: Pew Research Center, 2015. https://www.pewresearch.org/religion/2015/11/03/chapter-1-importance-of-religion-and-religious-beliefs/.

Pew Research Center. "Partisanship and Political Animosity in 2016." June 22, 2016. https://www.pewresearch.org/politics/2016/06/22/partisanship-and-political-animosity-in-2016/.

Pew Research Center. "U.S. Muslims Concerned about Their Place in Society, but Continue to Believe in the American Dream." July 26, 2017. https://www.pewresearch.org/religion/2017/07/26/demographic-portrait-of-muslim-americans/.

Pew Research Center. *When Americans Say They Believe in God, What Do They Mean?* Washington, DC: Pew Research Center. 2018. https://www.pewresearch.org/religion/2018/04/25/when-americans-say-they-believe-in-god-what-do-they-mean/.

Pew Research Center. "In U.S., Decline of Christianity Continues at Rapid Pace." October 17, 2019. https://www.pewforum. org/2019/10/17/in-u-s-decline-of-christianity-continues-at-rapid-pace/.

Pew Research Center. "Race, Ethnicity, Heritage and Immigration among U.S. Jews." In *Jewish Americans in 2020*, May 11. Washington, DC: Pew Research Center, 2021.

Pew Research Center. "Key Findings from the Global Religious Futures Project." December 21, 2022. https://www.pewresearch.org/religion/2022/12/21/key-findings-from-the-global-religious-futures-project/.

Pew Research Center. "Globally, Government Restrictions on Religion Reached Peak Levels in 2021, while Social Hostilities Went Down." March 5, 2024. https://www.pewresearch.org/religion/2024/03/05/globally-government-restrictions-on-religion-reached-peak-levels-in-2021-while-social-hostilities-went-down/.

Pew Research Center. "Government Restrictions on Religion Stayed at Peak Levels Globally in 2022." December 2024. https://www.pewresearch.org/religion/2024/12/18/government-restrictions-on-religion-stayed-at-peak-levels-globally-in-2022/.

Pew Research Center. "How the Global Religious Landscape Changed from 2010–2020." June 2025. https://www.pewresearch.org/wp-content/uploads/sites/20/2025/06/PR_2025.06.09_global-religious-change_report.pdf.

Pew Research Center's Religion & Public Life Project. "Religious Landscape Study." N.d. https://www.pewresearch.org/religion/religious-landscape-study/.

Philanthropy for Active Civic Engagement (PACE). "A Funding Guide for Faith and Democracy." N.d. https://form.jotform.com/PACEproject/faithguide.

Philanthropy for Active Civic Engagement (PACE). "Faith In/And Democracy." N.d. https://www.pacefunders.org/faith/.

Philanthropy Roundtable. Search results for "Faith." https://www.philanthropyroundtable.org/search/faith.

Phillips, C.H. *The History of the Colored Methodist Episcopal Church in America.* New York: Arno Press, 1972.

Pinkus, Arin. "Religious Stereotypes vs. Reality in Urban, Suburban, and Rural America." American Communities Project, April 15, 2022. https://www.americancommunities.org/religious-stereotypes-vs-reality-in-urban-suburban-and-rural-america/.

Platt, Elizabeth, Katherine Franke, Keisha McKenzie, and Katharine Henderson. "All Faiths and None: A Guide to Protecting Religious Liberty for Everyone," October. New York: Law, Rights, and Religion Project & Auburn Theological Seminary, 2020. https://lawrightsreligion.org/our-work/all-faiths-and-none.

Platt, Elizabeth, Katherine Franke, K. Shepherd, and Lidjia Hadjiivanova. "Whose Faith Matters: The Fight for Religious Liberty beyond the Religious Right," December. New York: Law, Rights, and Religion Project, 2019. https://lawrightsreligion.law.columbia.edu/content/whosefaithmatters.

Pope Alexander VI. "The Doctrine of Discovery, 1493." Gilder Lehrman Institute of American History. https://www.gilderlehrman.org/history-resources/spotlight-primary-source/doctrine-discovery-1493.

Pope John Paul II. "Encyclical Letter: Redemptor Hominis." March 4, 1979. https://www.vatican.va/content/john-paul-ii/en/encyclicals/documents/hf_jp-ii_enc_04031979_redemptor-hominis.html.

Pope Nicholas V. "Dum Diversas." F/CA, 2020. https://www.facechangealliance.com/dumdiversas.

Powell, John A., and Stephen Menendian. "The Problem of Othering: Towards Inclusiveness and Belonging." Othering and Belonging, 2016. http://www.otheringandbelonging.org/the-problem-of-othering/.

Price, J.F., C. Snorten, J. Wilson, C. Schall, M.A. Hasan, X. Luo, and S.M.A. Jahin. "Community Studies of Antisemitism in Schools (CSAIS) Community Typology Explorer." 2021. https://jeremyfprice.github.io/csais-dashboard.

Public Religion Research Institute (PRRI) Staff. "A Christian Nation? Understanding the Threat of Christian Nationalism to American Democracy and Culture." *PRRI* (blog), February 28, 2023. https://www.prri.org/research/a-christian-nation-understanding-the-threat-of-christian-nationalism-to-american-democracy and culture/.

Pucciarelli, Alexandra. "The Marvelous Mrs. Maisel' Gets Jewish Converts Totally Wrong." *Jewish Telegraphic Agency*, January 2, 2019.

Putnam, Robert. "E Pluribus Unum: Diversity and Community in the Twenty-First Century, the 2006 Johan Skytte Prize Lecture, 2007." *Scandinavian Political Studies* 30 (2007): 137–174.

Raboteau, Albert J. *Slave Religion: The "Invisible Institution" in the Antebellum South.* New York: Oxford University Press, 1980.

Rae, Noel. *The Great Stain: Witnessing American Slavery.* New York: Overlook Press, 2018.

Ralph, Allison K. "But What if They Preach? A Guide for Funding Faith-Inspired Grantees with Boundaries and Integrity." Aspen Institute Inclusive America Project, September 2021.

Ralph, Allison K. Personal communication with regional PSO, September 5, 2021.

Ralph, Allison K., Brad R. Fulton, and Samuel Allen. "Faith-Based Public Foundations: Identifying the Field and Assessing Its Impact." *Foundation Review* 14, no. 1 (March 1, 2022). https://doi.org/10.9707/1944-5660.1600.

Ramji, Rubina. "From Navy Seals to *The Siege*: Getting to Know the Muslim Terrorist, Hollywood Style." *Journal of Religion and Film* 9, no. 2 (2005): 1–15.

Rashid, Hussein. "Muslims in Film and Muslim Filmmaking in the United States." In *The Oxford Handbook of American Islam*, edited by Yvonne Yazbeck Haddad and Jane I. Smith, 259–273. Oxford: Oxford University Press, 2014.

Rashid, Hussein. "The Incidental Muslim: The Characters We Overlook." In *Muslims in the Movies: A Global Anthology*, edited by Kristian Petersen, 45–57. Boston: Ilex Foundation, 2021.

Razaki, Khalid, Anne Drougas, and Mohamed Askar. "Religion and Interfaith Dialogue: The Forgotten Pedagogical DEI Initiative in Business Education and Strategic Planning." *Journal of Higher Education Theory and Practice* 22, no. 10 (2022): 38–52.

Redding, Sean. "Witchcraft in Africa: Political Power and Spiritual Insecurity from the Precolonial Era to the Present." *Oxford Research Encyclopedia of African History*, March 26, 2019. https://oxfordre-com.proxyiub.uits.iu.edu/africanhistory/view/10.1093/acrefore/9780190277734.001.0001/acrefore-9780190277734-e-441.

Ressler, Robert, Brad R. Fulton, and Pamela Paxton. "Activity and Identity: Uncovering Multiple Institutional Logics in the Nonprofit Sector." Paper presented at the Association for Research on Nonprofit Organizations and Voluntary Action annual meeting, virtual, 2020.

Roberts, Bob, and Chris Seiple. "U.S. Senate Should Quickly Affirm Texan Rashad Hussain as Religious Freedom Ambassador." *Dallas Morning News*, October 21, 2021. https://www.dallasnews.com/opinion/commentary/2021/10/21/the-us-senate-should-quickly-affirm-texan-rashad-hussain-as-religious-freedom-ambassador/.

Rodriguez-Plate, S. Brent. "Seeing the Other in Cinema: Interreligious Connections through the Senses." *Journal of Beliefs & Values* 38, no. 3 (2017): 296–304.

Rosen, Sharon Leib. "Academy Museum of Motion Pictures Course Corrects on Jewish Founders." *The Forward*, January 28, 2022.

Rosenberg, Stacy. "Americans' Trust in Other Americans." Pew Research Center, May 30, 2020. https://www.pewresearch.org/politics/2019/07/22/the-state-of-personal-trust/.

Ross, Dorothy. *The Origins of American Social Science*. Cambridge: Cambridge University Press, 1991.

Roy, Arundhati. "The Pandemic Is a Portal." *Financial Times*, April 3, 2020. https://www.ft.com/content/10d8f5e8-74eb-11ea-95fe-fcd274e920ca.

Ruhee, Jaffer. "Los Angeles Holds 4th Annual Day of Religious Pluralism." *The Ismaili*, May 28, 2019. https://the.ismaili/usa/los-angeles-holds-4th-annual-day-religious-pluralism.

Rupert, Bethany. "The Sunday Rest Bill and the Battle to Keep the Civil Sabbath." *Seton Hall Legislative Journal* 39, no. 2 (2015). https://scholarship.shu.edu/cgi/viewcontent.cgi?article=1084&context=shlj.

Russell, Peter E. *Prince Henry "the Navigator": A Life*. New Haven, CT: Yale University Press, 2000.

Rymel, Tim. "Evangelicals Reaffirm Their LGBT Ignorance and Bigotry." *HuffPost*, August 31, 2017. https://www.huffpost.com/entry/evangelicals-reaffirm-their-lgbt-ignorance-and-bigotry_b_59a79affe4b096fd8876c0a0.

Saint-Cyr, Yosie. "Religious Diversity in the Workplace." HR Info Desk, November 2002. https://www.hrinfodesk.com/preview.asp?article=8835.

Salzberger, Joshua. Interview by Jody Hassett Sanchez, April 4, 2023.

Sansone, Livio. *Field Station Bahia: Brazil in the Work of Lorenzo Dow Turner, E. Franklin Frazier and Frances and Melville Herskovits, 1935-1967*. Leiden: Brill, 2023.

Saval, Malina. "Too Jewish for Hollywood: As Antisemitism Soars, Hollywood Should Address Its Enduring Hypocrisy in Hyperbolic Caricatures of Jews." *Variety*, June 18, 2021.

Savat, Sara. *Cultural Backlash: Is LGBTQ Progress an Attack on Christianity?* WashU, August 26, 2021. https://source.wustl.edu/2021/08/cultural-backlash-is-lgbtq-progress-an-attack-on-christianity/.

Schiappa, Edward, Peter B. Gregg, and Dean E. Hewes. "The Parasocial Contact Hypothesis." *Communication Monographs* 72, no. 1 (2005): 92–115.

Schnakenberg, Éric. "Treaty of Tordesillas, June 7, 1494." In *Encyclopédie d'histoire numérique de l'Europe*. https://ehne.fr/en/encyclopedia/themes/international-relations/europe-and-legal-regulation-international-relations/treaty-tordesillas-june-7-1494.

Schneider, Rachel C., Deidra Carroll Coleman, Elaine Howard Ecklund, and Denise Daniels. "How Religious Discrimination Is Perceived in the Workplace: Expanding the View." *Socius* 8 (2022). https://doi.org/10.1177/23780231211070920.

Seiple, Chris. "From Ideology to Identity: Building Communities of the Willing." In *Religion, Identity and Global Governance: Ideas, Evidence and Practice*, edited by Patrick James, 292–310. Toronto: University of Toronto Press, 2010.

Semmerling, Tim Jon. *"Evil" Arabs in American Popular Film: Orientalist Fear*. Austin: University of Texas Press, 2006.

Semmerling, Tim Jon. "Those 'Evil' Muslims! Orientalist Fears in the Narratives of the War on Terror." *Journal of Muslim Minority Affairs* 28, no. 2 (2008): 207–223.

Sen, Pirun. "Watt Samaki Temple." Pluralism Project Archive, Harvard University. https://hwpi.harvard.edu/pluralismarchive/watt-samaki-temple.

Sernett, Milton C. *Bound for the Promised Land: African American Religion and the Great Migration*. Durham, NC: Duke University Press, 1997.

Shaheen, Jack G. *Reel Bad Arabs: How Hollywood Vilifies People*. New York: Olive Branch Press, 2001.

Shaheen, Jack G. *Guilty: Hollywood's Verdict on Arabs after 9/11*. Northampton, MA: Olive Branch Press, 2008.

Shakman Hurd, Elizabeth. "The Politics of Secularism." In *Rethinking Religion and World Affairs*, edited by Monica Duffy Toft, Alfred Stepan, and Timothy Samuel Shah, 36–52. New York: Oxford University Press, 2012.

Sharpe, Christina. *In the Wake: On Blackness and Being*. Durham, NC: Duke University Press, 2016.

Shook, Ellen. "Stop Wondering if Faith Is a Workplace Issue. It Is." LinkedIn, October 28, 2018. https://www.linkedin.com/pulse/stop-wondering-faith-workplace-issue-ellyn-shook/.

Shortle, Allyson F., and Ronald Keith Gaddie. "Religious Nationalism and Perceptions of Muslims and Islam." *Politics and Religion* 8, no. 3 (2015): 435–457. https://www.cambridge.org/core/journals/politics-and-religion/article/abs/religious-nationalism-and-perceptions-of-muslims-and-islam/8FD27C85AEDE0B861040FC06E3DA2248.

Sikh Coalition. "Creating Safe Schools." April 21, 2023. https://www.sikhcoalition.org/ourwork/creating-safe-schools.

Singh, Simran Jeet. "Muslimophobia, Racialization, and Mistaken Identity." In *Muhammad in the Post-9/11 Digital Age*, edited by Ruqqayya Khan, 158–173. Austin: University of Texas Press, 2015.

Singh, Simran Jeet. "To Fight Racism, We Need to Confront Religion's Racist Past." *Religion News*, July 9, 2020. https://religionnews.com/2020/07/09/how-americas-religious-colonizers-brought-racism-with-them.

Singh, Simran Jeet. "Why Universities and the Rest of Us Need Religious Studies." *Religion News*, December 4, 2020. https://religionnews.com/2020/12/04/why-universities-and-the-rest-of-us-need-religion-studies/.

Singh, Simran Jeet. "How to Talk about Religion at Work." *Harvard Business Review*, September 16, 2022. https://hbr.org/2022/09/how-to-talk-about-religion-at-work.

"Six Guidelines for Teaching about Religion." *Education Week*, April 4, 2016. https://www.edweek.org/education/opinion-six-guidelines-for-teaching-about-religion/2016/04.

Smietana, Bob. "After 30 Years, Buddhist-Inspired Message of 'Groundhog Day' Still Holds Spiritual Power." *Religion News*, February 2, 2023.

Smith, Samuel. "Religious 'Nones' Now as Big as Evangelicals in the US, New Data Shows." *Christian Post*, March 20, 2019. https://www.christianpost.com/news/religious-nones-now-as-big-as-evangelicals-in-the-us-new-data-shows.html.

Society for Human Resource Management. "Religion and Corporate Culture: Accommodating Religious Diversity in the Workplace." Alexandria, VA: Society for Human Resource Management, 2008.

Somanathan, Rohini, and Danielle Allen, eds. *Difference without Domination: Pursuing Justice in Diverse Democracies.* Chicago: University of Chicago Press, 2020.

Stanwood, Owen. *The Global Refuge: Huguenots in an Age of Empire.* New York: Oxford University Press, 2020.

Stewart, W. Christopher, Chris Seiple, and Dennis R. Hoover. "Toward a Global Covenant of Peaceable Neighborhood: Introducing the Philosophy of Covenantal Pluralism." *Review of Faith & International Affairs* 18, no. 4 (Winter 2018): 1–17. https://doi.org/10.1080/15570274.2020.1835029.

Stockman, Robert H. *The Bahá'í Faith in America.* Vol. I. Wilmette, IL: Bahá'í Pub. Trust, 1985.

Stop AAPI Hate. "Two Years and Thousands of Voices." July 2022. https://stopaapihate.org/2022/07/20/year-2-report/.

Suleiman, Omar. "11 Hours of Prayer and Solidarity at the Colleyville Synagogue Standoff." *Religion News,* January 18, 2022.

Sung, Jung M. "Capitalism as Religion and Religious Pluralism: An Approach from Liberation Theology." *JSTOR* 34 (2014): 155–165. https://www.jstor.org/stable/24801361.

Sweet, James H. *Domingos Álvares, African Healing, and the Intellectual History of the Atlantic World.* Chapel Hill: University of North Carolina Press, 2011.

Swetnam Mathews, Mary Beth. *Doctrine and Race: African American Evangelicals and Fundamentalism between the Wars.* Tuscaloosa: University of Alabama Press, 2017.

Syed, Uzma, Olivia Kapera, Aparajita Chandrasekhar, et al. "The Role of Faith-Based Organizations in Improving Vaccination Confidence & Addressing Vaccination Disparities to Help Improve Vaccine Uptake: A Systemic Review." *Vaccines* 11, no. 2 (2023): 449. https://doi.org/10.3390/vaccines11020449.

Tajfel, Henri. "Experiments in Intergroup Discrimination." *Scientific American* 223, no. 5 (November 1970): 96–103, Experiments in Intergroup Discrimination on JSTOR.

Tanenbaum. *But, Where Can I Pray?* New York: Tanenbaum, 2018.

Tanenbaum. "10 Bias Danger Signs." Workplace Resources. N.d. https://tanenbaum.org/about-us/what-we-do/workplace/workplace-resources/.

Tanenbaum and Public Religion Research. *What American Workers Really Think about Religion.* New York: Tanenbaum, 2013.

Tanenbaum and Religious Freedom and Business Foundation. "Corporate Religious Diversity Assessment." https://crdatool.com.

Tavernise, Sabrina. "A New Country for Conflict Resolution Experts." *New York Times,* February 4, 2019. https://www.nytimes.com/2019/02/04/us/conflicting-experts-peacebuilders.html.

Taylor, Charles. *The Secular Age.* Cambridge, MA: Harvard University Press, 2007.

Tchen, John Kuo Wei, and Dylan Yeats, eds. *Yellow Peril! An Archive of Anti-Asian Fear.* London: Verso, 2014.

Teed, Paul E. "Interfaith Encounter and Religious Pluralism: J.T. Sunderland's Mission to Brahmo Samajes of India, 1895-96." *American Studies (00263079)* 50, nos. 1/2 (Spring/Summer 2009): 51–69. https://doi.org/10.1353/ams.2011.0091.

Teeman, Tim. "Let's Call 'Religious Freedom' by Its Real Name: Poisonous, Anti-LGBTQ Bigotry." *Daily Beast,* November 5, 2019. https://www.thedailybeast.com/lets-call-religious-freedom-by-its-real-name-poisonous-anti-lgbtq-bigotry.

Telhami, Shibley. "Measuring the Backlash against the Muslim Backlash." *Politico Magazine,* July 11, 2016. https://www.politico.com/magazine/story/2016/07/measuring-the-backlash-against-the-muslim-backlash-214034.

Tevington, Patricia. *Americans Feel More Positive Than Negative about Jews, Mainline Protestants, Catholics.* Washington, DC: Pew Research Center, 2023. https://www.pewresea

rch.org/religion/wp-content/uploads/sites/7/2023/03/PF_2023.03.15_religion-favorability_REPORT.pdf.

Thames, Knox, and Emily Scolaro. "Freedom of Religion or Belief and Cultural Heritage Protection: Synergistic Not Competitive." *Review of Faith & International Affairs* 20, no. 2 (2022): 49–60.

Thurman, Howard. *Jesus and the Disinherited.* Nashville, TN: Abingdon-Cokesbury Press, 1949.

Thurman, Howard. *The Luminous Darkness.* Richmond, IN: Friends United Press, 1965/1989.

Tisby, Jemar. *The Color of Compromise: The Truth about the American Church's Complicity in Racism.* Grand Rapids, MI: Zondervan, 2019.

Turkson, Peter, K.A., ed. "Vocation of the Business Leader: A Reflection," 5th ed. Rome: Dicastery for Promoting Integral Human Development, Vatican, 2018. https://www.humandevelopment.va/en/risorse/documenti/vocation-of-the-business-leader-a-reflection-5th-edition.html.

Turner, Henry McNeal. *Respect Black: The Writings and Speeches of Henry McNeal Turner.* New York: Arno Press, 1971.

Uddin, Asma T. *When Islam Is Not a Religion: Inside America's Fight for Religious Freedom.* New York: Pegasus Books, 2019. https://www.simonandschuster.com/books/When-Islam-is-Not-a-Religion/Asma-T-Uddin/9781643136059.

Uddin, Asma T. "Christian-Muslim Relations in a Tribalized America: Strategies for Healing." September 13. Washington, DC: Aspen Institute, 2021. https://www.aspeninstitute.org/publications/christian-muslim-relations-in-a-tribalized-america-strategies-for-healing/.

Uddin, Asma T. *Politics of Vulnerability.* New York: Pegasus Books, 2021.

United Nations. *Universal Declaration of Human Rights.* December 10, 1948. https://www.un.org/en/about-us/universal-declaration-of-human-rights.

Uplifting Words. "Robert Turner: Influential Baha'is: Baha'i Faith Articles." June 20, 2020. https://www.upliftingwords.org/post/robert-turner.

"U.S. Catholic Population Shows Growth, Especially in the South." Catholic News Agency, December 6, 2022. https://www.catholicnewsagency.com/news/252998/us-catholic-population-shows-growth-trends-southward.

USCIRF. "Religious Freedom Concerns for Followers of African Traditional and Indigenous Religions." Washington, DC: US Commission on International Religious Freedom, 2023.

US Commission on Civil Rights. "Recent Activities against Citizens and Residents of Asian Descent." Washington, DC: US Commission on Civil Rights, 1986.

US Department of Justice. "Kansas Man Sentenced to Life in Prison without Parole for Racially Motivated Shooting at Olathe Bar." August 7, 2018. https://www.justice.gov/opa/pr/kansas-man-sentenced-life-prison-without-parole-racially-motivated-shooting-olathe-bar.

"U.S. Is Polarizing Faster Than Other Democracies, Study Finds." Brown University, January 21, 2020. https://www.brown.edu/news/2020-01-21/polarization.

Vallone, Dan, Stephen Hawkins, Noelle Malvar, et al. 2021. "Two Stories of Distrust in America." More in Common. https://www.moreincommon.com/media/yfcbfmmp/mic_two-stories-of-distrust.pdf.

Venters, Louis. *No Jim Crow Church: The Origins of South Carolina's Bahá'í Community.* Gainesville: University Press of Florida, 2015.

Volf, Miroslav. *Flourishing: Why We Need Religion in a Globalized World.* New Haven, CT: Yale University Press, 2016.

Waggoner, Ellet Joseph. *The Blair Sunday-Rest Bill.* Oakland, CA: Pacific Press, 1889. https://m.egwwritings.org/en/book/1339.2#0.

Washington Adventist University. "The New Supreme Court and Religion: Constitutional and Prophetic Perspectives." YouTube video, September 17, 2022, 1:36:19. https://www.youtube.com/watch?v=_oy_2A6njK4.

Washington, James Melvin. *Frustrated Fellowship: The Black Baptist Quest for Social Power.* Macon, GA: Mercer University Press, 1986.

Weisbrot, Robert. *Father Divine and the Struggle for Racial Equality*. Urbana: University of Illinois Press, 1983.

Weisenfeld, Judith. *New World a-Coming: Black Religion and Racial Identity during the Great Migration*. New York: New York University Press, 2016.

Wenger, Tisa. *Religious Freedom: The Contested History of an American Ideal*. Chapel Hill: University of North Carolina Press, 2017.

White, Calvin. *The Rise to Respectability: Race, Religion, and the Church of God in Christ*. Fayetteville: University of Arkansas Press, 2013.

White, Ellen. *The Great Controversy between Christ and Satan in the Christian Dispensation*. Mountain View, CA: Ellen G. White Estate, 1911/2018.

Whitehead, Andrew L., and Samuel L. Perry. *Taking America back for God: Christian Nationalism in the United States*. New York: Oxford University Press, 2020.

White House, The. "By the President of the United States of America: A Proclamation." January 20, 2021. https://www.whitehouse.gov/briefing-room/presidential-actions/2021/01/20/a-national-day-of-unity/.

Williams, Duncan Ryūken. *American Sutra: A Story of Faith and Freedom in the Second World War*. Cambridge, MA: Harvard University Press, 2019.

Williams, Duncan Ryūken, Funie Hsu, Chenxing Han, Patricia Wakida, and Jhani Randhawa. "May We Gather." May We Gather. https://www.maywegather.org.

Willingham, A.J. "By 2040, Islam Could Be the Second-Largest Religion in the US." CNN, January 10, 2018. https://www.cnn.com/2018/01/10/politics/muslim-population-growth-second-religious-group-trnd/index.html.

Wills, David W., and Richard Newman. *Black Apostles at Home and Abroad: Afro-Americans and the Christian Mission from the Revolution to Reconstruction*. Boston: G.K. Hall, 1982.

Wilmore, Gayraud S. *Black Religion and Black Radicalism*. Garden City, NY: Anchor Press, 1973.

Wilson Gilmore, Ruth. "Where Life Is Precious, Life Is Precious." *On Being with Krista Tippett*, March 30, 2023. https://onbeing.org/programs/ruth-wilson-gilmore-where-life-is-precious-life-is-precious/.

World Economic Forum Global Agenda. "The Role of Faith in Systemic Global Challenges." June 2016. https://www3.weforum.org/docs/WEF_GAC16_Role_of_Faith_in_Systemic_Global_Challenges.pdf.

Yaccino, Steven, Michael Schwirtz, and Marc Santora. "Gunman Kills 6 at a Sikh Temple near Milwaukee." *New York Times*, August 5, 2012, sec. U.S. https://www.nytimes.com/2012/08/06/us/shooting-reported-at-temple-in-wisconsin.html.

Yang, Andrew, and Jonathan Greenblatt. "Yang and Anti-Defamation League CEO: Avoid Coronavirus Racism." *USA Today*, March 20, 2020. https://www.usatoday.com/story/opinion/2020/03/20/yang-anti-defamation-league-ceo-avoid-coronavirus-scapegoating-racism-column/2877976001/?fbclid=IwAR2cVVeepwUZHrkpYBltzDbsTvKGk-giWQtIiczwmrDWSA3Z4D4KQM1ugSk.

Young, Iris. *Inclusion and Democracy*. Oxford: Oxford University Press, 2002.

Index

For the benefit of digital users, indexed terms that span two pages (e.g., 52–53) may, on occasion, appear on only one of those pages.

A
acceptance, 64–65
accuracy (media representation), 116–17, 136
activism, 88–89, 107–8
analytical pluralism, 6, 61–62
anti-asian racism, 72–74, 76–78
antisemitism, 24–25, 123–25
assimilation (vs. integration), 21
authoritarianism, 50–51

B
belief (public expression of), 16–17, 146–47
belonging, 88–89, 152–53
  civic belonging, 33–34
  religious belonging, 88–89
  workplace belonging, 145–46
bias, 3–4, 23–24
  cultural bias, 27–28
  institutional bias, 49–50
  media bias, 115–17
bridge-building, 62–64, 152–53
buddhism, 18–19, 81–82, 135–36

C
calendars (religious structuring of time), 27–28
Christian nationalism, 50–51
Christian normativity/ Christian dominance, 22–24, 107
  cultural dominance, 107
  institutional forms of, 22–24
  legal implications of, 49–50
Christocentrism, 23–24, 94–95
  in public institutions, 23–24
  in U.S. history, 94–95
civic collaboration, 152–53
civic inclusion, 32–33
civic pluralism, 62–64
civil society, 3, 33–34
coalition building, 152–53
colonialism, 23–24, 94–95
community, 63–65, 160–61
  faith-based community, 63–65
  interfaith community, 152–53
conflict resolution, 16–17
creative representation, 136
cross-faith collaboration, 153
cultural erasure, 24–25
  through exclusion, 25–27
  through representation, 115–17
cultural omission, 25–27
cultural power, 23–25, 94–95
cultural stereotypes, 115–17, 124–25
cultural violence, 6–9
culture, 5, 27–28

D
decolonization, 94–95
democracy, 32–34, 50–51
  religious participation in, 32–34
  threats to, 50–51
democratic pluralism, 33–34, 50–51
dialogue (interreligious), 63–65, 152–53
diplomacy, 15–16
discrimination (religious), 25–27, 49–50
distributive justice, 87–88
diversity, 3, 135–36
  demographic diversity, 135–36
  internal religious diversity, 19
  symbolic diversity, 116–17
dualism, 93–94

E
education, 4–5, 27–28
embodied faith, 87–88
embodied religion, 87–88, 159–60
engagement, 16–17, 63–65
  civic engagement, 33–34
  institutional engagement, 145–46
  interfaith engagement, 61–64
equality, 22–23, 88
equity, 22–23, 160–62
  religious equity, 22–23
  structural equity, 160–62
ethical pluralism, 5, 38–40

ethics, 88–89
everyday religion, 26–28, 159–60
exchange (intercultural), 17
exclusion, 25–27, 49–50

F
faith, 17–18, 87–88
  embodied faith, 87–88
  lived faith, 26–28
  public expressions of, 17–18
faith and action, 88–89
faith-based coalitions, 170–72
faith-based organizations, 170–71, 178–80
first amendment, 48–49
freedom of religion. *See* religious freedom
funding, 170–72

G
global religious freedom, 32–33, 48–49

H
hate crimes, 74–78, 82–83
heterogeneity, 5–6
hierarchy, 93–95
Hinduism, 81–82
humanizing narratives, 116–17

I
identity (religious), 17–18, 62–63
  minority identity, 82
  racialized religious identity, 24–25
  religious identity, 17–18
illiteracy (religious), 22–23, 25–27
imagination, 38–40
inclusion, 88–89, 145–46
  civic inclusion, 32–33
  institutional inclusion, 145–46
  spiritual inclusion, 145–46
indigenous traditions, 94–95
inequity, 4–5, 22–24
integration (vs. assimilation), 21
institutional exclusion, 25–27
Institutional pluralism, 25–27, 49–50
Institutional power, 49–50, 107–8
interfaith, 61–64, 151–53
  collaboration, 152–53
  dialogue, 63–65
interfaith engagement, 61–64, 151–53
interreligious, 63–65
  partnership, 152–53
  understanding, 62–64
interreligious partnership, 152–53
intra-religious diversity, 19, 82
Islam, 49–50, 115–17
Islamophobia, 24–25, 115–17

J
Jainism, 19, 82
Judaism, 123–24
justice (religious frameworks of), 4–5, 87–88
  distributive justice, 87–88
  justice movements, 88–89
  restorative justice, 88–89
  social justice, 87–88
justice movements, 88–89, 107–8

L
law (religion), 48–50, 107
leadership, 170–71
legacy, 82–83
literacy (religious)
  as civic skill, 3
  cross-cultural, 15–16
  definition of, 5
  as a survival strategy, 22–24
lived experience, 3, 22–23
  religious lived experience, 3
  minoritized lived experience, 22–23
lived pluralism, 3, 61–63
lived religion, 26–28

M
media, 115–17
  narrative framing, 123–25
  representation of religion, 115–17
  stereotyping, 115–17
media bias, 115–17
media representation, 115–17, 123–25, 135–36
minoritization, 22–24
minoritized religions, 23–25
minority religions, 23–25, 82
moral formation, 5, 88–89
moral imagination, 38–40
multifaith, 152–53

N
narrative, 38–40
narrative change, 107, 136
neutrality, 28
normativity, 22–24

P
philanthropy (faith-integrated), 170–72, 177–79
pluralism
  covenantal, 15–16

definition of, 3
political dimensions of, 49–51
workplace, 160–61
polarization (religious), 61–62, 73–75
political pluralism, 49–51
political religion, 50–51
popular culture, 123–25
privilege, 22–24
pluralism, 3, 61–63, 160–61
public policy, 49–50
power, 23–25, 107–8
cultural power, 23–25
institutional power, 49–50
symbolic power, 115–16
power analysis, 94–95
power asymmetry, 23–25, 94–95
procedural justice, 48–49

R
racial justice (religion and), 87–88, 92–95, 106–7
racialization, 24–25
racism (religious complicity in), 94–95, 106–7
religious dignity, 25–27
religious discrimination, 49–50
religious extremism, 50–51
religious freedom
constitutional foundations, 48–49
definition of, 31–32
global dimensions, 31–32
legal frameworks, 48–49
threats to, 49–51
religious literacy, 5, 15–16, 22–24
as civic skill, 3
definition of, 5
in education, 27–28
representation (religious), 115–17, 136
resistance, 94–95
resilience, 76–78
restorative justice, 88–89, 95
ritual, 5–6, 87–88
ritual practice, 5–6, 87–88

S
sacred practice, 87–88
sacred space, 19–20, 159–60
sacred time, 27–28
secularism, 17, 28
Sikh identity, 3, 25–26
Sikhi, 3, 25–26, 72–74, 123–24
social cohesion, 39–40, 63–65
social transformation, 171–72
solidarity, 153
spiritual inclusion, 145–46
storytelling, 38–40, 116–17, 123–25
humanizing narratives, 116–17
narrative change, 107
popular culture, 123–25
structural racism, 94–95
structural violence, 6–8
symbolic power, 23–24, 115–16
systemic inequity, 4–5, 22–24

T
theological diversity, 19
tolerance (vs. respect), 20–21

U
U.S. history, 92–94
U.S. religion, 32–34, 50–51

V
Values formation, 18, 88–89
Violence
cultural violence, 6–9
religiously motivated violence, 74–78
structural violence, 6–8

W
Western bias, 27–28
White supremacy, 50–51
workplace (religion in), 145–46, 151–53, 159–60
world religions, 5